FIFTY KEY
MEDIEVAL THINKERS

Focussing on the individuals who shaped intellectual life in the middle ages, *Fifty Key Medieval Thinkers* is an accessible introduction to those religious, philosophical and political concepts central to the medieval worldview.

Entries include such diverse figures as:

- Boethius
- Hildegard of Bingen
- Thomas Aquinas
- John Wyclif
- Peter Abelard

- Anselm of Canterbury
- John of Salisbury
- Francis of Assisi
- William of Ockham
- Bede

Each entry presents a biographical outline, a list of works and a summary of their main theories, alongside suggestions for further reading. Chronologically arranged, and with an introductory essay which presents important themes in context, this volume is an invaluable reference resource and introductory guide for all those who wish to explore the thought of this fascinating period in European history.

G.R. Evans teaches medieval theology at Cambridge University. She is the author of *Philosophy and Theology in the Middle Ages* and *Law and Theology in the Middle Ages*, both published by Routledge.

ROUTLEDGE KEY GUIDES

Routledge Key Guides are accessible, informative and lucid handbooks, which define and discuss the central concepts, thinkers and debates in a broad range of academic disciplines. All are written by noted experts in their respective subjects. Clear, concise exposition of complex and stimulating issues and ideas makes *Routledge Key Guides* the ultimate reference resources for students, teachers, researchers and the interested lay person.

FIFTY KEY MEDIEVAL THINKERS

G. R. Evans

London and New York

First published 2002
by Routledge
11 New Fetter Lane, London EC4P 4EE

Simultaneously published in the USA and Canada
by Routledge
29 West 35th Street, New York, NY 10001

Routledge is an imprint of the Taylor & Francis Group

© 2002 G.R. Evans

Typeset in Times by Taylor & Francis Books Ltd
Printed and bound in Great Britain by TJ International Ltd,
Padstow, Cornwall

British Library Cataloguing in Publication Data
A catalogue record for this book is available from the British Library

Library of Congress Cataloging in Publication Data
Evans, G. R. (Gillian Rosemary)
Fifty key Medieval thinkers / G.R. Evans.
p. cm. – (Routledge key guides)
Includes bibliographical references.
1. Theologians–Biography.
2. Philosophers, Medieval–Biography.
I. Title. II. Series.
BR1702 .E93 2002
189–dc21
[B]   2001048457

ISBN 0–415–23662–2 (hbk)
ISBN 0–415–23663–0 (pbk)

CONTENTS

PREFACE

Is there a God? What is the purpose of human life? What is a person? For whose benefit should society be organised? Why should I believe what you tell me? What is real? How do words mean things? How do you know all this? The favourite problems of the thousand years of medieval intellectual endeavour have not yet been resolved. They have proved to be of perennial importance. Not only the topics with which medieval thinkers were concerned but also a number of the ways in which they addressed them, repeatedly come back into fashion as they are doing now.

This book is concerned not only with what medieval thinkers contributed to these long-standing debates but also with the interconnectedness of their work and its place in the heritage of western thought. For that reason, the focus is mainly upon the 'Latin West'. From the end of the Roman Empire, as Greek speakers and Latin speakers increasingly fell out of touch with one another, their two worlds of thought diverged. The Latins' 'Aristotelian grapple' with logic and science did not have its exact counterpart in the Greek-speaking East; the Greeks were more drawn to the exploration of Platonic principles, and in any case the Church in the East very early set its face against novelty. It is difficult to do innovative work where new ideas are heresy even if they are right. In the case of the dispute between East and West over the relationship of the Holy Spirit to the Father and the Son in the Trinity, the Greek objection to the Western 'addition' of the phrase *filioque* to the creed was first that it constituted an addition at all, and only secondly that they thought it was probably theologically unsound. Similarly, we shall look at the work of Arabic and Jewish scholars chiefly as it impinged on that Western world which was to draw it into its own internal debate. For Western thinkers argued with one another a great deal, as we shall see, and pointed backwards to the work of their predecessors and, often with a sense of daring, to the seductive non-

Christian authorities, among the secular authors of the classical world.

When a medieval teacher introduced his students to a new book, he would begin with an informal introduction, or *accessus*. This might take various forms. It might give the title of the work, its author, its subject matter (*materia*), its purpose (*intentio*) and the *modus tractandi*, or the way in which it dealt with its subject matter. The 'entries' in this present book are designed with a similar notion of making them an 'introduction' for the student or interested general reader who may want to go deeper into the subjects they touch on. They are starting points, but with hints of the directions in which these thinkers were looking. This present volume aims to be a resource book which will do more than enable someone coming new to it to begin to get inside the medieval world of thought. It tries to provide a glimpse of the tensions and the interplay. The links between the thinkers in this volume are important. Many of our authors made their contemporaries angry or admiring. Some formed chains of master and pupils or even 'disciples'. It is important that these writers are not looked at in isolation, for that was not the way in which they worked. To approach so complex a literature in this way by treating it in terms of brief studies of individual authors can be justified only if the result is to make the context of the thinking as well as some of the essential concerns of each author intelligible to the reader new to the field

Fifty is an arbitrary number, and we are concerned with interdependence as well as with the achievement of what must inevitably remain a sample of individuals. Readers familiar with the history of medieval thought may well call for entries which are missing, or point to areas of intellectual endeavour which are not included. The overflow of Latin learning into the vernacular is a story for which there has simply not been space, although Dante is included as an author able to do philosophy in Italian and through the medium of poetry.

The writers included here have been chosen for a number of reasons. Some of our authors would have been outstanding in any age. Anselm of Canterbury (1033–1109) is an obvious example. He is read today, not just because he was important in his time but because he had things to say which are still being taken seriously in their own right. Some authors are included simply because they were read a great deal in the Middle Ages and thus became influential upon the evolution of an intellectual world. The examples of late patristic scholars included are particularly important in that regard, but there are other examples in these pages. Some do not appear in these pages in their own right as writers, but as supporting players. In the aftermath of the fall of the Roman Empire, when books became hard to get and there was a danger that some texts would be lost for ever, Benedict Biscop travelled in search of new materials for others to study. Had he not brought texts back to Northumbria from the mother house of the Benedictine order at Monte Cassino in Italy, Bede would not have been able to write as he did, and those who read Bede would not have had access to the ideas and references he passed on. Many who were typical or representative are here in the background of others' stories. The tenth-century thinker Ralph Glaber reveals the mind of the historian and biographer or hagiographer (for the urge to record people's lives in the Middle Ages was most often fired by a perception of great sanctity and the exemplary character of a life). Others too were intellectual explorers. In the twelfth century, Peter the Venerable, abbot of Cluny and himself the author of letters and a treatise *Contra petrobrusianos*, against a sect of contemporary heretics, encouraged the making of a translation of the Koran. He wanted to understand how another faith worked. It was Peter the Venerable who chivvied Bernard of Clairvaux until he agreed to 'preach' the Second Crusade to rescue the Holy Land from the 'infidel'. Adelard of Bath, in the same century, is an example of a scholar with a different kind of mission. He heard that Arab scholars had written important works in the areas of mathematics and science, and he spent several years travelling in the parts of Europe and the Middle East where he could have direct contact with their work. The twelfth century also saw efforts to make translations of some of the works of Greek antiquity into Latin, on the part of a small number of individuals (such as James of Venice), whose Greek was of a sufficient standard.

These instincts of exploration and retrieval reflect in part the habit of regarding earlier authors with respect which is discussed in the introduction. But they also suggest an active curiosity, a desire to widen the sphere of knowledge.

Respect for the written word arose in more practical contexts. The papal administration consolidated its power from an early period partly by means of the keeping of records. In the third century Pope Fabian seems to have ensured that there were notaries in various parts of Rome. Papal letters and bureaucratic enactments were probably being enregistered before the fifth century, certainly by that time.[1] Such ecclesiastical record-keeping became pervasive, a habit. For example, a monastery usually kept any royal charters granted in its favour, a chronicle of the history of the world in which its own history, and local events, feature at appropriate moments. That kind of thing provided a framework of attitudes to books and records on which much of the work of our writers depends. It should not be forgotten that able people do not necessarily write books. It is important that in the medieval world so many of the best minds of the day chose to do so.

There is no sharp dividing line at the end of the Middle Ages. Despite his revolutionary ideas, Luther's education made him still in essence a mediaeval thinker, drawing upon such recent authorities as Gabriel Biel. In the 1530s, when the novelty of his reforming activities had already made him conspicuous and unpopular, and one might reasonably 'place' him in a post-medieval context, Luther was still conducting *disputationes* in the medieval way in the University of Wittenberg and still taking the text of the Vulgate to be the version of the Bible appropriate for analysis.

Nevertheless, something was changing, and this series of little studies, taken as a narrative of the intellectual life of a millennium, tells its own story.

Notes

1 Thomas F. Noble, 'Literacy and the papal government in late antiquity and the early Middle Ages', in *The Uses of Literacy in the early Middle Ages*, ed. R. McKitterick (Cambridge, 1990), pp. 82–108.

ABBREVIATIONS

PL	*Patrologia Latina*
CCCM	*Corpus Christianorum Continuatio Redievalis*
CCSL	*Corpus Christianorum Series Latina*
MGH	*Monumenta Germaniae Historica*

INTRODUCTION

Writers and readers

Augustine of Hippo (354–430) knew how it felt to be excited by a book. When he was very young, he was given Cicero's *Hortensius* (which now survives only in fragments). 'I was so fired with the love of philosophy', he reports, 'that I immediately thought of taking the subject up.' Augustine describes how he was disturbed and 'rerouted' in his thinking and filled with burning enthusiasm as he attempted a few of Plotinus's writings.[1] He wrote this recollection after his conversion to Christianity when he was discussing with a group of friends the nature of happiness. They discovered it was useful to know about the views of the Platonists and other philosophers when they were writing their own book (or, strictly, Augustine's book), on the subject.

Cassiodorus, late Roman Senator, describes how he gave up public life with its unsavoury secular cares (*noxio sapore conditis*) when he tasted the sweetness to be found in reading the Psalms. Avidly, he gave himself up to close reading (*avidus me perscrutator immersi*), thirsty for 'saving words' after his life of most 'bitter' actions. Here was the overworked executive of his day taking early retirement and starting seriously to read. At first the sensations are of pleasure and relief. He is filling his mind with something worth knowing. Then, as he gets deeper in, he begins to see difficulties. There are 'obscurities' and inconsistencies in what he is reading. He cannot merely enjoy. He wants to understand. He looks for a book by someone he respects to guide him. Augustine is, he knows, a most learned 'Father'. But Augustine's *Enarrationes* on the Psalms are so lengthy and detailed, and Augustine has so much to say, that Cassiodorus can hardly take it all in. He begins to realise that another book is needed, to meet the needs of a different kind of reader. He pauses, to ask himself whether it is not a presumption to write such a book, since Augustine is a very great author. But he comes to the conclusion that a short and accessible book of his own would be a help to others, and moreover, it would be something new. He is tempted from being a reader to becoming a writer. And he is able to recover in that way his own sense of the beauty of what he is reading and its calming effect on the spirit.[2]

These writers of the late antique world were sharing a modern experience. Readers still find their lives turned round by reading and become writers. Frankly prompted by sheer interest and curiosity, the writers in this book express a desire to give others assistance with a journey of comprehension they themselves have enjoyed.

Writing in the ancient and medieval world was more commonly a social activity than it is likely to be today. Plato's dialogues record the conversations Socrates had with the young men who were his pupils, as they explored together giant problems such as the nature of justice. Cicero looked forward to a retirement from political and public life to a leisure in which he and a group of friends could talk philosophy. When Augustine was converted to Christianity, the first thing he did was to retire with such a group to consider the implications. In the conversations which produced not only the book on happiness, the *De beata vita*, but further works, including the *Contra Academicos*, Augustine and his friends were discussing Virgil and other books they had been reading. They had their conversation recorded by a note-taker. Alypius asked to have read back to him a part of what Augustine had said when he had been out of the room.[3] A little later they were discussing Cicero as an 'authority' who corroborated the view that something was unacceptable. This was evidently a detailed analysis of what the ancient authors were saying.

In the same series of conversations, they talked about the concept of order in the universe. Here we glimpse Augustine recognising that sometimes books do not contain everything the enquirer needs to know. In a famous episode he thought out an explanation for the gurglings in the pipes which had kept him awake during the night. He did so, however, not alone, but by talking it through with his fellow students Alypius and Navigius, in what he jestingly calls 'our school', *schola nostra*. Then he wrote a book about it,[4] drawing conclusions about order in the universe.

The writing of books could be prompted by the exchange of thoughts in letters as well as in live conversation. In Letter 3, to Nebridius, Augustine comments on a question Nebridius had put to him in a letter. He says he did so while reading the letter reflectively by lamplight after supper in bed. It was nearly but not quite time to go to sleep, and in this period of leisure his interest was kindled and he spent some time in thought.[5] Such profitable exchange could be prompted by the reading of an author's existing books. Paulinus of Nola writes to Augustine to say that he feels he is getting to know him well through reading his books. It is like having a daily conversation with him.[6]

For many of the centuries with which we are concerned, the dialogue form was popular for the written records of such shared intellectual enterprises, and even where the individual contributions of 'speakers' have disappeared below the surface of the text it is possible to glimpse something of the quality of the exchange. There is often a pedagogic purpose in this working together on a problem, but it can also be a real exploration. Anselm of Canterbury wrote his first book, the *Monologion*, after many sessions of discussing the divine nature with his pupils among the monks of Bec, and later one of them reminded him that they had left a loose thread. They had forgotten to finish discussing 'truth'. So Anselm began to explore that theme in a new treatise, which led on to another and to another.

There was rarely anything of the isolated figure about a medieval author. Those who were 'outsiders' could make their mark, and some are in this book although they were never really 'accepted' by their contemporaries. But for the most part, the interconnectedness of the medieval intellectual endeavour is usually very obvious. Many of the writers in this book read one another. They form a chain or mesh of readers and writers, whose every instinct was to cross-refer. They wrote consciously within a tradition which was a *concatenatio*, or chain, as well as a 'handing on' (*traditio*). That is to say, it was important not only that what was said remained faithful to the truth as earlier articulated, but also that it could be seen where the warrants could be found for what was now being said. There is plenty of novelty and originality, but these tend to be by-products of an endeavour which set little store by them; which, indeed, regarded them with suspicion. The leading idea was to preserve, to develop understanding with a cautious eye on the work of others, to make sure that one was not sliding into error.

This had an effect on the aesthetic aspects of textual criticism. Augustine was put off reading the Bible for many years as a young man because his training in rhetoric made him fastidious about the simplicity of the writing. Bluntly, he found it crudely written. He rationalised this in the end in his *De doctrina Christiana*, where he discusses the role a knowledge of rhetorical devices ought to play in a Christian reader's approach to appreciation of what he is reading and to his own compositions. After him, authors such as Bede (*De schematibus et tropis*) pursued this relatively safe line of examining the beauty and usefulness of stylistic devices. But gradually, 'this is not well-written' gives way to 'this is dangerous' as a ground for discouraging the reliance upon a book. That is not to say that there was not a great deal of attention to style. Medieval writers often write with conscious artistry, and explain with pride that they are doing do. Sigebert of Gembloux remarks that he has improved the style of a number of saints' lives written by others. But there was no strong live continuing tradition of criticising an author for the *way* he wrote; only of asking what were his personal credentials and scrutinising the content of what he wrote for material to be used in support of the writer's present arguments.

We shall come to the personal credentials in a moment, for that became the heart of the matter. First we need to consider the notion of the 'support' one writer could give to another. A good place to begin is Peter Lombard's mid-twelfth-century *Sentences*, or 'opinions'. These constituted an important staging post on the way to the formation of a systematic theology for pedagogic and academic purposes. Peter Lombard collected supporting authorities for the points he wanted to make and that prompted him to say again and again something about what he was expecting of the authors he was using, and why he was bringing them into the discussion. For the most part he is 'leaning' on them, in the sense of speaking in accordance with them. 'According to the authorities of the catholic doctors' (*iuxta catholicorum doctorum auctoritates*), he will say. Sometimes the authorities support one another by 'agreeing'. In William of Ockham's *De corpore Christi*, we find: 'The canonical Scriptures agree with the aforesaid Scriptures: *praedictis etiam scriptoribus Scripturae canonicae consentiunt.*[7]

Another way of looking at what these texts do is to see them as 'witnesses', and especially as reliable and *authoritative* witnesses. Indeed, Augustine conjoins the two ideas of 'witness' and 'authority': *has ergo testimoniorum ingentium auctoritates ingenti studio scire desidero.*[8] Sometimes the authorities are seen as fortifications.[9]

This had little to do with taking care to ensure the survival of the texts. In some cases, texts we now have from the classical world were preserved only in a single manuscript,[10] and Cicero's *Hortensius* has had to be reconstructed from quotations from it in other authors. From early in our period the 'witnesses' tended to be 'quoted', with quotations collected for convenient reference. That could allow the full text to remain a comparative rarity.

We have not yet got it clear what 'authorities' are. On one reading they are individuals whose word may be relied on in these various ways.[11] Alternatively, 'authorities' may be simply the portions of the writings which are being cited in support of an argument or opinion. William of Ockham, for example, speaks of the *auctoritates sanctorum patrum*, the authorities of the Fathers which he is adducing to prove a point.[12] Similarly, he speaks of the 'many authorities of the truly learned' (*multas auctoritates doctorum authenticorum*) one can adduce to prove a certain point.[13] It is of course not always clear in such passages whether it is the author or the quotation which is meant, and the quotation would not be authoritative if it did not carry the author's authority.

The reliance on the Bible and on early and respected Christian authors was one thing. It was less clear that it was acceptable to treat as 'authorities' sources who were not Christian. In the earlier part of our period these 'alternative' writers were mainly the classical Greek and Latin authors who had lived before the time of Christ. There was a natural respect for them among educated people, for they were studied at school. They were also good reading, so much so that Jerome was not the only thinker to find them seductive. He described in despair in one of his letters his guilty recognition that he was in danger of being 'more of a Ciceronian than a Christian'. The position could be rationalised by saying that these authors had been guided by divine revelation working upon their reason. They fell into the category touched on by St Paul in Romans 1:18–9, of those who can be presumed to have been open to God's influence in this way even though they had no knowledge of the Christian faith.

It was less easy to know what to do with Jewish writers since the time of Christ and, in due course, with Islamic writers, for these could not be 'excused' on the grounds that they could not have been Christians if they chose. Nevertheless, the temptation to 'use' their work was strong. The Jews could be helpful with explanations of the meanings of terms in the Hebrew original of the Old Testament, as twelfth century writers such as Andrew of St Victor found. Among the Arabic thinkers who adhered resolutely to Islam were translators and interpreters of Aristotle and other Greek classical sources whose work was so invaluable that it made its way first into use and then into debate in the Latin West, especially from the thirteenth century. Sheer value and interest could achieve a great deal in overcoming reservations.

Famous and 'edifying' authors?

To the credentials of our medieval thinkers. Most have to be valued on their surviving writing. Unless a thinker in the Middle Ages was a writer, we are unlikely to know of his ideas. There are a few of whom this may not be true, such as the teacher Bernard of Chartres, who died in about 1130 and seems to have left only a reputation and the striking thought that the scholars of his own day were like dwarfs sitting on the shoulders of the giants of old.

The majority of the writers in the pages which follow were consciously 'Christian authors', *scriptores ecclesiastici*, aware that they were writing in a 'tradition', in the Christian sense of a 'handing on', of a body of thought and belief. The educational system, at least from the collapse of the system of secular schools at the end of the ancient world, was normally accessible only to 'clerics'. There were exceptions, such as the royal offspring who apparently studied alongside Fulbert of Chartres in the Rheims of the late tenth century. The 'sons of the nobility' are said by Orderic Vitalis to have 'flocked' to the monastic schools at Bec in the middle of the eleventh century when Lanfranc was master there. In the late twelfth century, the lay dissidents known as 'Waldensians' were apparently often able to match quotation for quotation when the Church's apologists tried to change their minds by pointing to the Bible. Later still, there was a demand from a new bourgeoisie for something improving or entertaining to read. There were notable laymen whose writings survive, especially towards the end of the Middle Ages, but the normative writer was the clerk or cleric.

The 'clerical requirement' was no bar to the writers' art attracting the most able and academically inclined; but it naturally encouraged an emphasis on the concerns of Christian theology. Some who had other interests, for example in what would now be called 'science', wrote about it from within this 'community of clerical scholarship', and from a theological perspective. That was not difficult to do. The story of creation in Genesis naturally raises questions of natural science as Robert Grosseteste and Henry of Langenstein saw.

In this heavily clericalised forum, Christian readers began early to want an answer to the question who it was 'safe' or 'acceptable' for Christians to read without putting their souls at risk. The need they recognised was not for 'representativeness' or variety, but for authoritativeness and reliability. This was so important an issue for the medieval centuries that we cannot reflect their concerns adequately without basing the choice of 'writers' in this volume to some degree on the answers they gave to the question, 'what should we read to improve ourselves?'

God's Word

The starting point was Scripture. In the period we are concerned with, the canon of Scripture was largely settled. It was not in dispute that there existed a body of texts which had been inspired by God himself and which were therefore the Word of God. There was still room for disagreement about the status of some of the apocryphal materials. As we shall see, Jerome was still considering that question at the end of the fourth century.

The meaning of 'inspired' prompted some discussion. The iconography of the four evangelists in the West shows them writing at the dictation of a dove, representing the Holy Spirit, which has its beak in their ears. The implication was strong that the Holy Spirit spoke the Word directly to the various authors of the books of the Bible, who simply wrote it down.

Something similar, though not exactly the same, could be entertained for the Old Testament prophets. In his *Prologue* to his reflections on the Psalms, which were paraphrased in the twelfth century by Peter Lombard and recast again about 1230,[14] Cassiodorus gave definitions to help his readers 'know where they were' with prophets. The matter proved quite knotty, once one got down to it. Was every prophet inspired in the same way? Some prophecy appears to be intellectual, some spiritual, some bodily. *Inspiratio*, it was suggested, involved direct input from the Holy Spirit. A mere dream or vision was not strictly 'inspiration'.[15]

Gregory the Great had been able to identify in Scripture examples of prophecies in all three main tenses, that is, referring to past, present or future. His notion was that prophecy is correctly to be identified not primarily as the prediction of the future, but as the ability to see what is hidden.[16] Gregory had also raised the question whether prophets are always prophesying in everything they say.[17] All these and other running questions interested writers involved in the thirteenth century debate about the nature of prophecy. Philip the Chancellor, William of Auvergne, Alexander of Hales look, among other points, at the claim of Amos (7:14) that he was not a prophet. When a prophet says 'I am not a prophet', he appears to be placing his reader in the position of the Cretan who says: 'All Cretans are liars'. If one tries to believe him one enters a paradox, for if he is truly a prophet and is prophesying truly, he is not a prophet, which cannot be true if he is truly a prophet. Intricate as this question became, it rests on a single strong presumption, that some writers in some circumstances have had a degree of divine assistance which places their utterances on a level of authority which is more than human.

Jerome encountered a further ramification of this assumption when he translated the Bible into the improved Latin version which won universal acceptance as the Vulgate. Was the translator himself inspired? Jerome was sure he himself was not, and said so, but the readers and commentators of the Middle Ages consistently took his Latin version to be 'the Word'. They analysed every turn of phrase exactly as they would have done if God had spoken into the ears of the evangelists and prophets in Jerome's Latin. *Interpres* also means 'interpreter'. A rendering into another language is itself an interpretation, presenting one face of an original text. But interpretation could also extend to making additional remarks by way of commentary.

Here several questions were also enormously important for medieval ideas of what guaranteed or pointed to 'authoritativeness' in writing. The first was how exegesis should be done, on what principles it should proceed. It took some centuries in the West for a common system to be adopted. In Augustine's day, in the absence of a better source or authority on exegetical method, it was still necessary for Augustine as a Catholic commentator to rely on the experiments of the Donatist Tichonius, whom he regarded as a heretic. Gregory the Great was successful in the sixth century with his division of the literal (or 'historical') sense from the three figurative senses. These figurative senses he identified as the tropological (which asked what moral lesson the passage carried); the allegorical (which asked what 'transferred' or 'spiritual' meaning the word might have); and the anagogical (the prophetic or eschatological).

The problem to which Tichonius and Gregory alike were trying to provide a solution was the fact that Scripture appears to be full of anomalies and opacities and contradictions, although that obviously cannot be the case if God is its author, and dictated every word. Many of the difficulties of interpretation disappear if some of the meanings 'intended' are not as they seem on the face of the page, but figurative.

Following on after Scripture: the idea of 'the Fathers'

The next question facing the reader and author was what use was to be made of authors writing after the closing of the canon. Jerome wrote a *De viris illustribus*, in which he listed the Christian authors who might be read by enquirers who wished to know who to trust for interpretation of Scripture, for moral guidance and for theological opinion.

It was not usual at first to speak of 'Fathers' at all except with reference to the *patres* of the Old Testament, the patriarchs. Augustine may have been the first to apply the word 'Father' to a writer who was not a bishop, when he used it of Jerome.[18] 'Fathers' gradually began to seem an appropriate term for the ancient, senior, most respected Christian authors. It carried with it the assumption that there had been at least two great ages of writing about the Christian faith, that of the composition of the books which found their way into the canon of Scripture and a later but still special age when writings of high authority came into being, possessing a reliability and an authority which could not be matched by the writings of more recent authors. If that was so, when did that age end? Or did it perhaps continue, with a few latter-day 'Fathers' still holding a distinct place in the scheme of things at the divine behest? Some twelfth-century collections contain extracts from Anselm of Canterbury, Bernard of Clairvaux, Hugh of St Victor, who have found a natural place alongside Augustine and Gregory the Great.

As Robert Grosseteste put it in the thirteenth century, later authors were *patrum vestigia sequentes*, 'following in the footsteps of the Fathers'.[20] If there came to be a special class of authors who could safely be followed in this way, what were the qualifications for membership? Were certain individuals down the ages favoured with divine assistance in their thinking even much later than the earliest period of the Church? Or was it merely a matter of seniority, orthodoxy, reliability? Was there a diminishing authority fading out gradually after the period when the canon of the Bible came into being? A clean break?

Did sheer antiquity count? Augustine makes some reference to this idea.[21] Isidore touches on the question too.[22] The notion that the earliest is the most reliable became stronger in the sixteenth century, when the cry *ad fontes*, 'back to the sources', was fashionable. For the Middle Ages another theme was perhaps more important, that of *antiqui et moderni*. By the late twelfth and thirteenth centuries there was a developing sense that some authors were respectable because they belonged to a former age whereas contemporaries were fair game for challenge or disagreement. To die might be to enter abruptly into the realm of the *antiqui* and thus to move out of the reach of the academic parry and thrust of contemporary rivals.

In Sigebert of Gembloux we find discussion of the *antiqui* and the *moderni*,[23] and also in Peter the Venerable, who lists *Ambrosium, Augustinum, Gregorium, antiquos et sanctos ecclesie doctores*, and *ad moderni temporis doctos et catholicos viros, Lanfrancum, Guithmundum, Algerum*. He suggests that the latter may be helpful for their sheer 'local' closeness and 'domestic' familiarity.[24] By Ockham's day there was consciousness of a division between *antiqui* and *moderni* ('although many modern doctors writing today contest that opinion')[25] because 'neither in the philosophers nor in the ancient Christian writers (*in antiquis sanctis*) or anywhere else is it found that they make that distinction'.[26]

De viris illustribus

A series of names emerged, who eventually formed a loose group known as 'the Fathers', ending roughly with Bede. We can begin to trace this evolution and its accompanying debate about 'standing' more systematically by looking at what happened to the tradition Jerome began with his *De viris illustribus*. Gennadius of Marseilles (late fifth century) continued Jerome's work with about a hundred extra names, taken mainly from the fifth century, drawn from both Eastern and Western halves of the Empire.

The *Decretum Gelasianum*, 'On books to be received and books not to be received' (*De libris recipiendis vel non recipiendis*) was usually held in the Middle Ages to have been a *decretum* of Pope Gelasius (492–6), and that gave it 'authority' on the subject of 'authoritativeness'.[27] It begins with a list of books of the Old and New Testaments which it identifies as those 'on which the catholic Church was founded (*fundata est*) by the grace of God'. It includes a list of writings whose use the Church does not prohibit. There are also references to works of Gregory of Nazianzen, Basil, Athanasius, John of Constantinople, Theophilus Alexandrinus, Cyril of Alexandria, Hilary of Poitiers, Ambrose, Augustine, Jerome, Prosper of Aquitaine, *gesta* of the martyrs and *vitae patrum*, Rufinus, Origen, Eusebius of Caesarea, Orosius, Sedulius and Iuvencus. There is a chapter on those works which are not to be received because they contain heretical teachings.

This text became the touchstone or reference point for the trustworthiness and Christian standing of early authors. The idea of bringing the list up to date proved attractive from time to time.[28] The

Libri Carolini, to which we shall come in a moment, already tend to prefer Western authorities such as Ambrose, Jerome, Augustine, Hilary and Gregory the Great, and they keep on the whole to the Gelasian list.[29] Sigebert of Gembloux wrote a latter-day *De viris illustribus* in the late eleventh century, consciously bringing to his own time what Jerome and Gennadius had done (vaingloriously placing his own works, at some length, at the end).

Flowers from the Fathers

A 'book' does not have to be the work of a single author, or even of contemporary authors. Medieval readers were happy with something very like scrapbooks. The notion that extracts from earlier writers are like flowers which can be put together in a posy and thus form a book in their own right is an ancient one. Clement of Alexandria uses the image in his *Miscellanies* (*Stromateis*),[30] to compare the variegated medley of flowers in a meadow to his own collection. Plutarch, Aelian, Athenaeus and the younger Pliny do something similar,[31] as does Aulus Gellius.

Aulus Gellius was born in the first quarter of the second century AD. His *Attic Nights*[32] is a miscellany, much of it taken from secondary sources and making no claims to be more than a derivative but entertaining notebook of anecdote and bits of philosophy. He used to jot down things which struck him as he read on winter evenings in Attica, he explains, although he evidently did not read many of his sources in the original. He discusses the genre somewhat portentously, finding thirty examples of appropriate titles for such miscellanies in both Greek and Latin. He admits that he himself has been selective. It is his principle (Preface, 12) that 'much learning does not make a scholar'. He has attempted to devise a way for busy people to avoid being ignorant. He says that he had in mind in writing it the creation of something improving for beginners to relax with, when they have a moment's leisure. That does not mean he has avoided difficult topics or presented only familiar materials; he hopes that some of his extracts will be new to readers. He expects those whose appetites have been whetted to follow up with serious study for themselves. His derivativeness did not discourage others from using him as a source in his turn. He was taken quite as seriously as he could have wished. Macrobius did so, and there is an approving reference to Aulus Gellius in Augustine's *The City of God* (IX, 4) as *vir elegantissime eloquii et facundae scientiae*.

There was thus both a serious pedagogic purpose and a

recreational purpose in drawing on earlier work. Two or three centuries into the Christian era there was, for pagan or Christian, already too much to read, certainly too much for it to be possible to own or have access to copies of everything which was available.[33] It became useful to be able to be selective, to have guidance about what was worth reading. It also became convenient to have the most striking or entertaining portions to hand. That could lead, as in Aulus Gellius, to an emphasis on light entertainment and memorable anecdote, or to the serious and important task of creating a reference book for those at the cutting edge of theology.

One way of knowing when an author has 'arrived' at patristic status in medieval eyes is to see what company he keeps in collections of extracts. Conversely, a development which strongly encouraged later writers to look for 'authority' in the writings of their predecessors was the habit of extracting from the texts short portions which could be quoted to support a particular viewpoint. Collections of such useful extracts were commonplace in the Carolingian period and beyond. The methodology remained in use throughout the Middle Ages. It kept a range of authors in play. But it unavoidably led to the breaking up into small pieces of what may have been an extended argument in the original.

It was about 700 that 'patristic texts' began to be seen in canonical collections in the West, for example, in the *Collectio Hibernensis*. The *Libri Carolini* is a useful example of a collaborative enterprise.[34] The Second Nicene Council of 787 had restored the Byzantine East to an iconophile position. This change, and with it the apparent ending of the iconoclastic controversy, was welcomed by Pope Hadrian. A copy of the proceedings of the Council (in Latin) came to the court of Charlemagne. The Emperor was unaware of the Papal approval of what had been agreed, and he set about having a rejoinder drawn up, on the assumption that the East was still in the wrong. This exercise of 'amassing headings against the synod', *capitulare adversus synodum*, was formally orchestrated by Theodulph, still in ignorance of papal approval, as a critique of the Council. Politically misconceived though it turned out the enterprise was, it had the value of causing Carolingian scholars to think out their position on the use of authorities. The *Libri Carolini* make the point that the Holy Spirit is not now given in the measure in which he was given in apostolic times: *secundum apostolicae mensurae gratiam* (IV.20).[35]

The ninth-century Sedulius Scottus's *Collectaneum miscellaneum* is a collection of excerpts of Biblical, patristic, classical materials, including ready-made *florilegia*, which it has been suggested were copied out perhaps as an aide-memoire rather than as a teaching aid. He speaks with respect of the wisdom of the Greeks, as 'like multicoloured precious stones', which he has brought together with care and effort.[36] Burchard of Worms has a significant proportion of patristic texts (247 out of 1,785). Ivo of Chartres speaks of *orthodoxi patres* (PL 161.47), including popes, councils and *scriptores ecclesiastici*. Gratian includes a good deal of patristic material (on the authority perhaps of Gelasius's list *De libris legendis et reiiciendis*).[37] So our writers are often used in extracted form with no expectation that the user will go back and read the whole book.

This system of collecting extracts largely provided the materials for the *Glossa ordinaria*, the standard commentary on the Bible which was brought finally into being in the twelfth century, on the basis of work stretching back several centuries. For certain books of the Bible a single patristic commentator tended to be dominant. For example, Gregory the Great is naturally very important on the book of Job, because of his much-read *Moralia*. The seventh-century Irish monk Lathchen abbreviated Gregory's thoughts on Job in his *Egloga* and that formed a 'work' in its own right, but one with a different purpose.[38]

The same habit of working from collections of extracts underlies the *Sentences* (*sententiae*, or opinions) of Peter Lombard, which became the standard theological textbook from the thirteenth century. It prompted Thomas Aquinas as late as the thirteenth century to put together a 'Catena Aurea', a 'golden chain' of quotations on the Gospels.[39]

When the authorities disagree

A result of the habit of collecting and collating extracts was that it became disturbingly clear that there could be contradictions between ostensibly reliable authors, that Christian 'authorities' disagreed with one another. That was hard to reconcile with the presumption that there was divine guidance (if not divine inspiration) behind what they had said, for it was upon that presumption that the authority of the texts ultimately rested. Not until very late in the Middle Ages was it really permissible to grade authorities for reliability except broadly, in descending order of trustworthiness, Scripture, Christian Fathers, secular classics.

Peter the Chanter, in his *De Tropis Loquendi* at the end of the twelfth century, tackled the problem of resolving contradictions by pointing out that if a statement is taken figuratively it may be possible for it to slide over other statements, which are being taken literally, or taken figuratively, but in another sense, without conflict arising between them. Robert Grosseteste explored still further ramifications of the problem in the first half of the thirteenth century. He says the problem is not in the texts but in our understanding of the texts. He took writers such as Augustine to be channels of the Holy Spirit's teaching (*Spiritus Sancti fistulae*). If we 'hear' them to be discordant, it is simply that we are not listening properly; we have not understood the deep harmony of what they are saying. We are spiritually tone deaf. Real 'spiritual musicians' would not be confused. 'There is a superficial discord and a hidden harmony'.[40] Wherever possible, the interpreter or later writer making use of these authoritative texts should seek to bring out that harmony.

Robert Grosseteste acknowledges that that is sometimes impossible. One explanation he offers is that when the Fathers seem to be stating facts they may actually be merely proposing possibilities. Another explanation involves resort to the 'prophecy' debate; just as prophets do not always prophesy in everything they say but have days or times when they are speaking simply as themselves (*propheta non sum*, Amos 7:14), so perhaps the Holy Spirit was not telling these important early Christian authors directly to write every word they set down. Perhaps sometimes he left it to them to use their own words, so that we might profit (*proveniret nobis aliquis utilis fructus*) from the disagreements.[41] But to say that is to emphasise the distinction between the canonical texts and those of later Christian writers who are becoming merely 'secondary' authorities.

Might a medieval writer presume to contradict the Fathers or other earlier authors himself? There was no hesitation about contradicting one's contemporaries. As we shall see, there is ample evidence of that in academic lectures and other products of the era of the first universities. Rupert of Deutz says that he attracted criticism in the early twelfth century because he had suggested that Augustine was not 'in the canon'.[42] It was late in the Middle Ages before one could say of an authority, 'but he was only a man'.[43]

'Borrowed or shared'

This respect for the authorities keeps company with a curious looseness about *meum* and *tuum*. Medieval writers did not share the modern notion of the dishonesty of plagiarism. Alcuin was capable of describing extracts from other authors' work as his own work: *haec mea dicta*. The medieval willingness to claim ownership of what has been written by others disturbs only the modern eye. When Alcuin does that, he is working on an assumption, which will be important throughout this book. The less a writer used his own words, the better and safer. It was, as we have been seeing, good practice for anyone seeking to make a contribution to Christian literature to collect extracts from earlier reputable Christian authors to rely on; and the best way to rely on the authorities was to quote them, stringing together a chain of quotations.

There was as yet no convention of punctuation which would make it possible to indicate by the use of inverted commas where one's own words ended and the borrowed ones began. There was no system of references which would make it possible to put the references in the footnotes. The 'weaving together' of the existing materials could therefore range from something very simple to something extremely sophisticated. In *florilegia* such as the *Liber scintillarum* of Defensor of Ligugé we find a simple scrapbook. Bernard of Clairvaux, by contrast, had plenty of eloquence of his own, but he so lived and breathed Scripture that it was impossible for him constantly not to refer to it or quote it, so his prose is actually a woven textile of the Word of God and his own words.

So these are the parameters within which our writers worked. They were deferential to the past, often challenging to their contemporaries, almost never writing in isolation. They form a 'company' of writers.

What can we learn from the fifty examples which follow, about the reasons this body of medieval thinking and writing came into existence? Writing a book is hard work. Even the most mechanical exercises of these writers cost them tremendous effort. Sheer dogged thoroughness characterises such enterprises as that which Johannes Altenstaig put together in his *Vocabularius theologiae* (Hagenau, 1517), a massive compilation of technical theological terms with references to the opinions and definitions of authors who had come to count as authorities.

How did medieval thinkers identify problems to write about and set themselves the various tasks on which we have seen them engaged? Modern thinkers often consciously discuss their 'positions' and 'schools of thought'. Labels such as 'deconstructionism' and 'postmodernism' have their medieval equivalents in 'nominalism and 'realism'. Modern 'schools' in the sense of 'followers of a leading thinker' also have medieval parallels. Yet few of the thinkers in this book approach their work in this way by consciously seeking to take forward a 'school of thought'. The stimuli which got them writing were different. On one level, they can claim that they were 'asked'. Sometimes they were commissioned to write by a royal or ecclesiastical patron, or made a dedication to such a person in order to suggest that they were. Frequently they claim that friends or pupils have pressed them to write, and sometimes no doubt that was true. They say that they write: 'to assist my brothers'; for edification; for the common good (*utilitas*); to fill a gap not covered by the ancients; to please a patron. But the modesty *topos* required the making of some such disclaimer, even if it was not true. Yet often the late Middle Ages saw thinkers writing in the fire of the moment, eager to make their contribution to a controversy.

Whatever his pretext for writing, an author has to make a decision about the *kind* of thing he is going to write. In the first Christian centuries there were natural 'Christian' genres, for example the exegetical homily, expounding the Bible to a congregation. Such homilies could be lengthy and could form extended series, as was the case for Augustine's *Ennarrationes* on the Psalms or his sermons on St John's Gospel. From that practice was to develop the commentary. There were other genres borrowed from the existing secular literature. For instance, the letter was well-established in antiquity as a literary form. Some of these *epistolae* were lengthy, forming books in their own right. It might be no small matter to arrange for a messenger to cross Europe with a letter so one would make the best use of the opportunity perhaps and send a short monograph, unless the messenger was capable of conducting the negotiation himself, in which case one might sent a flowery greeting and little more. There was the 'philosophical dialogue', the formal conversation on a philosophical or theological subject. There was the soliloquy, the private reflection of an individual. Both of these had ancient precedent. There was the prescriptive manual or handbook on how to do something. Cicero's little book on the way an orator could find arguments, much used in the Middle Ages, is an example.

Such genres had their imitators in the Middle Ages in the twelfth century, for example in the three 'medieval rhetorical *artes*'. The first of these, the 'art' of letter-writing, developed in the late eleventh century to meet the growing need for competent letter writers in the papal chancery and in the civil services of kings and emperors, as their mutual correspondence grew. The *ars dictaminis* drew on the rhetorical tradition for its teaching on the form a letter should take, the etiquette of salutation at the beginning and the need for a *captatio benevolentiae*. The second, the 'art' of poetry, concentrated upon the use of figures. The *artes poetriae* of the twelfth century were not all notable for their tautness of arrangement. They often ramble and appear to emerge from an oral tradition. Geoffrey of Vinsauf's *Poetria nova* is unusually orderly and rigorous. It is divided into sections dealing with such matters as the arrangement of a poem, amplification and abbreviation, style, memory and delivery. The arts of preaching, which reached their height of development in the thirteenth century, concentrated on the structure of a sermon, how to take a theme (a text from Scripture) and divide up its implications so as to treat them systematically one by one. The twelfth century also invented manuals for confessors, and, on the literary front, preachers' manuals. There was a new generation of encyclopaedias, such as Hugh of St Victor's *Didascalicon*; there were experiments with *summae*, a more advanced way of bringing together a great deal of knowledge or debate in a convenient and orderly form.

There was much that was experimental and even new: 'vices and virtues' literature; dream allegory, literary 'places' where the struggle between good and evil could be played out in drama. Poetry and spirituality, poetry and eroticism, might not be far apart. Dispute shaded into polemic on the page. Pathways were evolved to write about history and biography and science (the philosophical poem, such as Lucretius's *De Rerum Naturae*, has its medieval equivalents).

The intellectual interests of an age are reflected to some degree in its libraries. Through most of the period with which we have been concerned writings were predominantly in the hands of institutions such as monasteries and cathedral libraries, or being handled and taught in other institutions such as the developing universities. (University booksellers soon arose, who would hire out the portion of a text to be commented on by a lecturer at a given stage in the syllabus.)

It made a difference here that publication in the Middle Ages did not require acceptance of a book by a publisher, revisions, copyediting or marketing. A single copy was published as soon as it was circulated, and it might never be copied and multiplied beyond a small group of recipients. Where it was, later 'editions' could be put out by the author as often as he wanted to revise it, to the confusion of modern editors. Some of the literature of late medieval academe survives in the form of a *reportatio*, or students' notes of lectures taken at the master's wish, and more or less thoroughly reworked by him.

Towards the end of the Middle Ages, and especially with the invention of printing, there was a notable increase in private collections of books for personal use. This could be a matter of proprietorial vanity, even one-upmanship. It does not necessarily tell us how eagerly the owners read their books, but it does tell us that it was a matter of pride to be a book collector. After the invention of printing, manuscripts retained a certain snob value in such collections, even if it was only a respect for 'old' books in a new form. Pico della Mirandola and others made and exchanged inventories of their collections. He had nearly twelve hundred items, among them a hundred in Hebrew. So we are entering an age when writers might be 'collected'.

The advent of interest in Greek texts in this period is an important indicator of the changes which were to make the sixteenth century subtly different from its predecessors. Petrarch owned copies of Plato and Homer but did not have the Greek to enable him to read them. Others – for example Julius II in the period before he became Pope – seem to have collected Greek works in translation for preference. There are also books in the new private collections in the vernaculars, including translations from Greek into the vernacular.

The growth of respect for the vernacular as a vehicle for a man's lasting thoughts is another important indicator of change. Dante wrote *De Monarchia* in Latin, but he chose Italian for the *Divina Commedia*. Chaucer chose English for *The Canterbury Tales*. This was partly a result of the development of certain vernaculars to a point of sophistication where they could express abstractions and rival Latin in what they were able to say. But it is also an index of acceptance. Dante wrote the *Divina Commedia* with great hopes for its future.

The enticing novelty of the books which were being recovered from the Greek tradition at the end of the Middle Ages began to create a revolt against the old syllabus, the familiar authors. Lorenzo Valla, invited to deliver a panegyric in honour of Aquinas on 7 March 1457, chose instead to attack the edifice of late scholasticism at its foundations. Nicholas of Lyre, Ratramnus, Chrysostom, Alexander of Hales, Ambrose, Augustine, Jean Gerson, Anselm, Isidore, Gregory the Great, Gabriel Biel, Peter Lombard, William of Ockham, Aquinas, Duns Scotus, Petrus de Aquila, Aristotle, Bonaventure, Gregory of Rimini, Petrus de Palude, 'Hugo', John Damascene, Hrbanus Maurus, Durandus, Holcot, Jerome, Seneca, Panormitanus (Ivo of Chartres), Boethius, Hilary, Plato, Lactantius, Virgil, Pliny, Hostiensis: thus runs (with other names here omitted) the chronologically random hand-written list of authors cited in the front of Johannes Altenstaig's *Vocabularius theologiae*. That was the conservative list.

Even among the conservatives, a quite different way of thinking was beginning to emerge. The writers we have been looking at began to be read more as *fontes* (sources) than as *auctoritates*. For example, in the entry on whether any people should be given preferential treatment (*acceptio personarum*), Altenstaig cites a view of Alexander of Hales. Melanchthon and Johannes Eck have become reliable sources. In a similar exercise, the *Vocabularius* of 1511, Altenstaig collects extracts from grammarians on grammatical points. Here, too, there is no special elevation of authorities, just a workmanlike assembling of convenient material for reference. In 'Theologists in Council', by Johannes Jäger (1480–*c*.1545) may be read the spoof minutes of a faculty meeting chaired by Reuchlin's enemy Jacob Hoogstraten. 'I never approved of that "new" fashion and those "new" doctors', cries one ignorant speaker, grouping 'Jerome, Augustine, Athanasius and those poets, even though I don't know what they wrote and can't understand it'.[44]

For some time, it had been possible to detect changing fashions in the preoccupations of writers. In commentaries on Peter Lombard's *Sentences*, for example, there is a shifting of emphasis decade by decade and place by place through the centuries, as one topic of fashionable interest gave way to another. This academic game was not merely about ideas; we shall see it lead to heated controversy. But in the early sixteenth century some of those ideas became divisive in a more serious way. The discussion about where the *locus* of primary authority for the Christian faith lay led to the setting up of camps: *sola Scriptura*, 'Scripture alone' became the reforming cry, because it was argued that the institutional Church had been claiming too much. 'Faith alone', *sola fide*, was a counterblast to the teaching that it was necessary to salvation to do good works and to pay the penalty in kind, and by acts of reparation, for the 'bad' works which constituted sins.

So, at the end of the Middle Ages something altered. Luther's training and that of Calvin were essentially different. An approach to academic writing which had been becoming more constrained and even mechanical for some generations opened out again into experiment. It became possible to throw things away. Peter Ramus reconstructed the teaching of logic and made it much simpler; not very well, from a logicians' point of view, but persuasively for many of those who had to study the subject, because it was easier.

The *catena* scholarship of *florilegium* compilations had its ancient ancestry and it was not to come to an end with the sixteenth century.

But in its medieval phase it had had certain characteristics astutely observed by Mark Pattinson and John Henry Newman in the middle of the nineteenth century in the preparation of an English translation of Aquinas's *Catena Aurea*, the 'golden chain' of the commentaries on the Gospels. Pattinson suggests that until the time of Gregory the Great the Fathers were writing original commentaries, with 'a distinctive spirit and manner, by which each may be known from the rest'. But about the sixth to seventh century, 'this originality disappears'; 'it hardened', he suggests, 'into a written tradition, and henceforward there is a uniform invariable character as well as substance of scripture interpretation'. 'All later comments are in fact catenas or selections from the earlier Fathers'.[45] The exchange between Wyclif and Kennyngham illustrates a methodological truism of medieval debate. Authorities can always be marshalled on both sides. Reasoning can be seen as being used to weigh them,[46] or, more typically, to provide the framework in which they act as propositions supporting a position. The great achievement of the Middle Ages was the development of technical precision in the use of logic and language to conduct this weighing exercise. The ancient world had nothing to set beside this, largely because the education of citizens had a philosophical and rhetorical emphasis. But with the end of the fifteenth and the beginning of the sixteenth century the nature of the task changed, with the perception that there were books in the world with which one might make free, ideas one might conjure with.

Pico della Mirandola wrote a book on 'The dignity of man' (*De hominis dignitate*)[47] which begins with a pairing of Scriptural and classical tradition. 'Man is a great wonder, Asclepius'[48] 'What a piece of work is a man' (cf. Ps.8). He links the testimonies of Moses and Plato that God made man last in the order of creation, as its pinnacle. Now classical and Christian writing began a new relationship.

Notes

1 Augustine, *De beata vita*, I.4, CCSL.
2 Cassiodorus, Preface, *Expositio Psalmarum*, CCSL, 97 (1959), pp. 3–4.
3 Augustine, *Contra Academicos*, II.iv.10, CCSL, 29, p. 23.
4 Augustine, *Contra Academicos*, II.iv.10, CCSL, 29, p. 23.
5 Letter 3.1, CSEL, 34i, pp. 6–8.
6 Letter 25.2, CSEL, 34i, p. 79.
7 William of Ockham, *De corpore Christi*, 3, *Opera Theologica X* (St Bonaventure, NY, 1986), p. 94.

8 Augustine, *Epistulae*, 202A.4, CCSL, 57, p. 307.

9 *Deinde auctoritates inducit quibus haec sententia roboratur*, Peter Lombard, *Sentences*, III, capitula, p. 4; *Auctoritates ponit quibus suam muniunt sententiam*, Peter Lombard, *Sentences*, III, dist. 6.ii.2.

10 It is possible to get a picture of the pattern of transmission of a particular text by looking at the description of the 'family tree' or *stemma* of manuscripts on which a good modern edition has been based and the editor's introductory remarks on the relationship of the earliest one.

11 *Doctores egregii, sancti Patres scripturae Divinae expositores clarissimi ac a Romana Ecclesia authenticati.* William of Ockham, *De corpore Christi* 3, *Opera Theologica X* (St Bonaventure, NY, 1986), p. 94.

12 William of Ockham, *De corpore Christi* 4, *Opera Theologica X* (St Bonaventure, New York, 1986), p. 95.

13 William of Ockham, *De corpore Christi* 22, *Opera Theologica X* (St Bonaventure, NY, 1986), p. 140. Cf. *auctoritas alicuius doctoris authentici.*

14 *Prophetia est inspiratio vel revelatio divina rerum eventus immobili veritate denoncians.*

15 Cassiodorus's word was *aspiratio*. Cassiodorus, *Expositio Psalmarum*, CCSL, 97 (1958), p. 7, *Praefatio*, Chapter 1.

16 J.-P.Torrell, 'Théorie de la prophétie et philosophie de la connaissance aux environs de 1230', *Spicilegium Sacrum Lovaniense* 40 (1977), p. 5.

17 *Recte prophetia dicitur non quia predicit ventura, sed quia videt* [or prodit] *occulta*, Gregory the Great, *In Hiezechihelem prophetam*, I.i, CCSL, 142, p. 5; J.-P. Torrell, 'Théorie de la prophétie et philosophie de la connaissance aux environs de 1230', *Spicilegium Sacrum Lovaniense* 40 (1977), p. 7.

18 Gregory the Great, *In Hiezechihelem prophetam*, I.i.4, p.7 and I.i.16, CCSL, 142, pp. 7, 13.

19 J. Werckmeister, 'The Reception of the Church Fathers in Canon Law', Backus.

20 Robert Grosseteste, *De Cessatione Legalium*, ed. R.C. Dales and E.B. King (Oxford, 1986), III.i.30, p. 132.

21 *Si ergo nec scripturarum auctoritatis antiquitas Contra Faustum* XIII.6, p. 384.14: *Quod utique cavere debuit interpretum antiquitas, nisi etiam fidei haec esset antiquis, cui vestra coepit resistere novitas. Contra Iulianum* VI, col. 841.

22 *Cuius antiquior et potior extat auctoritas*, PL 83.901.

23 Sigebert of Gembloux, *Epistula de ieiuniis quattuor temporum*, Ep. 2.

24 *Vos mitterem, si saltem vel hos non pro maioris auctoritate sed pro temporis vicinitate et domestica cognitione dignaremini legere vel pateremini audire*, Peter the Venerable, *Contra Petrobrusianos haereticos*, ch. 153.

25 William of Ockham, *De corpore Christi* 37, *Opera Theologica X* (St Bonaventure, NY, 1986), p. 206.

26 Ockham, *De Quantitate*, Q.I.a.1, p. 34.

27 *Das Decretum Gelasianum de libris recipiendis et non recipiendis*, ed. E. von Dobschütz (Leipzig, 1912).

28 *Das Decretum Gelasianum de libris recipiendis et non recipiendis*, ed. E. von Dobschütz (Leipzig, 1912), pp. 66ff.

29 Otten in Backus, p. 18.

30 6.2.1 cf. 7.111.1–3.

31 Letter 1.i.1.

32 Aulus Gellius, *Attic Nights*, ed. J.C. Rolfe (Cambridge, MA, 1927/1961).

33 L. Holford Stevens, Aulus Gellius (London, 1988), pp. 21 and 115–6.

34 M.L.W. Laistner, *Thought and Letters in Western Europe, 500–900* (Ithaca, NY, 1931/1966).

35 *The Libri Carolini*, ed. H. Bastgen, *MGH Legum*, sectio III, *Concilia II, Supplementum*, ed. A. Freeman and P. Meyvaeart, *MGH Concilia II*, 1997.

36 Sedulius Scottus's *Collectaneum miscellaneum*, ed. D. Simpson, CCCM, 67 (1988), p. 3.

37 J. Werckmeister, 'The Reception of the Church Fathers in Canon Law', Backus.

38 Lathchen, *Egloga*, ed. M. Adraian, CCSL, 145 (1969).

39 Aquinas, *Catena Aurea in Quatuor Evangelia*, ed. P. Angelici Guarienti (Rome, 1952).

40 Robert Grosseteste, *De Cessatione Legalium*, ed. R.C. Dales and E.B. King (Oxford, 1986), IV.iii.165.

41 Robert Grosseteste, *De Cessatione Legalium*, ed. R.C. Dales and E.B. King (Oxford, 1986), IV.ii.165.

42 *At illi me ex hoc diffamare coperunt tanquam haereticum qui dixissem non esse in canone beatum Augustinum* (PL 70.495–6).

43 See my *Problems of Authority in the Reformation Debates* (Cambridge, 1992).

44 *Scheming Papists and Lutheran Fools: Five Reformation Satires*, trans. E. Rummell (New York, 1993).

45 Thomas Aquinas, *Catena Aurea* , trans. Mark Pattinson, reprinted with an introduction by Aidan Nicholls (Saint Austin Press, 1997), p. ii of 1841 edition.

46 *tum quia auctoritates pro utraque parte de facili possunt glossari, tum etiam quia scio quod tam profundus clericus non poneret opiniones extreaneas, nisi haberet pro illis multas rationes efficaces, immo quasi demonstrationes. Fasciculi Zizaniorum*, p. 12.

47 Pico della Mirandola, *De hominis dignitate*, ed. E. Barbaro (Rome, 1986).

48 Asclepius, *Hermetica*, ed. Scott (Oxford, 1924), I.294.

AUGUSTINE OF HIPPO 354–430

Life and times

The parameters

At the beginning of our story, many of Christianity's earliest battles had been satisfactorily fought and settled. Constantine the Great had made Christianity the established religion of the Roman Empire. During his reign the Nicene Creed had been framed (at the Council of Nicaea, 325). There was political acceptance that this was a religion which could not be drawn into the syncretistic contemporary mix of late classical polytheisms. A *modus vivendi* with its spiritual and intellectual rivals among the diverse faiths and philosophies of the late Roman world was precariously in balance, and Christianity was consciously trying to keep its balance and retain its integrity in making borrowings from earlier writing.

Some of the most intelligent and well-educated now embraced Christianity openly. Among them was Augustine, a North African who came to the faith slowly and reluctantly, but became probably the most important and influential of all Christian writers after St Paul, certainly during the millennium with which we are concerned.

Augustine is a giant figure in our story not only because of the immense quantity of his writings but also because of their influence. He looms large in all medieval academic and monastic collections of books. He became every writer's point of reference, helping to set the agenda for debate on almost every theological topic until the sixteenth century.

The leading question about Augustine must therefore be how he was able to do so much that appeared to his contemporaries and successors new or significant. A brief answer is that topics were coming to prominence which had not been properly examined before, especially in Latin, notably ecclesiology and the doctrine of the sacraments. Very little frightened Augustine intellectually.

We know a good deal about Augustine's life, partly from his own autobiographical account in the *Confessions*. Augustine was born in 354, in North Africa, to a pagan father and a Christian mother. His mother was ambitious for him and he received a good education, setting up as a teacher of rhetoric at Carthage. His mother also tried to persuade him to become a Christian, but to Augustine's eye as an up-and-coming young orator, the text of Scripture was written in no style he could admire, and he was especially offended as a young

1

man by the apparent crudities of the stories in Genesis. He spent his youth testing a variety of religious and philosophical positions. For ten years he was a Manichee. Manicheeism belongs to a group of 'dualist' systems, in which Gnostics and the later Albigensians, Cathars and Bogomils also fall. It had the great advantage of appearing to resolve the problem of evil. It postulated the existence of two opposed and eternal principles in the universe, the power of good (spirit) and the power of evil (matter). These were engaged in perpetual conflict, which made room for an extensive mythology of battle and many colourful characters for those who had a taste for such things. It also provided religious purpose for the followers who could see themselves as taking part in the war on the side of good, when they subjugated the flesh (matter); and for the 'elect', the leaders of the sect, who were deemed to have privileges and a special role in the cosmic story. Augustine abandoned that adherence only when he was able at last to hear the famous leader Faustus when he arrived in north Africa. Faustus proved not only unable to answer the lingering questions Augustine had eagerly waited for him to come and deal with, but also to be a far less accomplished speaker and a less educated man than Augustine himself.

The disillusioned Augustine decided about this time to go to Italy to better himself. Urged on by his ambitious mother, he sought a post as teacher of oratory which would be more prestigious than the one he had been holding at Carthage. He achieved his ambition in Milan, where, in a period of internal conflict and uncertainty about his future religious and philosophical direction, he went to hear Ambrose, the famous Bishop of Milan, preaching on Genesis. From 384 to the spring of 385, when his mother arrived to join him in Rome, Augustine continued occasionally to hear Ambrose preach. His general impression was that Ambrose knew more than Faustus the Manichee. Then, perhaps in the company of his mother, he began to go to hear Ambrose more regularly (*Confessions* V.xiii.23 and VI.iii.4). Now he found that he was impressed despite himself. Augustine still had a great deal of thinking to do to rationalise for himself the intellectual position in which he remained after withdrawing from the Manichees. Although he did not directly 'bring Augustine to Christ', Ambrose undoubtedly helped him to form his mature views on the nature of God, on evil and on the nature of Christ. In Holy Week 386, Ambrose was using borrowings from the Cappadocian Fathers to illuminate some of the very problems which had struck Augustine when he himself had earlier read Genesis, with some distaste. Moreover, these questions were being handled with a philosophical sophistication and literary eloquence which won his professional admiration. He went to try to talk to Ambrose, but he found than many others were waiting to see him too and that he had to take his turn. That whetted his appetite further.

Augustine's conversion to Christianity was no doubt prompted in part by this episode, and by the inner turmoil of his feelings. He was beginning to recognise that the Bible in its simplicity was able to teach the uneducated as well as the educated, and to conjure with the notion that higher truths may be explained to the simple in relatively unrefined language, stylistically speaking. His old intellectual snobbery about the text was undergoing modification. Now that his mother had joined him in Italy, she wanted him to become a provincial governor. A suitable marriage had accordingly been arranged, to a girl who was as yet very young, but as a token of good faith Augustine had had to send away his long-term mistress, the mother of his son Adeodatus. This distressed him profoundly. He also relates how he had arrived at crisis point over his attempts to resist such temptations as the theatre of the day afforded. He was in that state of resistance which classically precedes the decisive moment of conversion.[1]

One day as he sat in a garden he heard a child singing next door, 'take up and read'. He picked up the text of the book of Romans he had with him and his eye fell at random on the passage, 'not in chambering nor in wantonness'. This was a familiar device in the ancient world, the *sortilegium*, allowing fate to make a difficult decision. For Augustine, it became, rather, a moment of divine guidance, which brought him to an authentic 'conversion' experience, and from that moment in 386 he was a committed Christian.

He next did what he had always longed to do. He went into philosophical retirement with a few friends at Cassiciacum on Lake Como and thought his way through the implications of his new faith. Then he was baptised. He then returned to north Africa, his mother dying of a sudden infection as they were about to sail. On his home shores he set up a 'monastic' community with his friends. Despite his attempts at evasion of what he correctly foresaw to be a likely attempt to capture him for the office by physical 'arrest', it was not long before he was made Bishop of Hippo. He remained bishop there for the rest of his days, preaching and writing.

Work and ideas

In preparation for baptism, Augustine had to think out his faith, and the points at which he would have to change his ideas. That took him into fresh explorations of issues with which (he tells us in the *Confessions*) he had been struggling for years, but now he was approaching them with a new hope and in a new light. At Cassiciacum, Augustine wrote on themes of 'Christian philosophy', trying to reconcile his new faith with the schools of thought for which he had hitherto had respect. With the group of friends who accompanied him into philosophical retirement, he discussed happiness or the blessed life (*De beata vita*), order in the universe (*De ordine*), and wrote a book against the secular philosophers of the 'academy', *Contra academicos*.

Once he was baptised, and especially after he became Bishop of Hippo, Augustine continued to write. One of his early works, from about 389 (after his return to Africa), was the *De Magistro*, 'On the Master'. The book takes the form of a dialogue with his son Adeodatus, short-lived child of his long liaison with a beloved mistress. Adeodatus was a bright adolescent of fifteen or sixteen at the time. Augustine asserts that all the contributions in the book were what he really said. Together, father and son explore epistemological questions such as how we know what is true and how we link words with realities. Augustine developed two key ideas which were to appear in his later work: that words are merely signs, which point to realities; and that the knowledge of (and the test for), truth is internal, not a subjective evaluation, but a divinely in-built sense. *De Doctrina Christiana*, written in four books over a considerable period, contains Augustine's development of his theory of signs. These were to be ideas of immense importance for the Middle Ages, especially once they were conjoined with the work on logic and language which was to be developed out of Aristotle, by Boethius and by applying the work of the Roman grammarians.

A late antique education was a rhetorical education, creating in those who received it a sensitivity to language and habits of critical analysis. That made it important for Christian apologists to assist in discussion not only of the way the Bible was to be interpreted, but also of the hermeneutical 'method' to be used.

The Donatist heretic Tichonius was the first to compose a systematic work on exegesis. He emphasised the importance of spiritual interpretation and discouraged in his own commentary on the apocalypse the rampant millenarianism which is liable to flourish when the end of the world seems to be more than usually close at hand. Tichonius's work was of the utmost importance for the development of hermeneutics in the north Africa of the day. Augustine sensibly chose not to disregard it despite Tichonius's unfortunate affiliation with a group Augustine considered to have put itself outside the Church.

Tichonius sets out *regulae*, or rules, which he proposes as 'keys' to the meaning of Scripture. He suggests that these are universal rules, implicit in Scripture itself, and that they are provided by God in fulfilment of his promise that what is dark shall be illumined and what is closed shall be opened. Augustine adapted the principle to make the rules external to the text, to be applied to it so as to discover its meaning, rather than seeing them, as Tichonius had done, as mystical and inward. We find Augustine's adaptation of Tichonius discussed in later centuries, for example by Hugh of St Victor. But it was Gregory the Great with his fourfold exegesis who created a pattern which the Middle Ages was able to adopt for routine use.

Augustine's actual exegesis was mainly done in the form of preaching. He was a great success as a preacher. He could hold audiences for an hour or more, winning enthusiastic applause (allowable in Church under the conventions of the day). Various series of homilies by Augustine survive – on the Psalms and on St John – which show how he would explore a text at leisure over a considerable period. The study of the Bible was a persistent interest of Augustine's chiefly because he was such an active preacher. Exegesis and homiletic became one for a bishop such as Augustine in the exercise of his teaching responsibilities, especially in these extended series of *enarrationes* on the Psalms and his preaching on John's Gospel. But he also wrote about the theology embedded in Scripture.

Augustine's *De Genesi ad litteram* (393) is an example of the way in which exegesis could become the vehicle for systematic theology. Augustine confesses some bafflement in the course of his attempts to get things theologically clear, but he is confident and reassuring that the Bible will be worth reading even if it is not certain what is to be understood from it. Augustine's first five books of this treatise are concerned predominantly with the 'hints' or *vestigia* of the Trinity to be traced in the Hexaemeron or six days of the Creation; the actual meaning of the word 'days' used in connection with the

Creation, with the talk of 'morning' and 'evening'. Were the days successive, or were they more like points of division or distinctions between types of divine activity? Did God create only one day which was repeated seven times? What does it mean when it says that God rested on the seventh day? How does the divine governance of the world work? What is the nature of angelic knowledge? Books 6–11 deal with the creation of body and soul. Book 12 is on the meaning of Paradise, with an excursus into the types of vision described in Scripture; the nature of rapture and the state of the soul after death before it is rejoined with its body at the Last Judgement; Hell; what is meant by 'the bosom of Abraham'; and on need for the reunion of the soul with the body if there is to be enjoyment of perfect blessedness.

De genesi ad litteram takes an approach which illustrates the interest in and influence upon Augustine of another area of contemporary learning. Augustine describes in the *Confessions* how difficult he found it as a young man to learn to think in the abstract terms philosophy requires, and also bemoans his lack of fluency in Greek. Despite these two handicaps, his thinking became impregnated with Platonic assumptions. Genesis was a special test for him here. It was the superficial crudity of much of Genesis which had put him off Christianity when he was young and his mother was anxious for him to adopt the faith. When he heard Ambrose preach in Milan the sermons were on the Hexaemeron, the six days of creation in Genesis. Ambrose was making use of sophisticated ideas which he was drawing in part from the Cappadocian Fathers, but which had Platonism embedded in them. The 'Cappadocians', Gregory Nazianzen, Gregory of Nyssa, Basil the Great, fall chronologically outside our range, but they are important examples of the Platonising direction in which Greek-speaking scholarship was tending at the end of the ancient world.

A gloomy sense of decay and decline, the 'old age of the world' (*senectus mundi*) had already settled over the Roman Empire by the time of Augustine, with the recognition that the hegemony of Rome was weakening in the face of barbarian challenge. Did Christians have a responsibility to try to rescue the world from its decay? Or could they embrace the signs of the end with gladness, seeing therein the hope of heaven? Augustine favoured that view.

In *The City of God* (413–26), Augustine turned to providence and politics. He began to write it because educated pagan Romans were arriving in north Africa in flight from the barbarian invasion of Italy and putting to Augustine as the local bishop the very reasonable question of how, if the Christians were right about the omnipotence of their God, he could have allowed a Christian Roman Empire to fall. Augustine explained that it was necessary to take a larger view of God's providential purpose. In the divine plan for the salvation of the world the Roman Empire was merely an episode. He encouraged his readers to think eschatologically. God's people were citizens of the heavenly city, and those who were not among that number were citizens of another 'city' altogether. Neither city is visible; it is not possible to know who belongs to each. The baptised Christian is not necessarily among God's chosen and occasionally someone outside the Church may be among the predestined for heaven. But the Christian must go on in faith that he belongs to the heavenly city and get into the habit of thinking of his fellow citizens as including those who have already died and are dwelling there rather than as his next-door neighbours in this world, who may not belong with him at all in eternity.

The good Christian should be living the good Christian life. About 391, Augustine wrote *De Utilitate Credendi*, 'On the benefit of believing', a book mainly designed to help catechists teach able adult beginners in the Christian faith, who may well have awkward and sophisticated questions to ask. That took him eventually into discussion of 'faith and works' (*De fide et operibus*). There was a contemporary pastoral practice of which Augustine disapproved, which was to allow catechumens to attend classes to learn about the faith and arrive at the moment of baptism without any concomitant amendment of life being required of them. Augustine describes with disapproval in the *De fide et operibus* those who believe that God may be pleased by faith alone:

> This is that opinion which says that they who live most evil and disgraceful lives, even though they continue to live in this way will be saved and will gain eternal life, as long as they believe in Christ and receive his sacraments.

On the other hand, he did not approve of the Pelagian teaching that it is good behaviour which counts; on that subject he was vocal in his many 'anti-Pelagian' treatises against the adherents of Pelagius, a society preacher who was persuading the fashionable that they did not need to see themselves as infected by the 'original sin' Augustine said drove all human beings since Adam and Eve helplessly towards doing wrong. They merely needed to work hard at being good. This controversy helped Augustine to clarify his own ideas. He is very clear that the 'fallen human being' is hampered not only by the tendency to commit actual sins, but also by the guilt of this 'original' sin, which is inherited from Adam.

Pelagius appears to have had at heart mainly the reform of the behaviour and moral standards of Christians in Rome. He wrote a commentary on the Pauline Epistles, expounding them in the light of this objective. To tell people they could not help being sinners seemed to him unconducive to encouraging them to behave better. Pelagius came into Augustine's view after he left Italy in 409 with others fleeing into exile from the barbarian threat which culminated in the sack of Rome in 410. He went on to Palestine, where first Jerome and then Orosius challenged him and the nature of his 'heresy' became more visible.

Augustine's mature view of this important complex of problems seems to have been that what God looks for is faith expressed in love. But that, too, had its difficulties

The Augustinian dilemma itself stretched in several further directions. Under Pelagian influence confused and anxious Christians were uncertain what to do about baptism. If there was no original sin there was no need for the sacrament of baptism to remove the guilt and the penalty of original sin. On the other hand, if the Pelagian view was wrong, the risk of hell was terrible. Accordingly, Augustine found himself and his priests baptising the infants of Pelagian followers who were being brought to him for safety's sake. That caused him to think out his theology of sin and to clarify for himself and his readers and listeners the consequences for subsequent human nature of the sin of Adam.

All this made him consider whether the Church was necessarily coextensive with the community of the baptised. Strong though his doctrine of baptism and its importance were, it was also Augustine's view that baptism was not necessary for salvation, that only God knows who are his own and he may, by grace, admit the unbaptised to his favour. Equally, there are always sinners in the visible 'Church' who do not really belong among its citizens at all.

In *De Utilitate Credendi*, Augustine describes his own experience when he became involved with the Manichees: 'I fell among these people only because they said that they would put aside all authority and bring their hearers to God by pure reason'. He admits that he was attracted by the promise of rational explanations which did not require the act of trust inseparable from faith. He now sees things differently. Indeed, once he had left them and become a Christian, he was writing actively against the Manichees, as much to try to clear his own mind as to arm others against Manichee seductions. For he was left with the problem of evil when he abandoned the dualist system. To move to the Christian position was to be confronted with a paradox. Now there was only one power in the universe, a God both wholly good and omnipotent. How then could evil exist, for it could have no association with a perfectly good God, and an omnipotent God would surely not allow it? Augustine's explanation, and the one adopted by almost all Christian thinkers in the West after his time, was that evil is 'nothing', an absence of good, and that it derives from the free choice of rational creatures to turn away from God and disobey his will.

So when he wrote in the mid-390s on free will (*De libero arbitrio*), this was an issue important to him in connection with his continuing difficulty in freeing himself from Manichee suppositions and also – and here he was also to continue to struggle for clarity throughout his lifetime – because he saw that human free will and divine foreknowledge and predestination are no more easily reconciled than the presence of evil in the world with divine goodness and omnipotence.

This was one of a number of themes which recurred throughout Augustine's life, with some of his lengthier books being put together in episodes over as much as twenty years. He was to some degree aware of the dangers of this mode of composition, that it might lead to contradictions. Late in life he reviewed his works, and wrote the *Retractationes* to tidy up any anomalies. He found little that he wished to change. He also wrote his *Confessions* in 397–400. This is not strictly autobiography; nor is it a classical *epistola consolatoria*. It is a spiritual account of a life, interleaving prayer with narrative, exploring thoughts and events so as to build a theology. Its last three books are pure philosophical theology, concerned with such matters as time and memory.

Augustine was also important in the formulation of a number of further themes of Christian doctrine in Latin and within the Western tradition. One of the differences between Greek and Latin is that Latin is a much more concrete language than Greek. Augustine helped to expand its possibilities as a vehicle for the abstract reflection necessary in theology. In the preceding generations there had been a protracted controversy in the Greek-speaking world about the word which should be used for the divine 'substance', that 'same thing' which God 'is' in all three Persons. In *De Trinitate* (400, 406–7, 413–6, 418–21) Augustine tried out the available Latin vocabulary of *natura, substantia, essentia*.

He also experimented with the likeness between the human psyche and the God in whose image and likeness it was created (Genesis 1.28). It struck him that the mode of the relationship enjoyed by Father, Son and Holy Spirit must be in some way reflected in the mind of man, for man is made in the image of God. He therefore looked for psychological imagery to help explain how the one God is three Persons. In each human being 'memory', 'will', 'understanding' can be identified, or 'mind', 'knowledge' and 'love'; yet there are not three people. The individual remains one.

Influence

Augustine was widely read throughout the Middle Ages. In the sixteenth century debates of the Reformation period Augustine was quoted by both sides, for example, on the subject of 'faith and works'. Then the issue was the question Luther had forced everyone to confront: whether it was necessary to salvation to do good works or whether faith alone sufficed to justify the believer in the sight of God.

Note

1   A.D. Nock, Conversion (Oxford, 1993)

Bibliography

Many of Augustine's works are edited in Latin in the *Corpus Christianorum Ecclesiasticorum Latinorum* series and the modern *Corpus Christianorum Series Latina*, both of which should be found in most university libraries. There are also numerous translations, including: *Earlier Writings*, trans. J.H.S. Burleigh (London, 1953); *Later Works*, trans. J. Burnaby (London, 1955); *Augustine* in *Classics of Western Spirituality*, ed. M.T. Clark (London, 1984); *Confessions*, trans. Henry Chadwick (Oxford, 1991).

Further reading

The Augustine bibliography is immense. The following suggestions provide a starting-point, with further reading indicated in the bibliographies in each. General studies: Gerald Bonner, *St. Augustine of Hippo* (London, 1963, 2nd edn Norwich, 1986); Peter Brown, *Augustine of Hippo* (London, 1967); Henry Chadwick, *Augustine* (Oxford, 1986).

Augustine's world: R. Markus, *Saeculum: History and Society in the Theology of St. Augustine* (Cambridge, 1970); Carol Harrison, *Augustine: Christian Truth and Fractured Humanity* (Oxford, 2000).

Work and ideas: Christopher Kirwan, *Augustine* (London, 1989); Gillian Clark, *Augustine: The Confessions* (Cambridge, 1993); G.R. Evans,

Augustine on Evil (Cambridge, 1983); R.F. Evans, *Pelagius: Inquiries and Reappraisals* (London, 1968).

AMBROSE OF MILAN *c.*339–397

Life and times

Ambrose's father held a prominent position in the administration of the Roman Empire, and so Ambrose set out in life with some advantages. He was born at Trier in Gaul in about 339. Trier was quite an important city, where Athanasius of Alexandria had chosen to spend a period of exile from 335–7. There was a strong Christian community in Ambrose's birthplace. His own family may well have been Christian; for example, Ambrose's sister Marcellina consecrated her virginity to God on the feast of Epiphany in 353. Ambrose's own baptism was delayed until 374, when he was forty years old and about to become bishop of Milan, but late adult baptism was still the norm until the end of the fourth century, and that does not in itself indicate a late conversion to the faith on his part. Certainly, it was not now a matter of shame or embarrassment to be a Christian. At the beginning of the fourth century, the Emperor Constantine had made the Empire officially Christian. There was an interruption with the reign of Julian the Apostate, but in 364 a new law restored to Christians their right to teach in schools. Christian adherence was respectable thereafter, an acceptable non-syncretist position to adopt within the multiform society of the Empire, where all other religions but Judaism were prepared to mingle their gods in the common pool.

Ambrose began his own administrative career as a lawyer, in the prefecture. This was a modest civil service role from which he could hope to move on to a provincial governorship, the type of post Augustine's mother was to seek for her own, slightly younger son. In 370 Ambrose duly became governor of Aemilia-Liguria. That took him to Milan, from 370–4.

When the bishopric of Milan became vacant, a disputed election was foreseen and did indeed ensue. Paulinus, in his *Life* of Ambrose, describes an occasion when Ambrose was acclaimed as bishop by a crowd in the church, because a child called out 'Ambrose bishop' and those present took up the cry. Ambrose, bowing to the convention of the day, or perhaps out of genuine unwillingness, fled the appointment. He was captured and brought back and eventually consented.

It was necessary for him to be baptised in order that he might proceed through the orders and eventually be consecrated. He made it plain where he stood on one lively controversy of the day by insisting that he be baptised by a Catholic and not an Arian. (The Arians were followers of Arius (c.250–336), who had questioned the divinity of Christ and attracted high political support. Their teaching was condemned at the Council of Nicaea in 325, but their adherents continued to be politically influential as the Empire faced attack. Some of the invading tribes were Arians.)

Ambrose took his duties as bishop seriously. Paulinus notes his asceticism: there was 'much fasting, many vigils...chastising his body by daily denials'. 'His zeal in prayer was great night and day'.

Augustine, who was in Milan in 383 as the newly appointed professor of rhetoric, heard good reports of Ambrose's preaching. He went to listen to his weekly sermons, expecting, as a professional public speaker, to find much to criticise. However, Ambrose's subject was Genesis, and the apparent crudity of Genesis had been one of the reasons why Augustine had been so unmoved by the Christian Scriptures as a young man. Ambrose was giving a philosophically sophisticated account, making use of the Cappadocian Fathers. Augustine reports that he went to Ambrose's weekly sermons and was impressed by their quality and illuminated by their content. He wanted to meet Ambrose, and ask him for clarification of some of his own remaining difficulties.

Augustine describes how ready Ambrose was to see people. Indeed, they kept him so busy with their problems that Augustine was prevented from seeing Ambrose face to face. When he was not seeing people he spent his time in reading: 'Anyone could approach him freely and there was no formal announcement as a rule, so that when one came in one might well find him silently reading.' (Augustine found this a disincentive to pouring his heart out, which he judged would take some time.)

Work and ideas

Most of Ambrose's writings are exegetical. He left commentaries, which go through the text verse by verse, and monographs, which take a theme and explore it in the light of Scriptural passages. His method of interpreting Scripture included the use of two or three 'senses'. He worked out a number of practical lessons of exegetical method in the period before Gregory the Great established the use of the four senses (literal, allegorical, moral, anagogical) in the West and made it standard thereafter. Ambrose's monographs take, in turn, a series of Scriptural themes which were to prove important again and again in succeeding centuries.

Ambrose became bishop in contentious times, when there were adherents of counter-Catholic movements pressing unorthodox views on a number of points. He addressed himself to various issues and controversies, mainly through commentary on the Old Testament. Soon after he became bishop, Ambrose wrote *On Paradise*, exploring the relevant text in Genesis with the assistance of his reading of the prolific first-century Jewish writer, Philo of Alexandria. (Paradise is the human soul and its rivers are the cardinal virtues.) He took the opportunity to attack the Manichees and their close cousins the Marcionites. As he took the story forward, a study of *Cain et Abel* followed. The theme here is sacrifice, and again his debt to Philo is important. *De Noe* (which is not finished), was written between 378 and 384, and here Ambrose takes as his theme the allegorical interpretation of the human body. Once more, the borrowing is from Philo. He then moved on from Noah to Abraham. *De Abraham* was divided into two books, one for the beginner in the faith and the other for those who are more advanced. The first part concentrates on the literal interpretation and presents Abraham as a righteous man, an example. For those who are baptised, and therefore more advanced in the faith, Ambrose presents a discussion of the Covenant and an allegorical interpretation of the text. *De Isaac et Anima* contains an allegory of Christ's union with the Soul. *De bono mortis* deals with the idea of death: death to sin and death to the world and death of the body, which separates body and soul. *De Iacob et Vita Beata* (386) is about the pursuit of happiness. *De Patriarchis* (on Genesis 49.3) discusses the blessing of Jacob and the prophecy of the Messiah. There are reflections on abstinence in Lent, from Old Testament examples, and making use of the homilies of Basil the Great. *De Nabuthae* is on Naboth and Ahab, written against the rich who oppress the poor. *De Tobia* is on usury.

In Holy Week in 387–90 Ambrose preached nine sermons on the Hexaemeron, using the creation story as a basis for exploring ideas of man and nature. His was a device others were later to adopt. The creation story became the focus of scientific commentary for a number of later writers.

Ambrose made an attempt at a Gospel harmony in his major work on the New Testament, on Luke, which was composed in around 388–9. Once more he was helping to set a trend, for the reconciliation of the Gospel accounts was to be a need which repeatedly presented itself, and which indeed challenged Augustine to write his attempted harmony of the Gospels.

Ambrose contributed to a wide range of contemporary debates on points of classic theological difficulty. He wrote *On Virginity* and *On Widows*. Chastity and continence, like other ascetic practices, were highly respected in a late antique world unable to free itself of a mistrust of the body and its fleshly temptations. *De Paenitentia* was written against the Novatianists (rigorists who said that a baptised Christian who subsequently sinned could never be forgiven). In about 381 he was producing dogmatic works on the Trinity (380) and on the Holy Spirit (381), on Incarnation, on the Creed and on Sacraments.

There was also a series of ethical works about the practical living of the Christian life. Ambrose's interest in, and need to become familiar with, the requirements of his office may be a reason for his writing about Christian ministry, *De officiis ministrorum*. But the most important achievement is the synthesis of a Christian ethics from classical ideals. He tries to Christianise the Roman virtues, after the model of Cicero's *De officiis*. His idea is that virtue should be useful and pragmatic. For human beings have a duty to know God; that is what they were created for.

Among Ambrose's surviving letters are comments of political importance. To the Emperor Theodosius he wrote to insist upon the right of the Church's leaders to be able to speak their minds to secular rulers: 'It is not fitting for an emperor to refuse freedom of speech, or for a bishop not to say what he thinks' (December 388). In the Synodal letter to the bishops of Gaul at the Council of Aquileia (381) ('We give thanks to your holy unanimity'), he speaks of 'our adversaries, enemies of God, those defenders of the Arian sect and heresy, Palladius and Secundus, the only two who dared to come to the Council'. They have received their due sentences.

This is a wide-ranging output, the work of a serious scholar with a natural eloquence, but above all a working bishop, a teacher of his people.

Influence

Ambrose came to be accepted as one of the Fathers of the Latin West, and he is frequently cited alongside Augustine.

Bibliography

Many of Ambrose's works are edited in Latin in the *Corpus Christianorum Ecclesiasticorum Latinorum* series and the modern *Corpus Christianorum Series Latina*, both of which should be found in most university libraries.

Among the translations are Ambrose, *Selections*, trans. J.J. Savage, Fathers of the Church, New York; *Seven Exegetical Works*, trans. Michael P. McHugh (Washington, 1972); *Selections*, trans. E. de Romestin and H.T.F. Duckworth (London, 1868).

Further reading

F.H. Dudden, *The Life and Times of St. Ambrose* (1955), 2 vols; A. Paredi, *Saint Ambrose: His Life and Times*, trans. M.J. Costelloe (Notre Dame, 1964); G.R. Figueroa, *The Church and the Synagogue in St. Ambrose*, (Washington, 1949).

JEROME *c.*345–420

Life and times

Jerome, one of the most important of the Latin Fathers, was born near Aquileia. He was sent by an ambitious family to study at Rome under the famous grammarian Donatus, probably for the usual four or five years, which would have been followed by time spent at a school of rhetoric. This was the ordinary education of a prospective man of affairs in the Empire, and would have fitted him for prominence in the world. The content of this education was in many respects limited: the study of Virgil and Cicero was central, with some Terence and Sallust and other Roman literary authors. But, as in the cases of Augustine and Ambrose, this was not necessarily limiting.

Jerome was drawn to a life of extreme asceticism. That was a vocation also felt in the ancient world by many who were not Christians, and it could be followed as a 'philosopher's' way of life. This was an age when philosophy expected of its adherents not merely an intellectual grasp of a system of explanation of the world, but a pattern of behaviour too. Whichever particular philosophy was involved, it was likely to embrace many of the patterns of conduct considered to be 'religious' when they found their way into Christianity, such as self-restraint and moderation and uprightness of behaviour. In Jerome (who found the beauty of asceticism easier than the self-discipline of not losing his temper or his control) this was linked to a passionate desire to study Scripture and to live a dedicated Christian life. He did something unusual in presenting himself for baptism as a youth, before 366, in a period when it was common to leave baptism until late in life.

The difficulty of keeping to a Christian 'way' and staying clear of the seductive influence of secular reading proved to be a challenge to Jerome. Much later, in a letter he wrote to one of the well-born Roman women he encouraged in the same way of life, he describes how, when he himself began, he used to fast and then, in contradiction of this act of self-denial, pick up a secular 'classic' for pleasure (*Letter*, 22.xxx.1). 'After frequent night vigils, after shedding tears which the remembrance of past sins brought forth from my inmost heart, I would take in my hands a volume of Plautus's' (*Letter*, 22.xxx.2). Famously, he eventually faced up to the accusation touched on in the introduction: 'You are a Ciceronian not a Christian' (*Letter*, 22.xxx.4). This became a text of some importance as an anchor quotation for the continuing concern of educated Christians in subsequent centuries that they too might be open to seduction by the beauty and interest of secular studies, and indeed they felt the pull only too strongly.

Jerome returned to Aquileia as a young man. He set up a society of ascetics, but the community disintegrated after three years, apparently as a result of that 'abrasiveness' on the part of Jerome which was to be prominent throughout his life. He moved to Antioch with some of his friends, but this community also broke up. Jerome met an experienced and elderly hermit named Malchus and (on his advice?) decided to live in complete solitude. He went to the desert of Chalcis which was not far away; a number of hermits were already living there, under the rule of Theodosius. In an early letter (2.i), he describes the desert as 'the fairest city of all' and 'places empty of inhabitants but thronged by bands of saints – a true paradise'. For five years Jerome lived among them in extreme asceticism, studying the Bible.

In 379 Jerome went back to Antioch, where he was ordained priest by its bishop Paulinus and seems to have entered the latter's entourage for a time. It may have been in this way that he found himself in Constantinople. He was present at the General Council at Constantinople in 382, where he met the 'Cappadocian Fathers' Gregory Nazianzen and Gregory of Nyssa, whose influence on Ambrose was to prove one of the important points of contact between the increasingly divergent intellectual communities of Greek-speaking East and Latin-speaking West. He also spent time with Paulinus in Rome. The Pope of the day was Damasus, and

Jerome found himself becoming the Pope's 'adviser' in matters of Biblical interpretation.

In Rome, Jerome met others who were drawn to the ascetic life, notably the group of noble ladies already mentioned. Of these, Paula and her daughters Blesilla and Eustochium proved loyal allies, as did the rather older Marcella, the senior figure of the group, who provided a place for him and a party of followers or pupils to meet for the study of Hebrew, prayer and the singing of psalms.

Jerome's letters to these women are important evidence of the content and commitment of his teaching about the ascetic life, his championship of celibacy and especially of virginity. He urged them to self-discipline. Yet he encouraged them to keep clear of excess. To Marcella he wrote with warnings against the extremist Montanists and Novatianists. Letter 22 to Eustochium forms a treatise in its own right on the ascetic life. He seeks to teach Eustochium a sense of her own worth in the eyes of Christ, and a live sense of the companionship of Christ. 'Your Bridegroom is not arrogant. He is not proud. He has married an Ethiopian woman' (22.i.5). 'I do not wish you to become proud but to be fearful because of your decision [to live in this way]' (22.iii.1). He urges her to fight actively against sin (22.iii.3–4).

Pope Damasus died and his successor Siricius was less enthusiastic about Jerome, who found himself out of favour. Blesilla died, it was rumoured of too much self-denial. Rome became an uncomfortable place to stay. Jerome left, with Paula and Eustochium, to found a joint convent and monastery near Bethlehem on financial support provided by the wealthy Paula. Eventually that was exhausted and Jerome used up his own family's money to continue it. He kept the monastery going for the thirty-four years until he died in 420.

Work and ideas

The heart of Jerome's spiritual and intellectual life was the Bible. He was therefore concerned to get it clear what was really biblical, that is, what was included in the 'canon' of Scripture. The Bible at this date usually took the physical form of a 'library', that is, a set of distinct 'books'. The question what was inside it and what outside could not be settled by pointing to a single volume. Jerome's attitude to the questions which therefore arose about the content of the canon seems to have changed about 390. Before that time he gives, in a prologue to Samuel and Malachi, a list of Old Testament 'Biblical' books and 'whatever is extra to those and to be placed among the apocrypha', with an explicit rejection of Wisdom, Ecclesiasticus, Judith and Tobias. In a letter to Paulinus of 395 he gives a different list including the New Testament. There is a further list in a letter of 400–2 to Laeta, but its purpose was different; there he was mainly concerned to suggest an appropriate order of reading for a growing child to follow.

Jerome also wanted to be sure he was understanding the 'authentic text' in another sense. He was an excellent linguist, mastering new languages with comparative ease. He became fluent in Greek, and in his Chronicle produced a rendering of Eusebius's *History* with his own additions and extensions (382, Constantinople).

Jerome studied Hebrew, taught, he says, by a member of the Rabbinical school of Palestinian Jews. That interest is reflected in his writing on the subject of the Hebrew names in the Old Testament, as well as in his translation work. He also translated Eusebius on the sites and names of Hebrew places and wrote the *Questions on Genesis*.

It is his translation of the Bible which is historically perhaps Jerome's most important legacy. It became for the Middle Ages 'our translation' (*nostra translatio*); 'our usual version' (*nostra usitata editio*). During his period in Rome, Jerome was commissioned by the Pope to produce new Latin text for portions of Scripture. The Old Latin text (*vetus latina*) was in truth a number of different texts of mixed or inferior Latinity. Jerome says in his opening epistle on the New Testament that there are as many forms of the biblical text in circulation as there are manuscripts. One danger of this was that unregulated attempts were being made to harmonise the Gospels and the text was thus increasingly diverging from the original which was to some degree still retrievable. (Jerome had access to better Greek manuscripts than survive today.) The new standard version of the Gospels was mainly produced by Jerome from 382–5 in Rome.

For the Old Testament, Jerome came to realise that the Hebrew text was a better source than the Septuagint. In Jerusalem, from 391–404 Jerome was working on translation from the Hebrew. He translated the Psalms from the Septuagint. Tobit and Judith he rendered from the Chaldean about 398.

He was commissioned to tidy up the 'old Latin' translation. His new version of the Gospels proved controversial at first. There was a hostile reaction – as there perhaps always is to change in familiar wording in a holy book. His rendering of the Old Testament from the Hebrew was disparaged by Rufinus.

Jerome was also a commentator on a number of books of the Bible. Indeed, he died while still working on his commentary on Jeremiah. He did not confine himself to the Bible in his study and rendering of texts; he also translated portions of Origen from the Greek. He also wrote and translated Church history and stories and lives of exemplary Christians, as well as *De viris illustribus* (392, Bethlehem), *Lives* of the hermits (379, Antioch), and a translation of the *Rule* of Pachomius (404, Bethlehem).

Jerome's irascibility is visible in his letters and his treatises. He cannot have been a comfortable person to be with. His hot temper and controversial prominence made him an active polemicist, producing for instance *Against Jovinian* (393, Bethlehem), and *Against Rufinus* (402–4, Bethlehem). It was dangerous to get involved in controversy. To Mark, priest at Chalcis, he wrote in Letter 17 about the difficulty of making it clear where one stands on the doctrine of the Trinity, so as to avoid the charge of heresy: 'I am called a heretic for preaching that the Trinity is consubstantial. I am accused of the Sabellian heresy for proclaiming . . . that there are three subsistent persons' (*Letter*, 17.ii.2). He feels persecuted: 'I am not allowed even a single corner of the desert. Every day I am asked about my faith as though I had been "born again" without faith. I confess the faith as they require but they are not placated. I sign their form of words; they do not believe me' (*Letter*, 17.iii.1). He complains that he is suspected not only of unorthodox belief but also of heresiarch intentions: 'you are evidently afraid that I may go round the churches leading people astray and bringing about a schism' (*Letter*, 17.ii.4).

He became to some degree involved in the controversy over Pelagius. Here, he appears to have been slow to pick up on issues already in play in the writings of Augustine, perhaps because he was geographically somewhat out of the fray, perhaps because the bent of his mind was different from that of Augustine and he was not troubled by the same things.

In 415 he was visited by Orosius, who had been sent to him by an exasperated Augustine, whom he had been pestering with questions. He brought with him two letters from Augustine, each a treatise in its own right, in which Augustine asked Jerome's opinion. The first was on the origin of the soul and the second on the interpretation of James 2.10 (the assertion that whoever breaks one commandment is guilty of breaking them all). Both these topics were tangential to the

Pelagian questions, and the whole story usefully illustrates the interconnectedness of the work of many of our principal figures.

Influence

The 'Vulgate' became the accepted version of the Bible in the West (and remained so in the Roman Catholic Church until the second Vatican Council of the mid-twentieth century). Jerome made a distinction in the preface to the Pentateuch (PL 28.151) between a 'prophet' and an 'interpreter'. The prophet is inspired. The translator renders the text with the aid of his learning and a good vocabulary and his understanding of the meaning (*eruditio et verborum copia, ea quae intelligit, transfert*). God does not put every word of the translation into his mind. Despite Jerome's own assertion that he did not believe himself as a translator to be inspired, his translation was treated as the inspired Word, every nuance analysed as if breathed directly by the Holy Spirit.

Throughout the Middle Ages Jerome was steadily given credit for this remarkable achievement. Vincent of Beauvais said that 'Jerome, skilled in the three languages, revised the New Testament from the original Greek and translated the Old Testament from the original Hebrew' (*Speculum historiale*, XVI.xix). That does not mean that no one noticed that it contained errors. Roger Bacon was raising doubts about the translation in 1267, claiming that it was defective. When, towards the end of the Middle Ages, some Christian scholars such as Nicholas of Lyra learned Hebrew to a sufficient standard, they were able to point to numerous failures on Jerome's part to render correctly the *Hebraica veritas*. In *De rudimentis hebraicis*, Reuchlin finds two hundred places where he can correct the Vulgate.

The tide of criticism gradually mounted. It even became possible to ask whether the text in use as 'the Vulgate' for so long was in fact Jerome's work. It was observed that the Vulgate contains errors which Jerome had pointed out in his other writings and so was not likely to have committed himself.

Yet at the Council of Trent in the mid-sixteenth century, the Vulgate survived the challenge of the sixteenth century reformers despite many errors they were able to point out in it. It continued to be the official version of the Roman Catholic Church in the West. The reasons were partly political. By then the Church had a substantial 'investment' in the 'reformers' being proved wrong. And it was pointed out that if they were right the Holy Spirit had allowed the Church to use an unreliable text for a thousand years and that seemed inconceivable. The letters exhorting to the ascetic life survived as literary works of some influence in their own right.

Bibliography

A number of Jerome's works are in modern editions in Latin in *Corpus Scriptorum Series Latina*. Translations include Jerome, *Selected Letters*, ed. F.A. Wright (Boston, 1963); *Hebrew Questions on Genesis*, trans. C.T.R. Hayward (Oxford, 1995).

Further reading

J.N.D. Kelly, *Jerome* (London, 1975); *A Monument to St. Jerome*, ed. F.X. Murphy (New York, 1952); on Jerome's long-term influence, and his importance in the controversies about Bible translation in the sixteenth century, see Eugene F. Rice, *St Jerome in the Renaissance* (Baltimore and London, 1985).

PS-DIONYSIUS *c.*500

Life and times

The identity of 'Ps-Dionysius' is lost. He himself professes to be the first century Dionysius the Areopagite. His writings were relied on at a meeting in Constantinople in 533, and must therefore date from before that period. Indeed, he had been cited by Severus of Antioch two decades earlier. They cannot, however, be early enough to be authentically the work of the 'apostolic' Areopagite (the claim made by the Monophysites who wanted to raise his standing for use in their dispute against the position which had become officially orthodox at the Council of Chalcedon in 451).

Work and ideas

Ps-Dionysius's achievement was to bring together Platonic with Christian thinking about the order of the universe. He was particularly indebted to Proclus's mediation of late Platonist thinking. He wrote a book on *The Celestial Hierarchy*, describing the nine orders of angels. The lowliest are mere angels, who bring messages to men and women, and the next highest the archangels mentioned in Scripture, who bring really important messages, such as the Archangel Gabriel's announcement to the Virgin Mary. At the top stand the cherubim and seraphim who spend eternity in contemplation of God. In the middle are ranged Thrones, Virtues,

Dominions, Powers and Principalities, all capable, to medieval eyes, of being identified with their equivalents in the human hierarchy.

Ps-Dionysius also set out an *Ecclesiastical Hierarchy*, to medieval eyes really a book of spirituality, dealing with the modes by which human nature becomes more like the God in whose image and likeness it was made. The *Mystical Theology* takes this further, describing a system in which it is important to begin from what we cannot know of God, on the presumption that all we can know of him is what he is not. (He is infinite, immortal and so on, and human minds can understand only that which is finite and mortal.)

There is a Platonic 'overflow' theory within Ps-Dionysius's system. God is above even 'being', but he overflows in his generosity, and in this way multiplicity comes into the universe; and something resembling a relationship is formed by God with a created world which is full of mere existences and also embodies the universals of which all particular things form sub-species. There is thus a world of ultimate reality and a world to which it reveals itself, and in which we live and think.

Of particular future medieval interest was the *Divine Names*, in which Ps-Dionysius grapples with the difficulty for humans of using their creaturely language of a God it cannot possibly describe accurately. From the late eleventh century this question was to represent itself in lively new forms as scholars worked on the question of the way in which words signify things and concepts. 'Father', 'Son' and 'Holy Spirit' form a special category of names.

Influence

Perhaps the most important thing about Ps-Dionysius is his influence throughout the millennium with which we are concerned, on medieval authors themselves of considerable influence. The first of these was Maximus the Confessor (*c*.580–662), a Greek monastic theologian who became involved in the defence of the Orthodox position during the Monothelite controversy of the seventh century. (The Monothelites taught that the incarnate Christ had only one will, not both a divine and a human will.) Maximus was instrumental in getting this teaching – whose adherents had a contemporary political agenda – condemned in Africa and also in Rome, at the Lateran Council of 649. Through his commentaries, Maximus heightened the popularity of the writings of Ps-Dionysius. Maximus's own acceptability to the Latin West was strengthened by the availability of some of his writings in translation. His paraphrases of Ps-Dionysius helped to make his ideas known in the West. Ps-Dionysius's teaching on angels was used by Gregory the Great. In the Carolingian period, Eriugena took his ideas on hierarchy into his own work. Hugh of St Victor and other Victorines of the twelfth century also found him useful on angels (see p. 74). He was an important source for Bonaventure, Albert the Great and Eckhardt among many others. The chief difficulty in the way of his acceptance was the unusualness of his approach, which made some wary, and which perhaps prevented him from winning a secure place among the uncontroversial Fathers of the Church.

Bibliography

Ps-Dionysius, *The Complete Works*, ed. C. Lubheid; *Dionysiaca* (Latin translations from the ninth to the fifteenth centuries of works attributed to Ps-Dionysius) (Paris, 1937), 2 vols.

Further reading

Andrew Louth, *Denys the Areopagite* (London, 1989); Paul Rorem, *Ps-Dionysius: A Commentary on the Texts and An Introduction to Their Influence* (Oxford, 1993); C.E. Rolt, *Dionysius the Areopagite* (New York, 1920); Thesaurus, *Ps-Dionysii Areopagitae* (Turnhout, 1993).

CASSIODORUS 484/90–before 584

Life and times

Cassiodorus, born between 484 and 490, tells his own life-story in the little book *Ordo Generis Cassiodorum*, which is almost an intellectual genealogy.[1] He mentions Symmachus, a *vir philosophus*, whom he describes as a modern imitator of 'the Cato of old', but surpassing him in religion, for he is a Christian. He also mentions Boethius, eloquent in both Greek and Latin, and again the equal of the ancients in authorship and their superior in religion. Both, put to death in the 520s for political reasons, were probably relatives of Cassiodorus. The senator Cassiodorus, our Cassidorus's father, was 'a most learned man'.

This elder Cassiodorus was a provincial governor of Sicily; from *c*.503–7 he was praetorian prefect, while the young Cassiodorus worked as his aide. Cassiodorus was thus able to make his name and build his career from within the 'civil service' of the late Roman Empire, a world in which a man could still be, in the Roman meanings of those terms, a 'scholar and a gentleman'. From 507–11 Cassiodorus himself was a *quaestor*, then *consul ordinarius* (514), then the most senior 'civil servant' as *magister officiorum* in 523. In this post he was able to assemble the materials for his *Variae*, a collection of 'letters' of a senior civil servant.

Until 523, the position of *magister officiorum* had been held by Boethius, whom Cassiodorus describes as fluent in Greek as well as Latin (*utraque lingua peritissimus*). It is striking that he mentions this linguistic knowledge, for until comparatively recent generations it could have been taken for granted that educated Romans could read Greek. This was the period of the final linguistic division of the ancient Empire into two language groups which subsequently had difficulty in communicating with one another and gradually became two distinct cultures.

Boethius was arrested because he tried to defend someone accused of conspiracy, and he was eventually executed. Cassiodorus had kept out of the controversy. In the heightened politics of the time, that made him eligible to succeed Boethius in his desirable post. In 533 Cassiodorus became praetorian prefect.

Cassiodorus thus moved through a most satisfactory career in Roman public life, largely under the Arian Emperor Theodoric. Cassiodorus helped to influence him towards Catholicism. The importance of this imperial patronage to Cassiodorus's success is clear. After the death of Theodoric in 526 came a disturbed and war-torn period when Cassiodorus was frequently out of office. This experience encouraged in him (as in others) a gloomy sense that they were living in the old age of the world (*senectus mundi*), and like Boethius he began to see a need to rescue the learning and culture of his day and preserve it for the future. In the year when Benedict founded Monte Cassino, the Emperor Justinian closed the academy at Athens.

Cassiodorus turned visibly from public to religious life when the siege of Rome was lifted by the Goths. This took place after 538–40, although we do not know exactly when he was thus 'converted'. In the Preface to his work on the Psalms he writes: 'Some time ago at Ravenna I put aside the anxieties of office and the damaging enticements of secular responsibilities and began to read Scripture.' From 540–54 he was in Constantinople.

Cassiodorus also founded monastic houses. It was only in 529 that Benedict had founded Monte Cassino, so it was a notable move on Cassiodorus's part to follow his example. There was a double monastery on his estate at Scyllacium, the Vivarium for cenobites at

Mount Moschius and the hermitage at Mount Castellum. There is a hint in his exposition of the Psalms of the vision by which he was guided at this time. He describes (examining Psalm 100/1) how David cut himself off from wicked men and was united with the good, and by mental and spiritual struggle drove out the base desires of his heart and won a spiritual crown. That became Cassiodorus's own purpose.

Work and ideas

Cassiodorus's first work, around 519, seems to have been his *Chronicle* and *History of the Goths*. In 538 he published his *Variae* (letters) and about the same time his treatise on the soul (*De Anima*). The *Variae*, containing decrees and imperial edicts of the sort a Roman official such as himself drew up, was treated in the Middle Ages as a formulary, or book of standard letters to guide others faced with such routine but high-level secretarial tasks, though the altered context must have made it of doubtful value.

Cassiodorus describes in the work's preface (written about 537–8) how people have asked him to bring together his letters on public affairs. It is easy to find time for conversation, he observes, but the endless interruptions and distractions of a busy professional life make it difficult to find time to write. 'Persuasion ought to be resisted, for there is more danger than attraction in it,' he comments. But the friends and admirers have pressed him hard and he has given in. He moves on to discuss the three *genera dicendi* of antiquity, the three styles in which ancient rhetoricians learned to write and the need to adjust the style to the person, and settles happily to his authorial task.[2]

There is perhaps some nostalgia for a disappearing government machinery in the twelve books of edicts and model letters written between 506 and 538. Perhaps Cassiodorus was trying to leave a monument rather than a memorial, so that the old ways would not be lost altogether in changing times. His themes are topical: the defence of Italy, relations between Goths and Franks, the diplomacy of relations with Byzantium, criticism of the régime of the Emperor Justinian. His style is ornate, contrived, full of the devices of late antique Latin at its most affected, but then affectation was good style in some forms of epistle. He was a conscious stylist, commenting in his prefatory remarks that he had won favour because he was a good conversationalist and his friends appreciated his skills. He says that he hopes his examples will educate uncultivated men for the service of the state.

De Anima is derivative. Cassiodorus's work consciously reflects the influence of Augustine's *Enarrationes in Psalmos*. Cassiodorus added an emphases of his own, for example, on allegorical interpretation. He remarks in his Preface that when he set aside the cares of office and began to read the Bible closely he realised how great was the need to clarify apparent obscurities and difficulties in the text. He offers an account of what he feels he needs to 'add' to Augustine in that area.

A number of Cassiodorus's other interests emerge from the text. He explores familiar ideas about the cardinal virtues, giving them a social twist or emphasis. There is an emphasis on the unity of the Church and an anxiety to rebut the errors of Donatists, Pelagians and others who had famously challenged orthodoxy. His is, like so much contemporary commentary, consciously a vehicle for 'doing' theology.

In all his work, Cassiodorus is a civilised and cultured 'collector' rather than a pioneer. He says that he aspires only to collect the authorities, the *diversa lectio*, the Bible, the masters of secular literature, the *veraces doctores* (*De Anima*, 4.1,4). These are the established *auctores* and *veteres*. Augustine is *pater Augustinus* among them (9.21 and 11.54).

The *Expositio psalmorum* appears to be the product of his time in Constantinople. Cassiodorus wrote it for the sweet gathering, *suave collegium*, of his friends.[3] It is a defining marker of his turning from a secular to the religious life. He placed it at the end of the *Variae*, of which it forms Book XIII, and he ends it with the reflection that it is nobler to serve God than to rest one's ambitions in success in the kingdoms of this world.

Cassiodorus's most important work, from the point of view of its influence, was perhaps the *Institutiones*, written in his retirement (562). This was two works in one, first a syllabus of sacred reading and commentary by respected Christian authors, and second a survey of the liberal arts in the form of an encyclopaedia or convenient reference book. (The *Institutiones* recommend Hilary of Poitiers, Ambrose, Jerome and Augustine; Cassiodorus seems not to have had an interest in the Greek Fathers.)

The preface to Book I explains that the schools of the day were full of students who were expressing a keen interest to know more of secular letters. Cassiodorus has been struck with the thought that, for those who wish to get a similar grounding in the Scriptures, there are no such public teachers. He says that he worked with Agapetus, Bishop of Rome, to collect subscriptions so as to set up Christian schools. The political circumstances have made that impossible. The *Institutiones* is the next best thing; Cassiodorus hopes that it can in part take the place of a teacher.

In the part of the encyclopaedia which deals with secular learning he was also providing something not to be found in the schools. Here is a straightforward catalogue of the liberal arts of grammar, logic and rhetoric (the trivium or three 'ways') and the four mathematical subjects of arithmetic, music, geometry and astronomy, to which Boethius was to give the label the quarivium or four 'ways'. His last work, *De orthographia*, was written sometime between 577 and 584.

Influence

The *Institutiones* was immensely important as a standard medieval work of reference for centuries, surviving in numerous manuscripts, Book II on the seven liberal arts being particularly important. *De Anima* is widespread in medieval library lists. Cassiodorus himself is commonly mentioned.

Notes

1   CCSL, 96, p. v.
2   *Variarum*, CCSL, 96, pp. 3–6.n
3   CCSL, 96, p. 505.

Bibliography

Some of Cassiodorus's Latin works are available in the *Corpus Christianorum Series Latina* series. The *Ordo generis Cassiodorum – Excerpta*, was edited by L. Viscido (Naples, 1992). Translations are available of some of Cassiodorus's writings, for example, Cassiodorus, *An Introduction to Divine and Human Readings*, trans. L.W. Jones (New York, 1956); *Variae*, trans. S.J.B. Barnish (Liverpool, 1992); P.G. Walsh, *Explanation of the Psalms, Classics of Western Spirituality* (New York, 1990).

Further reading

J.J. O'Donnell, *Cassiodorus* (Berkeley, 1979).

BOETHIUS *c.*480–524

Life and times

Boethius was the son of Flavius Manlius Boethius, who was Consul in 487. Like Cassiodorus, Boethius was treated as friend and adviser by the Emperor Theodoric and was himself a consul in 510. He ended his life on an (apparently) undeserved charge of treason, which kept him under house arrest until his execution.

Work and ideas

The Consolation of Philosophy shows us Boethius in prison awaiting execution, discoursing with a personified Philosophy about how to come to terms with evil, freedom and providence. Boethius begins from a Stoic viewpoint, seeing the universe as proceeding inexorably from cause to effect, with no scope for more than an illusion of human freedom. He moves, with Philosophy's help, to a position in tune with a Christian Platonism. The soul is to seek its Creator, the One who is above all change, and who has nothing to do with evil. All goods are one and the pursuit of happiness is the pursuit of unity with the One who is the Good. Eternity he sees as the complete, simultaneous and perfect possession of endless life (*interminabilis vitae tota simul et perfecta possessio, Consolation* V.6). Boethius owes a substantial debt here to the first part of Plato's *Timaeus* (the only work of Plato which was easily accessible in the medieval West). Providence now begins to look different, a force which 'permits' things we do not perceive as good at the time, but which prove to be right for us in the end. Boethius thus comes to a different kind of acceptance from the Stoic, and to a Christian hope. Philosophy reminds Boethius that it is unwise to trust the notoriously unreliable Fortune. Boethius thus creates a systematic account of human destiny which leaves out the Christian elements of sin and its remission, redemption and eternal life. Boethius thought with Plato that the soul exists before the conception of the individual as a human body. But he does not hold a full-blooded doctrine of the transmigration of souls, and in fact there is probably nothing in his Platonism which is ultimately incompatible with Christian faith.

Boethius perceived the danger that the increasing linguistic separation of the Eastern and Western halves of the Roman Empire, and the encroachments of the barbarians upon its borders would put access to Greek philosophical culture at risk in the West. He set about translating the works of Plato and Aristotle into Latin, but only a small part of the logic corpus (the *Categories* and *De Interpretatione*) was completed before his death, together with a commentary on Porphyry's *Isagoge* and some logical monographs of his own.

With these should be grouped *De Arithmetica* and *De Musica*, both heavily dependent upon Greek sources, and especially upon the

Arithmetic of Nicomachus of Gerasa. Boethius coined the expression *quadrivium* (four ways), to go with the *trivium* (three ways) of grammar, logic and rhetoric. The quadrivium covered arithmetic, geometry, music and astronomy.

Boethius also wrote five short 'theological tractates'. *On the Catholic Faith* is a confession of faith, lacking the detailed philosophical analysis of the others. *Against Eutyches and Nestorius* was prompted when, in about 513, a Greek bishop wrote to Pope Symmachus to encourage the adoption of points in addition to the Chalcedonian formula. Boethius was there in person during the resulting debate. He learned of the 'Nestorian' view that Christ is both 'of' and 'in' two natures and the Monophysite view (Eutychian) that Christ is 'of' two natures, but not 'in' two natures. He addressed himself to the underlying questions about 'nature' and 'person' and their relationship. He defines 'person' as 'the individual substance of a rational nature' (*naturae rationabilis individua substantia, Contra Eutychen* 3) and argues, in accordance with the views of Maxentius, that Christ is indeed also one person of two natures; that there is one nature of the Incarnate Word; and that the incarnate Lord is 'one of the Trinity'.

Boethius believed that this could be said without implying that God can suffer or that there is plurality in the divine being. Here he had an eye to the Christological controversy which had been going on in the Eastern half of Christendom, and in Greek, and which was causing the arguments to be rehearsed all over again when its conclusions had to be put into Latin.

He was the first to attempt a comprehensive treatment in Latin. In 'On the Trinity', on 'Whether Father, Son and Holy Spirit are Substantially Predicated of the Trinity', Boethius explores concepts of form, unity and plurality, identity and difference. He makes the point that the Aristotelian 'categories' apply differently to God. In the Godhead all accidents are substantive. (God is not 'good', but 'goodness'.) Only relation exists absolutely between the Persons of the Trinity. Like Augustine, Boethius stresses that the persons of the Trinity are equal, but he takes further the question how equals can differ, for Father, Son and Holy Spirit are not identical.

The two 'trinitarian treatises' were probably written close together. *De Trinitate* is much more developed. *De Hebdomadibus*, on 'How substances are good in virtue of their existence without being substantial goods', takes the form of a series of axioms which can be applied, by those wise enough to comprehend them, to the resolution of the problem which is the subject of the treatise, the implications of Plato's belief that the good transcends being, so that everything which exists derives from the good. Boethius asks whether good things are good in the same way as the highest Good, or whether their goodness is merely an attribute.

Influence

Boethius was never a 'Father', because of a residual uncertainty about his Christian faith raised by his stance in *The Consolation of Philosophy*. Alcuin puts Victorinus and Boethius side by side with Pliny.

Boethius's most influential work throughout the Middle Ages was *The Consolation of Philosophy*: on Alfred the Great; Jean de Meun (French, thirteenth century); Chaucer (English, fourteenth century); and Jean Gerson in his *De Consolatione Theologiae*. It was first printed in 1471 and frequently after that.

The Boethian legacy of logic directly shaped the study of logic in the West until the twelfth century, when texts of the remainder of Aristotle's six books on logic were rendered into Latin, and this *logica nova* gave rise to a *logica moderna* which addressed itself to more advanced logical problems. Boethius's contribution encouraged the early medieval emphasis on problems of epistemology and signification, which was to shape many branches of thought in the Middle Ages.

The theological tractates were taken up with enthusiasm by scholars of the early twelfth century, when they became an important influence in the schools on the development of the use of logic in theology. *De Hebdomadibus* prompted an interest in demonstrative method which was to grow with the translation of Euclid and the reintroduction of Aristotle's *Posterior Analytics* into the West during the twelfth century. *De Trinitate* contains a version of the Platonic division of knowledge which places mathematics between theology and natural science. This encouraged twelfth-century attempts to classify the sciences, and, importantly, implicitly stressed the division between those aspects of theology which can be attempted by philosophical methods and those which are historical and depend on Biblical revelation (a division which we find taken up by Hugh of St Victor and others). Use was also made in the Middle Ages of what Boethius has to say about which of the Aristotelian categories apply to God, and the special ways in which they do so.

Bibliography

Patrologia Latina, ed. J.P. Migne, vols 63–4 (Paris, 1947) contains Boethius's collected works. Boethius's *De Consolatione Philosophiae*, ed. L. Bieler, is in *Corpus Christianorum Series Latina*, 94 (Turnhout, 1957); *Theological Tractates* and *De Consolatione Philosophiae*, ed. and trans. H. Stewart, E.K. Rand and S.J. Tester (Boston, 1973); *De Arithmetica* and *De Musica*, ed. G. Friedlein (Leipzig, 1986); *Commentaries on Porphyry*, ed. S. Brandt, *Corpus Scriptorum Ecclesiasticorum Latinorum*, 48 (Vienna, 1906); *Commentaries on Aristotle, De Interpretatione*, ed. C. Meiser (Leipzig, 1877–80); *De syllogismis hypotheticis*, ed. L. Obertello (Brescia, 1969).

Further reading

H. Chadwick, *Boethius: The Consolations of Music, Logic, Theology, and Philosophy* (Oxford, 1990); *Boethius: His Life, Thought and Influence*, ed. M. Gibson (Oxford, 1981); *The Medieval Boethius: Studies in the Vernacular Translations of the De Consolatione Philosophiae*, ed. A.J. Minnis (Cambridge, 1987).

GREGORY THE GREAT *c*.540–604

Life and times

Gregory the Great was born into the senatorial class. He became Prefect of Rome in 573. Then he gave his wealth to the poor, founding seven monasteries. In 574, he himself became a monk in his own monastic foundation of St Andrew's in Rome. A few years later the Pope made him one of the seven deacons of Rome. In about 578 he was sent to the Imperial Court of Constantinople as *apocrisarius*. There he continued to live a monastic life, expounding the book of Job to the community in the series of discourses which became the *Moralia in Job*. In the mid-580s, he returned to Rome and became abbot of St Andrew's. In 590 he was elected to the papacy. As Pope, he concentrated upon practical pastoral attempts to improve social conditions in a period of decline in the old Roman Empire. By Gregory's time the Papacy had largely taken over responsibility for the practical running of Rome; this gave it a temporal as well as spiritual authority which was to be important to its subsequent development in the long-running medieval power struggle between Church and State.

Gregory's pontificate was a turning point in several further ways. He was a significant figure in the process by which the Bishop of Rome came to claim and establish a hegemony among the five ancient patriarchates. Gregory refused to accept the claim of the

Patriarchate of Constantinople to be 'oecumenical' and argued for the primacy and supremacy of the See of Peter. The Papacy was growing increasingly autonomous as a result of disputes with both Western and Eastern imperial powers, and as Rome ceased to be considered as the capital of the Empire. It was now beginning to be perceived rather as the holy city, a resort of pilgrims.

Work and ideas

Gregory was not an original thinker, nor a natural philosopher, and although he probably had some Greek his direct access to the Greek patristic tradition was limited. His great achievement was to simplify and present for a popular audience much of Augustine's thought, and to integrate something of the spirituality of the Eastern tradition with that of the West, in a balance of the active and the contemplative in the Christian life. He worked for the most part through the exposition of Scripture, tracing patterns of imagery and drawing out spiritual meanings whose vividness gave them wide currency throughout the Middle Ages.

During his time at St Andrew's Gregory seems to have preached on the first Book of Kings, the prophets, Proverbs and the Song of Songs. Notes of the first and last of these survive. In about 591 he completed the *Moralia in Job*, probably the most widely-read of his works in the Middle Ages.

In 591, at a time when he was himself ill and unable to deliver them in person, Gregory composed sermons on the Gospels. While the Lombards were besieging Rome, he gave his homilies on Ezekiel, which he later published in two books (601).

Preaching was thus, for Gregory as for Augustine, the means by which the bishop properly fulfilled his function of guardianship and maintenance of the faith. He was largely responsible for the establishment of the fourfold pattern of exegesis with which medieval scholars subsequently worked in the West until the sixteenth century. Gregory distinguishes a literal or historical sense; an allegorical sense; an anagogical sense, in which the text is read as prophesying the heavenly future; and a tropological or moral sense, which gives instruction on the living of a good Christian life.

Gregory's use of Biblical imagery in speaking of Christ was highly influential. Christ as the Church's Bridegroom is the model for the intimacy which ought to exist between Christ and the soul. Christ is the door or gateway by which Christians come into the presence of God. Preachers imitate Christ in this, both opening the way for the faithful and preventing the entry of unbelievers. The Church herself is the gateway between this world and the next. She thus faces both inward and outward. Christ's headship of the Church is a paradigm for the bishop's leadership of the community. Christ is also the Judge who weighs men's merits with both justice and loving kindness. Christ came to us both as a man like us, and as a just man coming to those who were sinful, so that there was both 'likeness' and 'unlikeness' in his coming.

Gregory was responsible for the development of a theology of episcopal ministry in which there should be due balance between the spiritual and the practical, service and leadership. That was a balance he himself consciously sought to maintain, and he says that he found it difficult. In the early 590s he was working on the *Regula Pastoralis*, a handbook of spiritual and practical guidance for those in pastoral office.

He himself constantly felt the tension between the contemplative and the active life, and he links with it the bipolarity of 'inward' (spiritual) and 'outward' (bodily) in spiritual understanding. Outwardly all is distress and change and decay. Inwardly there is peace and tranquillity, the foretaste of a heaven Platonists as well as Christians could long for. The late antique preoccupation with the dichotomy of body and soul is thus developed by Gregory with a new richness of imagery. Also Platonist is the emphasis on illumination.

The *Dialogues*, a work of spiritual biography containing accounts of miracles, was written in 593–4. The *Dialogues* affect a style so different from Gregory's other writings that their authenticity has been doubted, but they may perhaps represent Gregory's attempt at a genre akin to the Eastern lives of the desert Fathers. For example, he describes (IV.xxxiv) a religious who saw as he was dying the prophets Jonah, Ezekiel and Daniel and others.

Of great importance is the *Life of Benedict* which forms the centrepiece of the *Dialogues*. Benedict of Nursia (*c*.480–550) was born of parents of middle rank. As a youth he travelled to Rome. He found the city decadent, and withdrew with a group of friends, rather as Jerome had done in an earlier generation, to try to live an ascetic life. He began to live as a hermit at Subiaco. He attracted disciples and that led him to give thought to the way in which the communities of people who wished to make a special commitment to the 'religious life' should be organised.

Benedict arranged at first for groups of twelve monks to live together in small communities. Then he moved to Monte Cassino where, in about 529, he set up the monastery which was to become the mother house of that 'Benedictine' Order which was to be vastly successful in the Middle Ages; there he composed his Rule for the use of this larger community.

The Rule of life drawn up by Benedict of Nursia in the early sixth century is not unique. It was a synthesis of elements in existing 'Rules'. But it 'held together' in a way which proved to provide a practical well-balanced pattern of life. The text known as the *Rule of the Master* was a particularly important influence on Benedict. About a quarter of Benedict's text was taken from it and a good deal more shaped or coloured by it. There was probably also some influence from the group of authors associated with Lérins from the fifth century onwards; Cassian and a series of bishops of Arles, notably Caesarius (d. 542) and Eucherius of Lyons and Faustus of Riez. These predominantly Western connections perhaps encouraged an emphasis on the cenobitic life as distinct from the eremitical and idiosyncratic patterns more usual in the eastern half of the Empire.

The idea of the Benedictine Rule was to encourage a life of dedication, but avoiding extreme asceticism, and lived in reasonable moderation. There is to be *nihil asperum, nihil grave*; the yoke is to be sweet, the burden light. It is a 'school' of the Lord's service, in which the baptised soul makes progress in the Christian life. It is a quiet and orderly life, spent in prayer and reading and manual labour. The monk 'learns' by painfully subjecting himself in obedience and by making reparation for the 'lazy disobedience of sin'. The *opus dei*, the time of prayer, is central:

> At the hour of the divine office, as soon as a monk has heard the signal, he shall immediately set aside whatever he has in hand and go with utmost speed, yet with gravity, so as not to give occasion for unruliness. Thus nothing is to be preferred to the work of God.
>
> (Chapter 43)

But there is also a balance of manual work and holy reading, and hospitality. Christ is the abbot of the Benedictine monastery, but he is also the brother, the guest, the sick person being cared for.

The Rule was a success. It was used in its early days not only at Monte Cassino and Subiaco but also at the Lateran in Rome, at the monastery of St Pancratius, to which the monks of Monte Cassino withdrew after their house was damaged in the late 570s. It may be that this temporary move to Rome ensured a diffusion of the Rule which it might not otherwise have had. The Rule appears in Gaul in about 620 and then in the Frankish Empire, where the disciples of Columbanus were using it. The movement northwards took place quite early. The oldest surviving manuscript of the Rule was written in middle England in about 700. The Rule met a steady need for almost all purposes, until at least the twelfth century, when the Augustinian Rule for canons gained a rival popularity, or the thirteenth, when the mendicant orders were founded.

There are discussions of philosophical and theological matters, too, in the *Dialogues*, in particular the Last Things and the nature of dreams, visions and *somnia* in general. It was important to be able to say when a vision was a revelation from God and when it was an illusion of the Devil (IV.xlviii), as we shall see when we come to the theme of prophecy.[1]

A substantial body of letters survives, forming both a key historical and an important ecclesiological resource for subsequent medieval thinkers.

Influence

The *Regula Pastoralis* was to influence medieval ecclesiology profoundly, in its portrayal of the role of a bishop, and also in its contribution to the development of thinking about the proper balance of action and contemplation. Bernard of Clairvaux used it in writing the *De Consideratione* for Eugenius III, and it thus affected theories of papal supremacy in the later Middle Ages.

Gregory's lifetime was a crucial period in ensuring the success of Benedictine monasticism which provided the Rule by which the Western religious were to live until the twelfth century introduced new experiments. The *Dialogues* were important here, as was Gregory's own patronage.

Gregory wrote to advise Augustine of Canterbury, his missionary to Britain, to make a sensible selection from the rites of the Roman, the Gallic, or any other Church, so as to construct an appropriate and acceptable rite for the new Christians of the island. A number of practices in the liturgy of the West, for example the use of the Lord's Prayer at the end of the Eucharistic prayer and before the Peace, seem to be indebted to Gregory's guidance. Much in the liturgy, was not accepted practice until Gregory's time. The text know as the *Gregorian Sacramentary*, which was sent by Pope Hadrian I to Charlemagne in about 790, and thereafter circulated widely in the Frankish Empire, goes back to Gregory's pontificate.

Notes

1 See pp. 161, 166.

Bibliography

Commentarie sur le premier livre des Rois, ed. A. de Vogüé, *Sources chrétiennes* 351 (Paris, 1989); *Dialogi*, ed. P. Autin and A. de Vogüé, *Sources chrétiennes* 260 (Paris, 1979); *Homiliae in Hiezechihelem Prophetam*, ed. C. Morel, *Sources chrétiennes* 327 (Paris, 1986); *In Canticum Canticorum*, ed. R. Bélanger, *Sources chrétiennes* 314 (Paris, 1984); *Moralia in Job*, ed. M. Adraien, *Corpus Christianorum Series Latina*, 143, 143A (Turnhout, 1979). The letters are also available in the *Corpus Christianorum Series Latina* series. Also *Regula Pastoralis*, ed. H.R. Bradley (Oxford, 1974); *The Earliest Life of Gregory the Great by an Anonymous monk of Whitby*, ed. B. Colgrave (Cambridge, 1985).

Further reading

C. Straw, *Gregory the Great: Perfection in Imperfection* (Berkeley, 1988); G.R. Evans, *The Thought of Gregory the Great* (Cambridge, 1986); P. Meyvaert, *Benedict, Gregory, Bede and Others* (London, 1977); D. Norberg, *Critical and Exegetical Notes on the Letters of St. Gregory the Great* (Stockholm, 1982); *The Rule of Benedict*, trans. P. Barry (York, 1997); A. de Vogué, *Community and Abbot in the Rule of St. Benedict* (Kalamazoo, 1978).

ISIDORE OF SEVILLE c.560–636

Life and times

Isidore's early life is obscure. His family seems to have fled to Seville before he was born. Isidore was educated in a local monastery, where his brother was a monk. His brother preceded him in due course to the See of Seville as bishop. About 589 Isidore himself became a monk. He became bishop of Seville in 600. He was involved in several Spanish Councils of importance, especially that at Toledo in 633.

Work and ideas

Isidore of Seville is important as an encyclopaedist rather than as an original thinker. The condensation of existing knowledge in an orderly way for beginners, or for convenient reference was nothing new. Indeed, Isidore's *Etymologies* is heavily dependent upon the *Institutes* of Cassiodorus. Yet we are beginning to be beyond the period of late antiquity when education still had much of its classical apparatus. The work involved in compiling an encyclopaedia was now less a matter of salvaging endangered but familiar materials and more something which required research.

The liberal arts had been *artes* worthy of the study of a free man;[1] but the old social patterns of the Empire had changed, and now it was the clergy who needed the knowledge. What Isidore seems to have tried to provide was something more than a crib to the essentials, and in particular, in offering an account of the derivation of terms, he was doing something medieval thinkers found very useful (unreliable though he looks to modern eyes).

A series of letters survives in which Isidore discusses the exchange of books and his work of research and preparation for writing his *Etymologies* with Bishop Braulionus. Letter V 'finds' him in Toledo, for the Council. 'I am disturbed over the Council', he comments; nevertheless, he has found time to send his friend Braulion of Saragossa the *Etymologies* and other codices.

Isidore seems to have had access to such contemporary and recent writings as those of Cassiodorus (whose lifetime overlapped with that of Isidore by two decades) and Gregory the Great; the degree of his access to other source materials is debatable. It has been suggested that Isidore's *Etymologies* show the influence of Varro in Visigothic Spain.[2] But Isidore could have borrowed Varro's idea that there are nine disciplines from Cassiodorus, and the striking image contrasting rhetoric and dialectic in *Etymologies* II.xxiii.1 is also in Cassiodorus, *Institutes* II.iiii.2 (rhetoric strikes like an open palm and dialectic like a clenched fist). It has also been suggested that Isidore's *De Natura Rerum* owes something to classical models such as Suetonius. The *Etymologiae* hints at a degree of joint authorship in another way. Braulion says that he divided the work into twenty books, where Isidore had merely arranged it under *tituli*.

The *Sententiae*, or collected sayings, appear to have a different purpose, closer to that of a *florilegium*, or collection of extracts. This collection is undoubtedly authentic Isidore. He says so himself in the text, and his friend Braulion of Saragossa cites the *Sentences*.[3] Their organisation reflects some topical grouping. Book I forms a commentary on the Apostle's Creed, with its built-in systematic theological sequence: Creator, creature, Trinity, Church, Last Things; then comes Book II on conversion, sins, vices and virtues; Book III on the living of the Christian life and in particular the monastic life; and Book IV on Christian life in the world, including criticism of clergy, princes and the exercise of power.

Like Ambrose, Isidore was concerned with questions of Church and ministry. He wrote *De ecclesiasticis officiis* before 615. He cannot have finished it earlier than 597–8 because he cites Gregory the Great's *Moralia in Job*, only parts of which had been completed by then. In his prefatory letter to Bishop Fulgentius, Isidore gives a clue about his reasons for writing it. He says: 'you ask me the origin of the offices in the Church...and so I have sent you a little book with a systematic treatment of the kinds of office, taken from the oldest authorities'. He identities (as types of authority), Holy Scripture, apostolic tradition and the custom of the universal Church.

Influence

Seventeen years after Isidore's death, the Eighth Council of Toledo spoke of him as outstandingly learned among the Church's writers, *doctor egregius ecclesiae catholicae*, and mentions the *Sentences*. Five hundred manuscripts survive from the eighth to the fifteenth centuries. The *Etymologiae* was successful enough to be used by the canon lawyer Gratian in the twelfth century, when he turned to it in search of definitions of key legal terms such as *ius* and *lex* to give at the beginning of his definitive *Decretum*. He evidently had no sense that this was a 'mere' encyclopaedia.

Notes

1   Jacques Fontaine, *Tradition et actualité chez Isidore* (London, 1988), V.
2   Jacques Fontaine, *Tradition et actualité chez Isidore* (London, 1988), III.
3   *Renotatio*, PL 81.15–6: *edidit...sententiarum libros tres quos floribus ex libris pape Gregorii moralibus decoravit.*

Bibliography

Isidore, *Etymologiae*, ed. W.M. Lindsay (Oxford, 1911); Isidore, *De ecclesiasticis officiis, Corpus Christianorum Series Latina*, CXIII (1989); *El Liber de haeresibus de San Isidor de Sevilla y el Codice Ovetense*, ed. P. Angel Custodio Vega (Escorial, 1958).

Further reading

Jacques Fontaine, *Tradition et actualité chez Isidore* (London, 1988).

BEDE 672/3–735

Life and times

We move now into a period when 'the ancient world', insofar as it owed its intellectual coherence in part to the political unity imposed by the Roman Empire, was by any definition a generation or two in the past and writers were often conscious that they were engaged not in trying to cherish and protect an existing world of thought which was being endangered by political change, but in salvage and rescue and reconstruction of learning. The old cultural support systems had largely shut down. The royal or imperial courts could give protection to the scholarly-minded and even provide a useful patronage. Charlemagne is especially important here, as a ruler who made sustained efforts in this direction and even used legislation to try to reform the clergy and foster education. There were admonitions to bishops to send out priests to preach sermons in the vernacular so that ordinary people (the *vulgus*) might get some real understanding of the Gospel.[1] Some archbishops and bishops were eager to keep up standards by creating teaching libraries. Hincmar of Rheims built up a good library of theological texts during his archbishopric. But for the most part, the burden lay upon the monasteries.

In the monastic world of the early eighth century lived Bede, the scholar who was the last to be routinely admitted as an 'authority' among the Fathers by later ages. Bede spent a quiet lifetime as a scholar, never moving far from his birthplace in north-east England. In the last section of his *Ecclesiastical History*, rather as Gregory of Tours had done in his *History of the Franks*, Bede gives a picture of himself as its author. He describes his childhood; how he was given as a child oblate at the age of seven to Benedict Biscop, founder of the new monastery at Wearmouth, which had begun in 674. Bede also helpfully provided his own list of his writings at the end of his *Ecclesiastical History*.

Around 681 a sister house was founded at Jarrow. Bede was sent there with twenty-two monks, with Ceolfrith at their head. Plague swept the house, and all but Bede and Ceolfrith died. The two of them, the small boy and the man, continued to observe the Rule. The house survived and a double community persisted throughout Bede's lifetime.

Bede was made a deacon at the age of nineteen (six years before the age which was canonically allowable), and in 703 he became a priest. That was the sum of the 'promotions' of his lifetime.

This was not a place or a time in which one might expect to find a leading author. Bede had to make his way intellectually without much by way of the stimulus of live debate with fellow scholars. But Benedict Biscop made it possible for Bede to be bookish. He brought back from Monte Cassino, the house where the Benedictine Order had begun, a supply of key sources for the library of his own monastery. Without these resources Bede's own work would not have been possible.

Work and ideas

The strongest marks of Bede's scholarship are the solidity and reliability of his deployment of the work of earlier authors whom Christian readers could regard as 'safe to read'. That is not to say that he lacks originality. He was a salvager, synthesiser and consolidator in ways which were themselves original.

The *Ecclesiastical History* itself Bede finished at the age of fifty-nine, a few years before his death. In his preface he was careful to establish the authoritativeness – in a more homely sense – of the witnesses on which he had depended. The first was Abbot Albinus, who had been educated by Archbishop Theodore of Canterbury and Abbot Hadrian, 'both of them respected and learned men'. It was from this source that he says he has obtained his information about the conversion of the English to Christianity by Augustine of Canterbury at the end of the sixth century. Nothelm, a London priest, passed on a good deal of this material to Bede, and he himself had visited Rome and, with the permission of the then Pope, looked into the archives. He brought back (for Bede to incorporate) letters of Pope Gregory I to Augustine. Albinus also made sure that Bede had been provided with information about the Church in Northumbria and elsewhere. Bede had applied to Daniel, Bishop of the West Saxons, for materials about the history of the Church in his area and the isle of Wight. From the monastery of Lastingham he had obtained information about the conversion of Mercia. In this systematic way he did his best to check his facts. So he had relied on those who were knowledgeable about the local events he was describing.

Historiographically speaking, this was novel. Bede saw (with unusual clarity for his time) the distinction between the creation of an accurate 'record' and 'explanation of events', and history as a 'story' from which Christians might learn for their edification. This last purpose of history was in the forefront of his mind, at least alongside the need to be accurate, of which he was so conscious. He begins his preface thus, pointing out that if history records good things of good men, the thoughtful hearer is encouraged to imitate what is good; if it records evil of wicked men, the pious reader is led to avoid evil and behave well. To the modern reader the juxtaposition of elements of the miraculous with hard-headed political comment can make it difficult to read the *History* as a unity, because it seems to alternate two entirely different kinds of story, the ordinary event and the miraculous. But for Bede, that too was important. He may have had different criteria of reliability for miracles, but saw them as indispensable to the creation of an edifying picture.

The *History* Bede himself describes as an 'ecclesiastical history' of our island and race: *nostrae insulae ac gentis*. That bespeaks a striking sense of national or racial identity for its time, as well as a consciousness of the unity of the 'island'. These notions are remarkable and need to be interpreted in the light of the fact that Bede was well aware that he did not live in a unified kingdom and can have had only a limited sense of the extent of the main 'island' of Britain.

The list of Bede's own works in the *Ecclesiastical History* also includes saints' *Lives*, of Felix, Anastasius and Cuthbert, and a history of the abbots of his own monastery (Benedict, Ceolfrith and Hwaetberht), as well as letters and hymns.

Bede's main work was on Scripture. He comments in his exposition of the Acts of the Apostles that he knows that in his maturity Augustine wrote *retractationes*, of works he had composed when young. With the passage of time and wider reading (*ex lectionis usu*) and with divine assistance, Bede, like Augustine, believes himself to have come to a better understanding,[2] and so composes his own *retractatio*.

Bede was not without a sensitivity to language both as something beautiful and as raising philosophical questions. He wrote a *De orthographia*, in which he provides something more than a straightforward account of the rules of correct spelling. He explains the differences between *verbum, sermo, sententia, loquela* and *oratio*. Anything said by tongue and voice is a 'word'. A *sermo* has more precision of articulation. A *sententia* enables a meaning to be grasped. A *loquela* adds eloquence. By the time we get to the *oratio*, he thinks, we have a developed art form. In *De schematibus et tropis*, Bede imitates Augustine in *De doctrina Christiana*, but at a more pragmatic level, exploring the use of figures of speech in Scripture and asking what is their purpose (one of 'clarification' or 'adornment').

Bede's *De rerum natura* is a book about what we should now call natural science. Here he chose a genre for which there were classical precedents. Pliny had written in a similar vein in prose, and there was material in Seneca and even Lucretius. Each of these classical authors relates, often anecdotally, observations of the behaviour of things in the natural world. Bede was attempting it in a Christian context, where the natural world is perceived differently, as the creation of the Christian God.

De temporibus is a pioneering work about chronology, which contemporary debate had made a burning topic. The lack of fixed points of reference for the dates from which to begin calculations of the moveable feasts of the Church's year was causing difficulty, most significantly over calculating the date of Easter each year. The importance of the work on calculating dates was heightened in Bede's day by the controversy over the date of Easter which divided Europe and threatened to divide the Church. It was important that all Christians should be able to celebrate Easter on the same day. This was regarded as a token of the very unity of the Church.

The problem was especially urgent in England because there was a division of usage there between Christians of the 'Roman' conversion, when Gregory the Great had sent Augustine of Canterbury to England, and those of the older Celtic tradition, who had brought Christianity across the sea from Ireland. Different local churches were celebrating Easter at different dates, to the domestic embarrassment of royal personages, where one member of a married couple adhered to one system and the other to the second.

Bede realised that if all the days have twelve hours the hours will be different lengths at different seasons of the year, whereas if the hours are all the same length, each day will have more of them in summer, fewer in winter.

Influence

Bede was read for his *History* and for his Biblical commentary, which was chiefly what brought him recognition as one of the Western 'Fathers'.

Notes

1 W. Ullmann, *The Carolingian Renaissance and the Idea of Kingship* (London, 1969), p. 36.
2 Bede, *Expositio Actuum Apostolorum et Retractatio*, ed. M.L.W. Laistner (Cambridge, MA, 1939), p. 93.

Bibliography

Bede, *Ecclesiastical History*, ed. and trans. B. Colgrave and R.A.B. Mynors (Oxford, 1969). Bede, *Opera de Temporibus*, ed. C.W. Jones (Cambridge, MA, 1943). Some of Bede's exegetical writings are in modern Latin editions in the *Corpus Christianorum*. There is a further translation of Bede, *Ecclesiastical History*, by L. Sherley-Price revised by R.E. Latham and D.H. Farmer (London, 1990).

Further reading

Peter Hunter Blair, *The World of Bede* (Cambridge, 1990, 2nd edn); Benedicta Ward, *The Venerable Bede* (London, 1990, second edn 1998).

PASCHASIUS RADBERTUS *c.*790–860

Life and times

With Paschasius we move to a group of near-contemporaries, many of whom knew and influenced each other, who can loosely be called 'the Carolingians'. Paschasius Radbertus was a Benedictine monk at Corbie under Abbot Adalhard, and went to Saxony with Adalhard in 822. He himself became Abbot of Corbie in about 844, resigning in 853 so that he could study in peace and without the responsibilities of high monastic office, with its occasional outside duties such as attendance at councils of the Church. He is recorded as being present at the Council of Paris in 847.

To get a picture of this world, we need to begin with Alcuin (*c.*740–804). He was born of noble parents in Northumbria. His interest in education continued steadily throughout his life. He himself was educated at the cathedral school at York, where he had access to a good library and was a pupil of Aelbert and Egbert, both of whom later became Archbishops of York. Alcuin became a master in the school in 766. He then travelled on the continent of Europe with Aelbert until the latter succeeded to the see of York. Around 781, he met Charlemagne and was adopted as the imperial 'educational adviser'. He established a library in the Palace; he became the royal 'tutor', officially teaching the young princes and the women but often listened to by a curious Charlemagne himself. Alcuin found congenial scholarly company at Aachen. Then in 796 he became Abbot of Tours, where again he set up a school and library.

Charlemagne's interest in the things of the mind seems to have been genuine. An example is a letter (*Letter* 144, of 798) written on behalf of Charlemagne to Alcuin enquiring about the method of dating arithmetically (*per campos arithmeticae artis*) the moveable feasts of the Church's year. Alcuin's reply, *Letter* 145, includes a response to another letter he had received enquiring about the phases of the moon. Alcuin had evidently done some research.[1] He has applied his powers of reasoning, he says, and collected the views of mathematicians, so as to give Charlemagne a full and reliable answer. Letter 148 (in 798) was sent to Charlemagne to thank him for gifts which had been relayed to him by Fredegisus, a minor Carolingian author now known chiefly for his reflections on the nature of nothingness (*De nihilo et tenebris*). Alcuin takes the opportunity to discuss astronomy. He points out that the philosophers were not the founders (*conditores*) but the discoverers (*inventores*) of these arts. It was the Creator who founded astronomy, by making nature as he chose. Astronomers merely try to discover how the universe works.

Perhaps stimulated by conversations with Charlemagne himself, Alcuin gave some thought to the role of a king. He drew on Isidore in making a list of the tasks which fall to a monarch: to govern the kingdom; to do justice; to renew the Church; to correct the people; to make fair decisions about individuals; to defend the oppressed; to make laws; to comfort the exile; and to show forth to everyone everywhere the way of equity and eternal life (*Letter* 177). He wrote to Charlemagne (in the mode of Gregory the Great) to tell him that he was *rector* and *praedicator*. He uses both the sword of power and the trumpet of catholic preaching (*Letter* 41). This is startling. The drawing of a line between the priestly function and that of the lay ruler later became very important, and the ministry of the Word was settled firmly on the Church's side of this line.

Alcuin's *Letter* 131 (796–8), written to the young men of St Martin at Tours, exhorts them to sedulous confession of their sins. They are encouraged to study hard, to live soberly, chastely and modestly, and to confess their sins, because sins are particularly tempting in adolescence. The Devil will not succeed in tempting you, he reassures them, if you are vigilant about confessing your sins. All sins are venial if they are confessed and if penance is done for them.

God knows all that you do in secret. He has provided a place for self-accusation (confession), *a locus accusandi nosmetipsos in peccatis nostris coram sacerdote Dei*, so that we may accuse ourselves rather than being accused by Satan before the judgement seat of God.

The letters are important. The little exhortatory passage about confession in the letter to the young monks of St Martin is of special interest because it shows Alcuin to have been up to the minute on contemporary developments in the penitential system. This was a period of significant change, when the old public penance for serious sins in the face of the congregation with exclusion from communion and lengthy public penance until eventually absolution was pronounced by the bishop, gave way to regular private confession of even small sins to a priest. Alcuin's writing on virtues and vices is also a significant staging-post in the literature.

Alcuin's *Rhetorica* is derivative; most of it comes from Cicero's *De inventione*. Alcuin was attracted to the Ciceronian idea that a great man could lead by his eloquence and domesticate his people by the use of his tongue. But the work's very existence is striking, for it was to be several centuries before serious academic work was to be done in rhetoric again.

Alcuin's *De virtutibus et vitiis* was popular in the Middle Ages, but Alcuin's chief influence was largely a personal one, upon the generations of writers we are now concerned with. He stimulated others. Among his pupils was Hrabanus Maurus (*c.*780–856), who was educated at the leading monastery of Fulda, where he was an oblate, and then at Tours, to which he was sent with a friend, Hatto, for further study, partly under Alcuin. When he returned from Tours (before Alcuin's death), he was made master of the school at Fulda, where Walafrid Strabo became his pupil. He was made deacon in 801 and priest in 814.

Hrabanus was made Abbot of Fulda in 824. He was a successful abbot and the abbey throve both intellectually and in terms of its prosperity. But he did not enjoy the politics, and in 842 he resigned the abbacy (much as Paschasius was to resign his) and withdrew to Fulda to study. His involvement in various political and theological conflicts did his career no harm, and he was not able to pursue his quiet scholarly life for long. In 847 he rose to be Archbishop of Mainz. During his tenure of the see three synods were held at Mainz in 847, 848 and 852.

Hrabanus can be seen in correspondence maintaining a network of scholarly exchange. To the Bishop of Lisieux, Frechulfus, he writes of the *magnorum virorum conamen antiquitus*, the endeavour

45

of the 'great' of the past to keep one another intellectually on their toes by letter writing and encouraging each other to write books.[2]

Hrabanus's friendship with Hatto persisted and he sent the latter an early work (*c*.814), the *Opus in laudem sanctae crucis*. Holy Scripture exhorts us to bring gifts to God and it makes an exception of no one, he says in the accompanying letter. He has tried an experiment, setting out the text in the form of a Cross and putting in special marks to make the material accessible and easy to read. (There are figures of the Seraphim and Cherubim standing round.) If anyone feels offended by this novelty, he should be reminded that Hrabanus has done it on purpose, to make things clearer, *ut lucidior sensus et loquutio in eis fieret*. He refers Hatto to the practice of the *veteres*, older writers, particularly Prosper of Aquitaine and Sedulius (he does not mention Boethius by name), of alternating prose and verse in a composition, to make it more fun to read and also more profitable to the readers: *quo iucundiora simul et utiliora sua legentibus forent ingenia*.[3]

Hrabanus was influential in the evangelisation of Germany. That led him to write a handbook for the clergy, *De clericorum institutione*, to explain the principles and theology of the liturgical acts for which they were responsible. He comments in *Letter* 9 on the link between this task and the study of Scripture. In Exodus, for example, 'almost all the sacraments by which the present Church is founded, nourished and ruled, are touched on figuratively'.[4]

In the same spirit of providing for the pastoral necessities of a growing ecclesiastical community, he was a prominent exegete. He wrote commentaries on the Pentateuch, the Wisdom literature, St Matthew's Gospel and the Pauline epistles. A glimpse of the strong pastoral motivation of this work is to be had in *Letter* 5.[5] Hrabanus sends his commentary on Matthew with the letter, explaining that his brother monks have complained that they do not have a sufficiently full commentary (*tam plenam et sufficientem expositionem*) of this Gospel, as they do for other Gospels, where Augustine, Ambrose and Bede have provided materials. Hrabanus says he has looked carefully at the resources in Cyprian, Eusebius, Hilary, Ambrose, Jerome, Augustine, Fulgentius, Victorinus, Fortunatianus, Orosius, Leo, Gregory Nazianzen, Gregory the Great, John Chrysostom and 'other Fathers'. This must raise the question of how far he had been able to consult these in the original and *in extenso*, but the main point here is his use of them as authorities. He seems to have found the exegetical tasks thus pressed on him a tall order. He complains that Frechulf has asked him to do something beyond his powers in requesting him to digest the Fathers sufficiently thoroughly to enable him to provide both a literal and a spiritual interpretation of the Pentateuch.[6]

Hrabanus was an encyclopaedist, too, composing a *De universo*, or *De rerum naturis*, which is heavily indebted to Isidore's *Etymologiae*. The predestination controversy also drew him in. Hrabanus's 'encyclopaedia' continued to be read surprisingly late in the Middle Ages; Nicholas of Cusa admits to having used it.[7] (For Hrabanus on the *glossa ordinaria*, see p.57.)

Next we must bring in Walafrid Strabo (*c*.809–49). Strabo (which means the 'Squinter') was born in south-west Gernany. He was an oblate at the monastery of Reichenau, where he was taught by Wetti and subsequently by Tatto. At about the age of fourteen he met Gottschalk and they became friends. This was to remain a loyal friendship, despite the fact that Gottschalk moved beyond the pale of intellectual responsibility and became one of our 'outsiders'. Gottschalk of Orbais (born *c*.806/8) and Walafrid Strabo were oddly paired as friends, the one prominent for dangerous opinions, the other careful not to offend. Gottschalk began at Fulda as a *puer oblatus* in 814. At some time in the next decade he studied at Reichenau, where the friendship began.

Gottschalk was at Fulda under Hrabanus Maurus when he was abbot. Walafrid too moved on to Fulda to study under Hrabanus, who did not much like Gottschalk. The situation was perhaps somewhat tense, and Walafrid moved again from Fulda to Aachen, where he seems to have been in the spring of 829. In the early summer of that year he was appointed royal tutor to the young Charles. He let it be understood that he could not account for this preferment (*quo nescio casu*), but there is evidence that he had assiduously sought patronage, acquiring as a new patron Grimald, chaplain of the imperial court. When there were two rebellions in royal circles, in 828 and 832–3, Walafrid behaved characteristically, keeping a low profile – possibly at Weissenburg – and letting his quiet loyalty to Louis and his family make itself felt. He was duly rewarded once Louis was reinstated; the twenty-nine-year-old Walafrid was given the abbacy of Reichenau.

Letters between the two strangely matched friends survive from 848, when Gottschalk had been condemned for heresy at Mainz and sent to Orbais under a sentence of 'life imprisonment'. In the spring of 849, Gottschalk was brought for retrial before Charles and the Frankish bishops, but he was not willing to recant. Walafrid was accidentally drowned in 849 while on a mission from Louis the Emperor to Charles the Bald.

A group of poems survives from after Wetti's death in the *Visio Wettini*, which seems to have been finished when Walafrid was eighteen. It takes the form of a vision Wetti had on the day before he died (3 November 824). The monk Heito had made a prose account of the vision as Wetti related it, and Walafrid turned this into verse. It is a long and complex example of a genre of literature which was to become popular throughout the Middle Ages. It is also a self-conscious genre, often involving a philosophical discussion of the whole subject of visions. The poet visits the abode of the blessed. There is an angelic guide in the *Visio*, who has political comments to make: 'A great many priests strive for worldly gain, and they cling to that obsessively. They behave obsequiously at court to get ephemeral rewards. They are adorned with fancy garments rather than a shining and exemplary life. They are more interested in goods than in good living.' The model on which Walafrid is likely to have depended was the section on visions in Gregory the Great's *Dialogues*, Book IV. Indeed, Wetti calls out for the last words of Gregory's *Dialogues* to be read out to him as he lies dying.

A notebook of his extracts from Isidore, Bede and Alcuin also survives, containing portions on natural phenomena and portents.

As abbot of Reichenau Walafrid wrote a book on gardening, *De cultura hortorum*. There is no evidence that his example was directly influential, but it illustrates a trend: 'A man instructed in both cultures sees ahead of him the things of heaven and he watches out behind him for the things of this world.' More importantly, this work stands in the tradition of guided visits to the supernatural world, in which we shall later find Dante writing. The anti-clerical comments are to be met with among the Waldensians in the twelfth century, and in Wyclif and the Lollards in the fourteenth and fifteenth centuries.

Work and ideas

Paschasius Radbertus is thus a representative of a series of Carolingian and post-Carolingian scholars who took onwards the work of Bede and others on the interpretation of Scripture.

In his Biblical commentary, Paschasius gave some thought to the question how to balance brevity with completeness (*In Matthaeum*, p. 470). He says that he has written on Matthew's Gospel to assist his brothers (p. 463). He describes the Gospels as a *quadriga*, a four-wheeled chariot in which Christ the celestial Charioteer quarters the world (*In Matthaeum*, p. 464). Christ is 'always' with the Father (in eternity), but in the temporal world he 'goes about' in this 'vehicle'. The four animals which symbolise the Evangelists are linked with this image (*In Matthaeum*, pp. 465–6).

Paschasius, who had read his Augustine, was well aware of the problem of the apparent lack of harmony of the Gospels. He gave the matter fresh thought. He does not see them as complementary, which might have provided a relatively simple solution to many of the failures of the Gospels to agree in their accounts of events, but as coinhering in one another in a deeper way. He takes the view that though each has its own qualities as a narrative (*suam . . . proprietatem*), that does not mean that 'faces' or aspects will be found in one which are actually lacking in the others. They are all complete (*In Matthaeum*, p. 467).

The deeper – also Augustinian – exegetical question of the relationship of 'words' and 'things' preoccupies Paschasius too (*In Matthaeum*, p. 470ff). This, he explains, is what most characteristically underlies the allegories of Scripture. Here again, he was helping to keep consciously in the minds of scholars matters of the utmost importance in medieval thought.

Paschasius also became involved in the Eucharistic controversy of the age. His *De corpore et sanguine Domini* (831, revised 844) is the earliest attempt at systematic clarification of the doctrine of the Eucharist. He was attacked over this work by Ratramnus of Corbie and Hrabanus Maurus. In his prologue, addressed to Abbot Warinus, Paschasius gives a preliminary list of authorities. His preface (addressed to Charlemagne) offers the Emperor a 'little book', small in size but 'great' in what it has to teach about the sacrament of communion. Paschasius's starting point is that there can be no doubt that in the Eucharist the *verum corpus*, the true body of Christ, is present. None of the faithful can afford to be unsure about that. He defines a sacrament as 'whatever is given us as a token of salvation in divine worship, when a visible thing had a quite different invisible effect. He distinguishes within this broad definition a range of 'mysteries': the sacraments of Christ in the Church; the *sacramentum iuris* (the taking of an oath); mysteries such as the birth of Christ; and any situation in which the Holy Spirit acts inwardly by grace. Here, too, he was putting up the fenceposts of later debate, in which the idea of a sacrament would gradually become controversial. It was the Church's wish to emphasise that the sacraments, which were valid and efficacious only within the Church, were necessary to salvation; anti-establishment dissidents from the twelfth century onwards were moving in a direction which was eventually to lead to some sixteenth-century reformers' insistence that the sacraments, though helpful, were not indispensable.

Influence

See under Remigius.

Notes

1 *Epistolae Karolini Aevi*, ed. E. Dümmler, MGH, II (Berlin, 1895).
2 Hrabanus Maurus, *Epistolae*, 8, ed. E. Dümmler, Epistolae Karolini Aevi, 3 (Berlin, 1899), p. 393.
3 Hrabanus Maurus, *Epistolae*, 2(a), ed. E. Dümmler, Epistolae Karolini Aevi, 3 (Berlin, 1899), p. 382.
4 Hrabanus Maurus, *Epistolae*, 9, ed. E. Dümmler, Epistolae Karolini Aevi, 3 (Berlin, 1899), p. 385.
5 Hrabanus Maurus, *Epistolae*, 5, ed. E. Dümmler, Epistolae Karolini Aevi, 3 (Berlin, 1899), p. 389.
6 Hrabanus Maurus, *Epistolae*, 8, ed. E. Dümmler, Epistolae Karolini Aevi, 3 (Berlin, 1899), p. 393.
7 London, BL, Ms. Harley 3092, fol.1r, Elisabeth Heyse, *Hrabanus Maurus' Enzyklopädie 'De rerum naturis'* (Munich, 1969), p. 3.

Bibliography

Epistolae Karolini Aevi, ed. E. Dümmler, MGH, II (Berlin, 1895); *Rhetores Latini Minores*, ed. C. Halm (Leipzig, 1863). Paschasius Radbertus, *Expositiones in Matthaeum*, ed. B. Paulus, CCCM, 56A–B (1984); Paschasius Radbertus, *De corpore et sanguine Domini*, ed. B. Paulus, CCCM 57 (1969); Paschasius Radbertus, *Vita Santi Adalhardi*, trans. Allen Cabaniss (Syracuse, NY, 1967); Hrabanus Maurus, *In Honorem Sanctae Crucis*, CCCM (1997); Hrabanus Maurus, *Epistolae*, ed. E. Dümmler, Epistolae Karolini Aevi, 3 (Berlin, 1899), p. 389.

Further reading

Eleanor Shipley Duckett, *Alcuin, Friend of Charlemagne* (New York, 1951); C.J.B. Gaskoin, *Alcuin: His Life and Work* (New York, 1966); A. Kleinclausz, *Alcuin* (Paris, 1948); L. Wallach, *Alcuin and Charlemagne* (Ithaca, NY, 1959); Elizabeth Heyse, *Hrabanus Maurus' Enzyklopädie 'De rerum naturis'* (Munich, 1969); Howard R. Patch, *The Other World* (Cambridge, MA, 1950); H.D. Stoffler, *Der Hortulus des Walahfrid (Sic) Strabo* (Sigmaringen, 1978); David A. Traill, *Walafrid Strabo's Visio Wettini* (Frankfurt, 1974); M.-L. Weber, *Die Gedichte des Gottschalk von Orbais* (Frankfurt, 1992).

JOHANNES SCOTUS ERIUGENA *c.810–c.877*

Life and times

Several Irishmen were working on the continent of Europe in the ninth century. One of the best-known was Sedulius Scottus. Another, Martinus, was Master of the cathedral school at Laon for a time. Johannes Scotus Eriugena was the most notorious of this group. Before 846, Eriugena had won the patronage of the Emperor Charles the Bald; was living at the royal court and was entrusted with the running of the palace 'school'. The palace under Charles the Bald was still equipped with a school, alongside the cathedral schools Charlemagne had fostered with such determination

Work and ideas

In one area, Eriugena's work was of an originality which perhaps neither he nor others fully appreciated at the time. Eriugena was commissioned by the Emperor Charles the Bald to translate the writings of Ps-Dionysius which had been given to the court of Louis the Pious by the Greek Emperor Michael Palaeologus in 827, including a treatise on the heavenly hierarchy. A negative or apophatic theology developed from this tradition, placing an emphasis on what we cannot know about God rather than upon his recognised 'attributes'. For example, we do not know his immensity, only that he is infinite. Eriugena also translated Gregory of Nyssa's *De hominis opificio*. For these purposes, Eriugena had to learn Greek very quickly. He made errors, and his modest invitation to others to put him right if they notice errors may be in keeping with the presumption that there were other Greek speakers locally.[1]

The *Periphyseon*, On Nature was written between 860 and 866, late in Eriugena's career. He moves from the application of reasoning in the first three books to an exegetical approach at the end, with the final part of Book II concentrating on literal interpretation and Books IV–V on allegory.

John Scotus Eriugena was principally influenced by Ps-Dionysius in the *Periphyseon*, along with Maximus the Confessor and Gregory of Nyssa's *De hominis opificio*, from which he quotes a great deal in the *Periphyseon*. He is unusual in the development of his ideas in this work, in thinking beyond collating his sources. He does not merely paste them together but works them into the deeper levels of his argument.

Eriugena's *Periphyseon* proposes a division of nature. Nature he takes to include 'everything which is and is not'. He divides it into what creates and is not created (God himself); what is created and creates (primordial causes); what is created and does not create (times and places, the subject-matter of cosmology and the genre of the hexaemeron); what neither creates nor is created (a philosophical treatise and commentary on Genesis 1.24–3.19.

Eriugena was asked by Hincmar of Rheims to refute Gottschalk's theory of predestination. He was thus to be involved in the other leading controversy of the day, on 'double' predestination (whether, if God predestines the damned to hell as well as the blessed to heaven, he is the author of an evil). In about 850 Eriugena wrote *De divina praedestinatione*. This kind of stimulus of a writer joining in illustrates very well the intellectual interdependence of this group of scholars.

In his gloss on Martianus Capella's *De nuptiis Philologiae et Mercurii*[2] from the mid-fifth century, we see Eriugena's scientific interests again. This account of the marriage of Mercury describes how he failed in his earlier attempts to court Sophia, Mantice and Psyche. Then Apollo suggests he should try Philology. Mercury, Virtue and Apollo undertake a journey to see Jupiter and get his permission for the marriage and to ask for the gift of divinity to make the previously mortal Philology a fit consort. From Philology's mouth come the books which are gathered up for their use by the arts and sciences and the muses. This tale may have got him interested in cosmology, for the journey in *De nuptiis* carries the characters through the heavens. Eriugena also uses Macrobius on Cicero's *Somnium Scipionis* as a jumping-off point for cosmological reflections.

Influence

Heiric of Auxerre got to know Eriugena's work in the 860s. He borrows from Eriugena in his own *Homily on St John* and the *Vita S. Germani*. See, too, under Hincmar of Rheines.

Notes

1 Otten in Backus, p. 5; J.J. Contreni, *The Cathedral School at Laon from 850–930*.
2 See S. Gersh, *Middle Platonism and Neoplatonism: the Latin Tradition* (Notre Dame, 1986), 2 vols.

Bibliography

Johannes Scotus Eriugena, *Periphyseon*, ed. E.A. Jeauneau, *Corpus Christianorum Continuatio Medievalis*, CLXI–CLXII (1996–7).

Further reading

G.-H. Allard, *Jean Scot Écrivain* (Montreal and Paris, 1983); J.J. Contreni, *The Cathedral School at Laon from 850–930*; John J. O'Meara and Ludwig Bieler (eds), *The Mind of Eriugena* (Dublin, 1970); W. Otten, 'The Role of the Fathers in Carolingian Theology', in *The Reception of the Church Fathers in the West*, ed. Irena Backus (Leiden, 1997); R. Roques, *Libres sentiers vers l'érigénisme* (Rome, 1975).

HINCMAR OF RHEIMS *c*.806–882)

Life and times

Hincmar was educated at the monastery of St Denis. In 822 he accompanied his abbot and teacher Hilduin to the Court of Louis the Pious. He entered the royal service in 834 and remained there under Charles the Bald. Charles's influence got Hincmar elected to the archbishopric of Rheims in 845. In his letter on his accession, he confidently identifies the Councils of Nicaea, Constantinople, Ephesus and Chalcedon, and reassures his readers that he holds their decrees and the orthodox faith.[1]

Hincmar proved a somewhat aggressive archbishop, energetically reforming his diocese and tangling with the Emperor Lothar I, to the point where Lothar attempted to have him deposed for seeking to nullify the ordinations of his predecessor. In *Letter* 12 Hincmar complains that many contradictory and untrue things are said about him, and he asks his correspondent to bear in mind Proverbs 29.12, the rule that those who are ready to listen to lies will have impious ministers.[2]

Work and ideas

Hincmar was prominent in the debate over Gottschalk's teaching on 'double' predestination. He wrote against Gottschalk in *Letter* 37, which is addressed to the *simplices* of his diocese, whom he wishes to save from being misled. He also mentions Remigius of Auxerre as his archbishop.

Satan is prowling about, Hincmar warns, seeking to introduce error in order to break up the unity of the Church. If they saw Satan as he really was, people would flee from him. He therefore puts on the appearance of an angel of light. Such false Christs and false prophets are not new in the history of the Church. But here is one arisen in this very diocese. He is confusing the foreknowledge and predestination of God, teaching that there are those who are predestined to hell (who cannot avoid it whatever good they do) and those predestined to glory (who cannot fall from grace however badly they behave). The implication is he points out, that God did not die for all, and that baptism does not purge from sin those who are not predestined.[3] That is, a dangerous doctrine. Hincmar has two writings of Gottschalk's in his possession, and he urges that if they come into anyone else's hands they should be destroyed. In a spirit of pastoral care, Hincmar himself has provided some extracts from the Fathers to be used by anyone who finds himself persuaded by what Gottschalk is saying. He gives a series of definitions. *Praescientia* is foreknowledge, which knows what will happen beforehand, or where that which is known beforehand will actually happen. Predestination is a fore-ordering or preparation by grace. The great error, in Hincmar's view, was that it implied that God is the author of evil, which must follow if he predestines to hell as well as to heaven.[4]

Hincmar got a sharp rejoinder from some of his contemporaries, including Ratramnus of Corbie. He was instrumental in bringing Eriugena into the debate, seeking an ally. Eriugena's *De divina praedestinatione* created a storm, with a backlash against Hincmar. Hincmar wrote his own rather untidy *De praedestinatione Dei et libero arbitrio*. Two synods, at Quiercy in 853 and at Valence in 855, went opposite ways in ruling on the controversy. A formal statement was produced 'gagging' Gottschalk.[5] Hincmar was, however, more impressive in the knowledge of legal texts he displayed in the running of the diocese. He was a good practical bishop.

Influence

The predestination question was to become important again in the fourteenth century and most strikingly with Calvin in the sixteenth century. Calvin was a strong advocate of a doctrine of double predestination, and he coupled it with an idea which Augustine had resolutely resisted because of its worrying pastoral consequences, that those who were to be saved knew it. This had the unfortunate pastoral implication that those without this certainty could only despair and those with it need make no further effort to be good.

Notes

1 Hincmar, *Epistolae* 1, *MGH Epp. Karolini Aevi*, Tome VIII, Fasc.I (Berlin, 1939).
2 Hincmar, *Epistolae* 12, *MGH Epp. Karolini Aevi*, Tome VIII, Fasc.I (Berlin, 1939).
3 Hincmar, *Epistolae* 37, *MGH Epp. Karolini Aevi*, Tome VIII, Fasc.I (Berlin, 1939), pp. 12–3.
4 Hincmar, *Epistolae* 37, *MGH Epp. Karolini Aevi*, Tome VIII, Fasc.I (Berlin, 1939), pp.14–20.
5 *Frater Gotescalc, sacrosanctum sacerdotalis misterii officium, quod inregulariter usurpasti... perpetuum silentium ori tuo virtute aeterni verbu imponimus.*

Bibliography

Hincmar, *Epistolae*, MGH Epp.8i (Berlin, 1939); Hincmar, *De divortio Lotharii Regis et Theutergae Reginae*, ed. L. Böhringer (Hanover, 1992); Hincmar, *Collectio de ecclesiis et capellis*, ed. M. Stratmann (Hanover, 1990); Hincmar, *De ordine palatii*, ed. T. Gross and R. Schieffer, MGH Fontes, 3 (Hanover, 1980).

Further reading

W. Otten, 'Carolingian Theology', in *The Mediaeval Theologians*, ed. G.R. Evans (Oxford, 2001), pp. 65–84.

REMIGIUS OF AUXERRE *c.*841–*c.*908

Life and times

Remigius was probably of Burgundian stock. He was one of a group of prominent scholars who emerged from the monastic school of St Germain d'Auxerre in the Carolingian period. He was a student of Heiric of Auxerre, who had been taught by Lupus of Ferrières, himself a student of Hrabanus Maurus. He became master of the school at Rheims when Heiric died. Later he taught again at Rheims, when Archbishop Fulk sent for him to raise the standards in the cathedral school there. After Fulk died in 900 it is probable that he then taught in Paris. Remigius disappears from view after 908.

Work and ideas

Remigius was commenting on works his pupils were studying. He was writing pragmatically for their use, and much of what he says is unashamedly derivative. There is commentary on Latin grammarians (Donatus, Priscian, Phocas), on Cato's *Distichs*, Boethius's *Consolation*, Juvenal, and on Bede's *Ars metrica* and *De schematibus et tropis*.

Remigius's commentary on Martianus Capella's *De nuptiis Philologiae et Mercurii* is based on the vast commentary of Hrabanus Maurus, and it concentrates prosaically on the literal rather than the figurative interpretation. In his rendering, Mercury presents the seven liberal arts as handmaids to his bride Philology. This is a quite different type of 'encyclopaedia'.

His exegetical works include commentary on Genesis and the Psalms. There is also a commentary on the Mass. The 'school' of Auxerre is important as a staging-post in the endeavour which eventually created the *glossa ordinaria*. Remigius was not the only master of the school of Auxerre in the late Carolingian period to have a claim to the authorship of surviving commentary; Haimo of Auxerre has also been credited with a commentary on Genesis. The essence of these commentaries is their derivativeness. They were shared work. They were on their way already to becoming an 'ordinary gloss' in the sense that they were less a unitary literary work than points taken from a bundle of authorities convenient for the elucidation of a given passage.

They were shared work too in the sense that they reflect an intimacy between Auxerre and Fleury and other houses. From Adrevald of Fleury (active between 850 and 875) Remigius took large slices of text for his own commentary on Genesis, concentrating on the literal interpretation. Haimo of Auxerre had probably already finished his own period of active work in exegesis by this time and Adrevald's text was copied alongside Hamo's in two surviving manuscripts. In framing his own commentary on Genesis, Remigius also took a good deal from Angelomus of Luxeuil, who had in his turn incorporated much of what Alcuin had had to say. The dominant source for Remigius on Genesis was Hrabanus Maurus.

Remigius is nevertheless notable for the degree to which he integrates his sources into the discussion, identifying them only where they are so uncommon as to make it necessary for him to provide a prompt for the user. The commentary on Martianus Capella[1] may owe something to John the Scot or the Dunchad, possibly by Martin of Laon. There is little acknowledgement, but the remarks are often from this common pool.

Influence

Sigebert of Gembloux includes Remigius in his *Liber de Scriptoribus Ecclesiasticis.*[2] He says that Remigius is *nominatus in exponendis saecularibus scripturis, notificavit se utilius divinas etiam Scripturas exponendo.*

There was a more general achievement and influence of this group of writers, which it is convenient to touch on here. For some centuries it was to remain the case that some portions of Scripture attracted more attention than others from commentators, for example the Pauline Epistles and the Wisdom books of the Old Testament. Thus there remained gaps in the routine exegetical coverage of the Bible. These centuries of work on commentary on the Bible were brought together, apparently largely as a result of a systematic endeavour by the brothers Ralph and Anselm teaching at Laon, into the *Glossa ordinaria*, which became a more or less standard text during the twelfth century. The bringing together of the authorities was a bigger and more complex task for books on which there was a great deal of commentary to review.

The task was different for different books of the Bible. For example, the Psalms and the Pauline Epistles had been very commonly commented on, but other books much less so. The Carolingians, for especially – Remigius of Auxerre (on the Psalms) and Hrabanus Maurus (on the Wisdom literature) made interim contributions to the compilation. The main sources used to provide authorities were the major Fathers. In the case of certain books of the Bible one Father is dominant, for example – not surprisingly – Gregory the Great for the book of Job.

Notes

1 *Remigii Autissiodorensis Commentum in Martianum Capellam*, ed. Cora E. Lutz (Leiden, 1962), 2 vols.
2 *Patrologia Latina* 160.573.

Bibliography

Remigius, *Expositio super Genesim*, ed. Burton Van Name Edwards, *Corpus Christianorum Continuatio Mediaevalis*, 136 (Turnhout, 1999); *Remigii Autissiodorensis Commentum in Martianum Capellam*, ed. Cora E. Lutz (Leiden, 1962), 2 vols; Remigii Autissodorensis, *Expositio super Genesim*, ed. Burton Edwards, *Corpus Christianorum Continuatio Mediaevalis*, CXXXVI (1999).

Further reading

Burton Edwards, in *L'école carolingienne d'Auxerre: 830–908*, ed. D. Iogna Pratt, C. Jeudy and G. Lobrichon (Paris, 1989).

GERBERT OF AURILLAC (*c.* 940–1003)

Life and times

Gerbert of Aurillac (Pope Sylvester II) began his career as a young monk in Aquitaine. The Omayyid Caliphate of Cordova was at the height of its dominance in Spain. In that southernmost region of France there was perhaps a sufficient geographical closeness to the Moslem scholarship of Spain to make it feasible that something of the learning of Islamic scholars was accessible to him. Gerbert was able to teach in the school of Hatto, Bishop of Vichy, a cathedral school where the mathematical subjects of the quadrivium were taken seriously. Nearby was Sainte Marie de Ripoll where there was a library with notable scientific holdings. These chance factors may have encouraged in him a mathematical and scientific interest.

In 970 Gerbert went to Rome, where he met Pope John XIII. But his early bent was for scholarship, not ecclesiastical politics, and he returned to his academic work. From 972–80 he studied at Rheims. From 980–3 he was abbot at Bobbio, but returned to Rheims from 983–9. There was a good library at Bobbio, but Gerbert seems to have been driven (or frightened) away by disturbances there and went back to Rheims where he was able to carry on studying under the protection of Archbishop Adalbero. The movement to and from monastery and cathedral schools we observed in earlier authors of these centuries appears still to have been not uncommon together with and the pattern of periodic 'retreat' into scholarly peace and quiet.

From the historian Ralph Glaber we can get a view of the personalities in this 'learned society' of the early eleventh century. Glaber knew of the scholarly reputation of Gerbert of Aurillac, 'with his keen mind and outstanding knowledge of the liberal arts': *ingenio acerrimus, artium liberalium studiis plenissime institutus*, and that of Fulbert of Chartres, and he lived into the era of Lanfranc and Berengar. He seems to have spent a good deal of his monastic life at St Germain d'Auxerre (*c.*990–1010). He was surprisingly peripatetic for a Benedictine monk. Behind his journeyings may lie a story of discontent and being a misfit. He admits that he was driven out of St Germain because of his intolerable behaviour. He took refuge at

St Bénigne de Dijon around 1024–30, possibly even from 1016. He then spent a period at Cluny (*c*.1030–1034/5). From *c*.1036/7 to his death in about 1046 he was back at St Germain d'Auxerre.

Ralph Glaber is an example of a medieval author who, himself living out his life in the limited geographical area and range of human contact of a series of Benedictine houses, nevertheless had grandiose ideas of the scale and purpose of his work. It was the calling of a monk to practise living, intellectually as well as spiritually, in an eschatological dimension. Ralph set his histories in eternity, with small theological excursions. For example, he discusses an episode (which he places in about the year 1024), when the Bishop of Constantinople and the Emperor Basil, with others among the Greeks, discussed how the Church of Constantinople might make good its claim to be considered *universalis in suo orbe, sicut Roma in universo*. Ralph's *History* traversed the first millennium and also the anniversary of a thousand years since the *passion* of Christ, which he recognised as a millennium in its own right. Historiographically, his approach was to seek to extend the history of the world since the creation onwards through the existing record, into the events of which he himself had knowledge, and there to offer something new. So he explains, 'We intend to narrate the story of all the great men who have lived since the year 900 of the Incarnation of the Word' (*History*, I.i.4). He also claimed a special knowledge of events in contemporary France and Germany. 'We are going to tell only of those events at which we were present or of which we have had certain report' (*History*, I.i.4). He speaks in the *Vita* of 'the many things which we have seen and the many more garnered from truthful narrators', which 'will shape the course of this narrative'. In fact his knowledge was patchy. He was unreliable on Britain and not well-informed about Normandy, but he knew a good deal about wars between Brittany and Anjou.

He wrote hagiography, the distinctive form of biography common in these centuries, in which a life is celebrated for its sanctity and portrayed as an example to others. The *Vita Domni Willelmi Abbatis* displays features of the conventional hagiography of the century to come, at the end of which it was even possible to hire a writer to compose a *Life* according to the accepted requirements. William's mother was not only of noble stock but also outstanding in virtue. Moreover, she had the prophetic dream about her son common to mothers of future saints. She used to relate how she had dreamed that she was wearing a dalmatic, when a ray of the sun lit up her right breast. Angels appeared and they bore her infant upwards, bathed in light. She was terrified and cried out that she committed him to the Mother of Christ. The child grew up notable in every way, and at the age of seven he was given to the monastery of Lucedio, which was dedicated to the Virgin and St Michael. There William readily outstripped his fellows.

We can get another view of the intellectual world of monastic and cathedral schools in which Gerbert was scholar and educator, and another glimpse of Gerbert himself, from Fulbert of Chartres (*c*.970–1028). Cathedral schools such as that at Chartres had a special importance because of their continuity and their independence of the unreliable favours of royal or imperial patronage. Charlemagne had required each cathedral to maintain a school and take the education of its canons seriously. These cathedral schools were also open to the world, to a 'passing trade' of scholarship, in a way which was only intermittently the case for monastic schools, with their (normally) internal students and their resulting natural focus on the education and religious formation of young men who were to spend their lives in the house to which they had been given as oblates. As we saw in looking at the previous few centuries, it was by no means as tidy as that, and there was plentiful exchange.

Fulbert was born, probably in Picardy in 960–70, of humble parents. It is likely that he studied with Gerbert at Rheims in the 980s and went to Chartres about 990. It seems probable that he was not a monk. But he was respected for his holiness of life. Fulbert's own letters and poems survive. In a letter to Abbo of Fleury, *c*.1004, he asks where the troubled Christian soul (*afflicta Christiana anima*) may be able to find rest. The answer used to be, 'within the cloister', but Fulbert laments that thieves can now get in there too, and nowhere is really safe, spiritually speaking. The preoccupation with the notion of the soul's need for a safe place to conduct its interior pilgrimage is associated from this period with a growing monastic literature of such calls to 'withdrawal'. Some *opuscula* also survive. There is a *Contra iudaeos*, in which Fulbert develops the idea of a kingdom, needing a king, people and land, as a building needs its roof, walls and foundations. This work was a polemic, intended to convince the Jews of the truth of the Christian faith by appealing to their reason (*rationabiliter convincere*). This too belongs within a line of work which was to run strongly on into the twelfth century, as we shall see in looking at Hermannus Judaeus (p. 85). There is also –

evidence of Gerbert's influence perhaps – an Arabic–Latin glossary of terms relating to the astrolabe.

Gerbert of Aurillac's relative peace and quiet in this world of monastic and cathedral learning and millennarialist preoccupation was to be interrupted. In 1999, he was elected pope and took the name Sylvester II. This was a deliberate echoing of the choice of Sylvester I, pope to the first Christian Emperor, Constantine the Great, in the first quarter of the fourth century. The year 1000 was approaching, and if the end of the world was at hand it seemed appropriate that the Pope should bear the name Sylvester again as the Christian Empire came to its end in the eschaton.

Work and ideas

Gerbert's personal interest as a thinker seems to have been mainly in mathematics. A number of Gerbert's letters touch on mathematical questions, such as, for example, a letter to Adelbold on the triangle. It is difficult to be sure which Arabic works Gerbert had access to, but he had a knowledge of the Arabic numerals. The Arabs had already devised a way of signifying zero with an '0'. This was known, but its implications were not immediately grasped. It was to transform numerical notation and methods of calculation only a generation or two later when Roman numerals were widely replaced with Arabic ones. Gerbert wrote on the abacus, a calculation device which involved the placing of counters in columns (hundreds, tens and single units). The abacus was now attracting new interest because it allowed for the use of Arabic numerals on the counters and, importantly, for the use of a blank disc, the 'sipos', to represent nought. The abacists were slow to move from the Roman numerals, but the principle was now in their hands.

But Gerbert's great interest was in geometry, for he had encountered Euclid. 'In the four mathematical subjects the natural place for geometry is third after arithmetic and music', he remarks. He describes how the Egyptians discovered the laws of geometry because it had a practical usefulness in measuring fields. Then some students began to find it intellectually interesting and enjoyable (*exercitio iocunda*). The subject has a *utilitas* to all who are lovers of wisdom, he claims, with the authority of the text most often used for this purpose, which asserts that God made everything by number, measure and weight: *omnia in numero, mensura et pondere* (Wisdom, 11.21).

Influence

Gerbert's best-known pupil was Richer de Saint-Rémi de Rheims. He describes Gerbert's studies in his *History*, and says that he attracted many pupils. Among them may have been Fulbert of Chartres.

Bibliography

N. Bubnov, *Gerberti Opera Mathematica* (Berlin, 1899); *Historiarum Libri Quinque and Vita Domni Willelmi Abbatis*, ed. and trans. J. France (Oxford, 1989); *Aelfric's Colloquy*, ed. G.N. Garmonsway (London, 1939); *The Old English Version of the Heptateuch*, EETS (Oxford, 1922); *Exameron Anglice*, ed. S.J. Crawford (Hamburg, 1921); Aelfric, *Lives of Saints*, ed. W. Skeat, EETS (Oxford, 1890, repr. 1966); Aelfric, *Homilies, A Supplementary Collection*, ed. J.C. Pope, EETS (Oxford, 1967); Fulbert of Chartres, *Contra judaeos*, *Patrologia Latina* 141.305ff; *The Letters and Poems of Fulbert of Chartres*, ed. F. Behrends (Oxford, 1976).

Further reading

Loren C. MacKinney, *Bishop Fulbert and Education at the School of Chartres* (Notre Dame, 1957); P. Riché, *Les écoles et l'enseignement dans l'occident chrétien de la fin du ve siécle au milieu du xi siècle* (Paris, 1979); P. Riché, *Gerbert d'Aurillac, le pape de l'an mil* (Paris, 1987); B. McGinn, *Antichrist* (San Francisco, 1994).

BERENGAR OF TOURS *c.*before 1010–1088

Life and times

The forbears of Berengar had supplied canons to serve St Martin's at Tours. Fulbert of Chartres's personal influence as an educator may be apparent again here, though it is possible that he has had credit for more here than he really deserves, since the evidence is that he was mainly a busy bishop (from 1006), much preoccupied with the problems of the Church in a feudal world, and it is not clear that there was a real school at Chartres at which Fulbert himself actually taught. The first reference to the school at Chartres is to a schoolmaster of the tenth century, who seems also to have been Chancellor of the cathedral. Nevertheless, the reputation itself is important, as are the links with other known names. If Fulbert was perceived to be a great teacher, Chartres would benefit from the rumour alone.

Berengar of Tours may have received some teaching at Chartres. Guitmund of Aversa, writing about Berengar's schooldays at

Chartres, says that he was full of levity, careless of his master, took no notice of his fellow scholars either, and despised the textbooks of the liberal arts.[1] Adelman of Liège salutes Berengar as a 'school-mate' (*collectaneum*) and describes how he enjoyed sweet fellowship with him when they were both pupils of Fulbert, 'our venerable Socrates, more worthy of our respect than Plato' (*in academia sub nostro illo venerabili Socrate*).[2] He describes private discussions in the garden in the evening, when Fulbert would exhort them to work hard and keep to the narrow way of righteousness, weeping with earnestness and the desire to save them from Satan's snares. Hugh of Langres was a canon of Chartres before he became bishop of Langres. He was deposed on charges of simony and went to Verdun as a penitent. He reappears as an opponent of Berengar.

Angelram the scholasticus of St Riquier prefaces his *Vita S. Richarii* with a dedicatory letter to Fulbert as his master. He says that he was gifted with all wisdom, human and divine.[3] The *Vita Angelranni* refers to Fulbert as *praeceptor* and Angelram as *discipulus*.[4] These testimonials may be exaggeration or formality, but they are circumstantial and they add up to a substantial 'reputation' for Fulbert.

Berengar himself set up in life as a professional 'teacher'. He became secretary to the Count of Anjou, enjoying a patronage which gave him a certain position and notability.[5]

Work and ideas

By 1049 the content of Berengar's teaching was attracting attention. Theoduin of Liège wrote to tell the King of France that Berengar was introducing ancient heresies into modern times (a stock accusation when unorthodoxy was suspected); he said that Berengar and others were destroying legitimate marriage, and discouraging the baptism of infants. He saw it as imperative that they be publicly confuted.[6] He accused Berengar of saying that the consecrated bread and wine of the Eucharist was not 'really' the body and blood of Christ, and further of attacking the very efficaciousness of the sacraments. Moreover he was arguing, said Theoduin, that the handing over of the episcopal staff did not convey the authority of the office.[7]

Berengar wrote angrily in his own defence. He was well aware of the connection of what he was saying with the debate of a generation or two earlier about the Eucharist, in which the Carolingian scholars Paschasius Radbertus and Johannes Scotus Eriugena were involved. He mentions their names in a letter to Lanfranc;[8] Paschasius he also mentions in writing to Adelman.[9]

Berengar was sensitive to the accusation that he had been a stumbling block to the faithful. Anyone who thought for himself might prove to be doing likewise because he was not submitting to the general consensus. Hugh of Langres says that a thinker should not presume to think for himself (*singulariter sentire*); he has a duty to concur with Christian and canonical faith. He insisted that he was not a troublemaker but speaking as his conscience made him.[10] Yet in taking that line he was setting out on a road which was ultimately to lead to the debates of the Reformation about the balance between individual conscience and the duty to submit to the teaching of the Church.

It was partly Berengar's own fault that the controversy did not subside. He thrust himself purposefully into arguments with the higher clergy. To Adelman of Liège he wrote indignantly to say that he had been falsely accused of Manicheism. He tried to find allies. He wrote a letter to Lanfranc, seeking to stir him into taking an interest in some of the turning points of Eucharistic controversy.[11]

In 1059 Berengar was summoned by the Pope to answer for his views at a Council at Rome. At a plenary session, he was presented with the demand that he should swear to a confession of faith on the Eucharist which had been drawn up by Cardinal Humbert. His writings were condemned and burnt. That gave the Church authorities a document with which they could hope to bring the discussion to an end and suppress Berengar's contentious views. Berengar objected that an oath taken under duress is not binding. He became still more indignant. Portions of a treatise of this period survive, attacking the Pope and Humbert personally.

As a contribution to this crisis, Lanfranc wrote his own treatise *On the Body and Blood of Christ* in the early 1060s, while he was Abbot of St Stephen's, Caen, and that began to clarify the issues in ways which were to lead into the formulation of the doctrine of transubstantiation. New in this phase of debate was the application to the Eucharistic debate of Aristotle's *Categories*, which recognises that although, by definition, accidents may alter (for that is the nature of accidents), the substance does not, or else it would become a different substance. In the Eucharistic change, when bread and wine 'become' the body and blood of Christ, the accidents, the appearance and smell of the bread and wine, remain the same but the substance is believed to be changed, from that of bread and wine to that of the body and blood of Christ. There is *trans-substantio* (to use the terminology of the twelfth century).

Influence

Berengar's opponents, and the generation after them, travelled a long way down the road of definition and clarification of what became the doctrine of transubstantiation. That was, ironically, Berengar's chief legacy. He was a thinker memorable for having forced the Church to define its position. He stimulated the work of others in this way: Hugh of Langres, Alger of Liège, Durandus of Troarn, Lanfranc, Guitmund of Aversa all wrote and debated aspects of the controversy begun by Berengar.

Notes

1 PL 149.1428.
2 PL 143.1289.
3 PL 141.1423
4 PL 141.1405
5 Margaret Gibson, *Lanfranc of Bec* (Oxford, 1978), pp. 64–5.
6 PL 146.1439–42.
7 PL 146.1439–42; Theoduin of Liége, Letter to Henry I of France.
8 PL 150.67–8, 63.
9 J. de Montclos, p. 533.
10 Berengar, *Rescriptum contra Lanfrannum*, ed. R.B.C. Huygens, CCCM, LXXXIV, A, B, p. 40.
11 PL150.63.

Bibliography

Berengar, *Rescriptum contra Lanfrannum*, ed. R.B.C.Huygens, CCCM LXXXIV, A, B.

Further reading

Margaret Gibson, *Lanfranc of Bec* (Oxford, 1978); J. Macdonald, *Berengar and the Reform of Sacramental Doctrine* (London, 1930); J. de Montclos, 'La controverse eucharistique du xi siècle', *Spicilegium Sacrum Lovaniense* 37, pp. 393–4.

PETER DAMIAN 1007–72

Life and times

Peter Damian was born in 1007 at Ravenna. In his youth, he became a secular master. In about 1035 he took the decision to become a monk and entered the monastery of Fonte Avellana. There he became so noteworthy as a teacher that he was moved by the Order to Pomposa, where the monks apparently stood in need of a good schoolmaster.[1] He became Cardinal-Bishop of Ostia in 1057. In this movement from one world of teaching to another, and ultimately into high office in the Church, Peter Damian illustrates the growing public recognition that an 'academic' career could be a good starting point for moving on into public life. Lanfranc and Anselm, one resigned, one reluctant, followed similar progressions in becoming successive Archbishops of Canterbury.

Work and ideas

Peter Damian became above all a 'monastic' scholar, writing on topics of spirituality as well as on what was to become 'academic' theology. There are letters, sermons, saints' lives, prayers, poems and treatises which he sent to his contemporaries,[2] in an age when 'publication' might be no more than such friendly exchange. He was also interested in the politically heated issues of the time, the debate on simony and the controversy about clerical celibacy, on both of which he had things to say. On simony, which he characterises as a dragon 'spewing forth its venom', he sees the Archbishop of Ravenna as a dragon-slaying knight of Christ.[3]

Peter Damian's *Letter* 1 is addressed to Honestus. It purports to be in response to a request from him for material with which he may meet the arguments of the Jews. The result is one of those dialogues with Jews which were to become a popular form of composition in the next generation. The main topic in dispute between Jews and Christians was whether Christ was the incarnate Son of God. But Peter Damian also discusses ceremonies, circumcision, the Sabbath and unclean foods.

Peter Damian's *On Divine Omnipotence*, addressed to Desiderius, Abbot of Monte Cassino, is the first book of the Middle Ages on divine power. The question whether an omnipotent God can restore lost virginity was, it seems, a teaser used to entertain students in the schools; it is to be met with quite frequently.

Peter Damian was conservative about the new fashion for dialectic. In his book on divine power, he says that he is angry with contemporary 'dialecticians' whose challenges seem to place the Virgin Birth in question. Present in 1059 for Berengar's confession, he 'stood for' sacramental realism against Berengar.

Notes

1 I.M. Resnick, *Divine Power and Possibility in St. Peter Damian's De Omnipotentia* (Leiden, 1992).
2 Peter Damian, *Letters*, ed. Owen J. Blum (Washington, 1989–92), 3 vols; Vol. 1, Letter 12, to a bishop called John.
3 Peter Damian, *Letters*, ed. Owen J. Blum (Washington, 1989–92), 3 vols; Vol. 1, Letter 3.

Bibliography

Peter Damian, *Letters*, ed. Owen J. Blum (Washington, 1989–92), 3 vols, and material in the *Corpus Christianorum*.

Further reading

I.M. Resnick, *Divine Power and Possibility in St. Peter Damian's De Omnipotentia* (Leiden, 1992).

ANSELM OF CANTERBURY 1033–1109

Life and times

Anselm was born an Italian, at Aosta, in 1033. His father died when he was a young man, and he set off, as others of his generation were doing, towards the north in search of what we should now call a 'higher' education.

At the new abbey of Bec in Normandy, Lanfranc, a fellow Italian from Pavia, had opened a school to which the sons of the local nobility came flocking. This was an unusual development, since it ran counter to the usual practice under which the 'schools' run by monasteries were internal. (Most such schools simply helped those who entered the monastic life to understand the liturgy so that they could do the 'work of God' (*opus Dei*) in worship, and for *lectio divina*, the reflective 'holy reading' of the religious life.) To this uncommonly 'open' monastic school came the young Anselm, after he had been wandering for about three years in Burgundy. He discovered that Lanfranc was lecturing on works of classical logic and rhetoric, as well as teaching the study of the Bible.

Anselm decided to be a monk. There was a period of indecision while he wondered whether he ought to choose Cluny with its reformed Benedictine rigour but lack of intellectualism. He decided in the end to stay at Bec. In due course Lanfranc left for the monastery at Caen and then to become Archbishop of Canterbury. Anselm took over the school, and it reverted to being an 'internal' school, strictly for the monks of Bec, but it became unusual in a different way.

Within that sheltered place, with opportunities for extended influence, Anselm developed in the Bec monks capacities which made them all appear to the historian Orderic Vitalis like 'seeming philosophers'. His method of teaching them had been to hold a form of debate with them of the 'Socratic' sort, in which the participants in the dialogue argue out the issues. Meanwhile, Anselm was reading the books in the Bec library, and steeping himself in Augustine.

Anselm became in due course Abbot of Bec and then Archbishop of Canterbury in succession to Lanfranc. He made no bones about the fact that he did not want to be Archbishop. He was thrown into a world of politics where he lacked the pragmatism and the necessary skills, as well as any taste for such a life as he now had to lead, involved in confrontation with King William Rufus. The King, for his own reasons, wanted Anselm to acknowledge the anti-pope as the true Pope. But Anselm had already given his loyalty to Urban II and he was not prepared to change it. That would, in his eyes, have been a breach of 'right order' (*rectus ordo*). The quarrel took him into exile, and led to further disagreements with the next King, Henry I.

Work and ideas

Anselm's first book was the *Monologion*.[1] He describes it as a meditation on the divine being. His chief model at this early stage of his authorship remained the works of Augustine, and it is apparent throughout the *Monologion* that Anselm had been borrowing from Augustine's work *On the Trinity*. But he was able to take a fresh approach, beginning from the experience of the good each person has, and moving 'upwards' in thought to higher and higher goods, until he could help his pupils to glimpse the Highest Good.

When he had finished the *Monologion* he sent a copy to Lanfranc (who was by now Archbishop of Canterbury), to ask him for his comments. Lanfranc took the view that it was inappropriate for him to be putting so much into his own words. He said that he should be quoting Augustine's authority and keeping close to the text of his source. Anselm clearly came to his own conclusions about this advice, because the *Monologion* was put into circulation as it stood, without Lanfranc's suggested amendments. Thereafter Anselm continued to write his books in his own way.

Anselm was confident that any reasonable person, presented with a clear explanation of the truths of faith, would be able to accept them. Indeed, he says as much in his next book, the *Proslogion*. He was conscious that in the *Monologion* he had constructed 'a chain of many arguments' and that appeared to him to be untidy.[2] So he began to search for 'a single argument' which would prove not only that God exists but all the other things Christians believe about him.

This led him to the ontological proof which is unique among the arguments for the existence of God. (Aquinas placed this in a category of its own because he said it really depended upon the sheer self-evidence of God's existence.) His discovery excited Anselm and he says that he believed it would give others the same joy.[3] In the remainder of the *Proslogion* he went on to use the argument to show that all the divine attributes – goodness, mercy, justice – can be arrived at by the same reasoning, and he concludes with a reflection on the nature of heaven in which he suggests that it must, by definition, involve a continuation of the legitimate joys of earth. Thus, someone who runs fast in this life will still enjoy running fast in the next.[4]

In Bible study, Anselm's idea was to teach a method, an alertness to questions of language and logic, which would enable the student to understand whatever portion of the text he was reading. It was thus a quite different method of exegesis from that which was to evolve in the twelfth century into the *Glossa ordinaria* (p. 57).

Anselm's transition from Bec to the Archbishopric of Canterbury, as Lanfranc's successor, coincided with his first encounter with criticism. In Roscelin of Compiègne, Anselm encountered for the first time academic controversy and personal attack upon his orthodoxy and integrity. Roscelin had started a rumour that Anselm was teaching heresy. He was to write his treatise *On the Incarnation of the Word* as a consequence of the need to rebut Roscelin's accusations, but so rattled was he that it took him, uncharacteristically, several attempts.

There followed the period of Anselm's mature writing. A former pupil, Gilbert Crispin, was now Abbot of Westminster, and it seems possible that during the time when he rightly feared that he might be chosen as Lanfranc's successor, Anselm may have spent some time staying at Westminster with Gilbert (1092–3), perhaps hoping to keep out of sight and avoid a preferment he did not want. At the time, Gilbert himself was writing a book on a topical subject, a *Disputation* between a Jew and a Christian. This winter's conversation may have prompted Anselm to begin the *Cur Deus Homo*, a treatise seeking to show that when God became man he was doing the only thing which would save mankind and also God's own honour. He took a draft with him into exile.

Anselm begins the *Cur Deus Homo* by asking what problem was created by the fall of Adam and Eve. God could not simply forgive them, Anselm argues, because his own 'honour' was diminished by what they had done. This assumption was much coloured by the fact that Anselm had lived most of his adult life in a feudal world in northern Europe. Could God himself have intervened? But he was not the debtor. To pay oneself a debt someone else owes is not to discharge the obligation of the other person. Could God have used an angel? But the angel would, again, not have been the debtor. Could God have used a human being? There the difficulty was that all human beings, who were indubitably in debt to God, were now tainted with original sin, and were simply not able to do what was required. And so we come back to the incarnate Christ, who was indeed the only solution, because he both owed the debt and was able to pay it.

In 1098, while he was in exile at the papal court, seeking the Pope's backing for his stand against the King of England, Anselm was called upon by Pope Urban II to frame a rebuttal of the arguments of the Greeks who were attending the Council of Bari. In 1054 a schism had divided the Eastern and Western Churches and the Pope wanted it mended. There was a great deal of politics involved in this schism, but the leading theological bone of contention was the debate about the inclusion of the *filioque* clause in the creed. The original version of the creed had said that the Holy Spirit proceeded from the Father. The Western version added a phrase which suggests that the Holy Spirit proceeds from the Father *and the Son*.

Anselm asked for a few days to prepare a defence of the Western formulation. The result was a speech at the Council and, four years later, his treatise *On the Procession of the Holy Spirit*. He approached the problem straightforwardly as one of reason. His argument turns on symmetry. Only if the Spirit proceeds from the Father and the Son do we have a situation in which each Person of the Trinity has an attribute peculiar to himself and each has an attribute which he shares with the other two. Only the Son has a Father; only the Father has a Son; only the Spirit does not have a Spirit proceeding from himself. But both the Father and the Spirit 'do not have a Father'; both the Spirit and the Son 'do not have a Son'; and both the Father and the Son have a Spirit proceeding from themselves.

In these last years of his life Anselm also returned to the 'most famous question', as he calls it, of the relationship between human freedom of choice and divine foreknowledge and predestination and the action of grace.

On his death bed, Anselm was still hoping to complete a book on the origin of the soul, for, if he did not do so, he was not sure than anyone living would be able to do it if he could not live long enough.

Influence

Anselm's influence in the Middle Ages was chiefly in the area of his spiritual writings. There are many manuscripts of his devotional works and a vast body of spurious imitative spiritual writings attributed to him. His theological and speculative writing endured in a different way. The sheer durability of his ideas meant that philosophers and theologians have kept his arguments in play not for their antiquarian interest, but for their intrinsic value and importance.

Notes

1 *Proslogion, Prologue*, S I, p. 7.
2 *Proemium*, S 1, p. 93.
3 *Proemium*.
4 Chapters 24–6.

Bibliography

The Works of St. Anselm, ed. F.S. Schmitt and R.W. Southern (Rome and Edinburgh, 1938–68), 6 vols; *Memorials of St. Anselm*, ed. R.W. Southern and F.S. Schmitt (Oxford, 1969); *The Works of St. Anselm*, ed. and trans. G.R. Evans and Brian (Oxford, 1998).

Further reading

R.W. Southern, *St. Anselm and his Biographer* (Cambridge, 1963); R.W. Southern, *St Anselm: A Portrait in a Landscape* (Cambridge, 1997); G.R. Evans, *Anselm and Talking About God* (Oxford, 1978); G.R. Evans, *Anselm* (Chapman, 1989); *Anselm, Aosta, Bec and Canterbury*, ed. David Luscombe and G.R. Evans (Sheffield, 1996).

HUGH OF ST VICTOR *c.*1096–1142

Life and times

Hugh of St Victor's origins are obscure. We find him among the Victorine Canons of Paris at the beginning of the twelfth century, at a time when this mode of religious life was increasingly attractive. Canons differed from monks in their vocation. The monk gave himself up to a life of prayer and the slow reflective 'holy reading' of *lectio divina*. The canon was a priest who might go out into parish ministry or serve a cathedral, and he needed an adequate education, a higher level of schooling than was routinely to be found in Benedictine houses.

Hugh himself was first and foremost an elementary teacher. His work has spiritual depths, but intellectually it is deliberately unambitious stuff. Hugh does not tangle with the leaders of thought of the day. Indeed, William of Champeaux retreated to quiet St Victor precisely so that he could escape the strains of combat with such contentious figures as Peter Abelard in the lecture room (see p. 87).

Work and ideas

Hugh tried hard to be helpful to beginners (for example, he describes how to memorise the Psalms by their coloured initials). These elementary works should not be despised. It was no easier then than it is now to reduce a mass of scholarship to a brief compass.

Hugh's *Didascalicon* was an early work, which forms his contribution to the corpus of 'encyclopaedia' literature. This perhaps represents his attempt to bring conveniently into a single compass for his students the essential things they needed to know about the study of the liberal arts and the interpretation of Scripture. For that, he borrows from Augustine's use of Tichonius in *De Doctrina Christiana*, helpfully summarising the key points. The whole work appears to be designed to give students basic tools of study. His *Epitome Dindimi in Philosophiam* is a further abbreviation of this modest encyclopaedia.

De sacramentis ecclesiae is a systematic treatise on theology, and here Hugh covers a certain amount that is new. The ground rules of the 'lay-out' of the discipline of systematic theology (which was still referred to as 'the study of Holy Scripture') were being established in this period. It will be remembered that Boethius had used *theologia* for the branches of antique philosophy concerned with the being and nature of God and the creation of the world. That corresponds with the 'work of creation' in Hugh's scheme. Hugh made an innovative division between the *opus creationis* (the work of creation) and the *opus restaurationis* (the work of restauration). The 'work of restoration' is concerned with the reasons for the incarnation and death of Christ and the consequences for the salvation of mankind.

These matters would not be considered 'philosophically' in the same way as the first group, because they depend upon the evidence of revelation. They are historical events. They cannot be arrived at by reasoning alone.

The modest independence of Hugh's work can perhaps best be seen in an illustration of the way he liked to tackle problems. Like Anselm of Canterbury and Anselm of Bec and Peter Abelard, Hugh was interested in the question of the Devil's position in the story of the redemption of humanity, but the emphasis is his own. He envisages a hearing in court. God, man and the Devil are present. The Devil is convicted because he injured God by abducting his servant man by fraudulent means and held him by violence (not, it is to be noted, by right). The Devil is convicted of injuring man, because of his deception in seducing him and the harm he did by bringing evil on him afterwards. Man is convicted too, because he submitted himself to the Devil and spurned the command of God to whom he owed his service. In pointing out that in this 'court-room' man would need an advocate, and the only advocate available to him would be God, Hugh then follows Anselm of Canterbury in accepting that there are tasks here which man could not discharge for himself. But his account of the divine intention and purpose is quite different. 'In order, therefore, that God might be placated by man, God freely gave man what he had a duty to repay to God' (I.viii.4). 'The Son was sent so that he could show his agreement to the adoption of humanity by God' (I.viii.6). Hugh, unlike Anselm, is clear that God did in fact have other 'options' and could have redeemed humanity in a different way if he had chosen (I.viii.10).

Hugh's thinking is perhaps influenced here by the centrality of his personal conviction that the institution of the sacraments was a generous act of God to assist humanity in its difficulties. Anselm's explanation of the reason why God became man does not carry over in the same natural way into an ecclesiology and sacramentology. This was a remedy for a sickness, as Hugh saw it.

These versions and reconfigurations of familiar elements will recall the topics which were engaging interest in the eleventh century. There is the same balancing of the themes which respond to reasoning against the ones which are dependent on 'revelation', the written story to be found in Scripture.

Hugh's other great interest was in 'spirituality', writing designed to help the soul in its search for God. That was to be an important Victorine tradition, carried forward especially by Richard of St Victor. Hugh's spiritual and mystical writings include two on

'Noah's Ark', interpreted mystically and for its moral lessons (*De arca Noe morali et mystica*); one on the vanity of the world, *De vanitate mundi*; and others on contemplation, *De contemplatione et eius speciebus*. All these reveal a spirituality as much intellectual as emotional.

Hugh's *Heavenly Ladder* (*Scala caeli*) describes the fifteen rungs of the heavenly ladder. It contains a division into aspects or stages or steps, of a type very familiar in spiritual writings of the twelfth century. In this way the author attempts to provide the would-be spiritual athlete with step-by-step instructions. There are 'thrones' and 'chambers', each historically or spiritually interpreted. There are three *piscina*. The first has five entrances. There are three water-courses or floods, three conduits or arches, three new floods, seven wells. There is a table of seven vices opposed to seven gifts of the Holy Spirit or graces; there is mention of seven columns, seven eyes, seven lamps, seven days, seven years, seven breads. There is a second *piscina* with five entrances and a third, also with five entrances. In this third one there is *afflictio carnis, labor, abstinentia, continentia*; there is *utilitas operis*; there is the *habitus paupertatis*; there is despising of praise and *appetitus extremitatis*. Here is Hugh offering homely food for the reader in search of spiritual sustenance.

Hugh was also – unusually for his time – interested in the Ps-Dionysian literature, with its discussions of the hierarchy of the universe. This fifth-century material, in Greek, had been attributed to Dionysius the Areopagite and was held in some reverence for that reason. The most usual means of access to it in the Latin-speaking West was through the work of Johannes Scotus Eriugena. Hugh wrote a commentary on the *Hierarchia* of Ps-Dionysius by Johannes Scotus Eriugena (see p. 23).

Influence

Hugh's work was used with respect; he is occasionally even quoted in *florilegia* of the Fathers. He also gave an impetus to future work at St Victor. Richard of St Victor was to be a pioneering writer in the field of spirituality, exploring the Trinitarian theme. Andrew of St Victor was to be important as an exegete trying to make use of an acquaintance with Hebrew.

Bibliography

Hugh of St Victor, *Didascalicon*, trans. Jerome Taylor (New York, 1961, 1991); Hugh of St Victor, *De Sacramentis Ecclesiae*, trans. R.J. Deferrari (Cambridge,

MA, 1951); Hugh of St Victor, *Practica Geometriae*, trans. F.A. Homann (Milwaukee, 1991); *Six opuscules spirituels*, ed. R. Baron (Paris, 1966).

Further reading

R. Baron, *Études sur Hugues de Saint-Victor* (Angers, 1963).

ADELARD OF BATH early twelfth century

Life and times

Adelard seems to have been of mixed English-Norman descent. There is no reason to doubt the authenticity of the linking of his name with Bath. He began his teaching career in England, at a date when it is hard to identify any institutional school where he may have taught. It is worth setting the English experience in the context of the preceding century to try to get a sense of the extreme limitation of educational opportunity, despite which Adelard made such notable progress. His English predecessor of the previous century, Aelfric (*c.*955–*c.*1020), was a writer of a relatively limited life-experience. Aelfric lived in comparatively peaceful times under the English King Edgar. He says he appreciated that. He grew up in the monastery at Winchester while Aethewold was bishop of Winchester (963–84). In 1005, Aelfric became abbot of the abbey of Eynsham. Aelfric had no higher ambition that to make a modest learning widely accessible. He was influenced by Abbo of Fleury and by Bede. He wrote for the tastes and needs of a monastic readership. The monastic world was evidently in need of simple aids, preferably in its own language. Aelfric translated parts of the Pentateuch and Joshua and other portions of the Old Testament into the vernacular, and also rendered Alcuin's questions on Genesis. He also translated Bede's *De temporibus* into Anglo-Saxon. That does not mean that he did not take seriously the need to teach the Latin language to the monks. Aelfric's *Colloquy* is a delightful simple introduction, with conversation lessons about the 'jobs' of country people brought in to provide practice and enlargement of vocabulary. There is a grammar and glossary in simple, clear Latin, which is nevertheless a long way removed from classical standards. There is a verse *Lives of the Saints* and a *Life of Aethewold*. For this sort of composition, Aelfric favoured alliterative verse, made up to rules of his own.

Aelfric's more adventurous work was connected with the millennium. A book of his *Homilies* survives, containing striking material on the apocalypse. His contemporary Adso, in a letter on Antichrist written to Gerberga, sister of the Emperor Otto I, had prophesied that Antichrist would arise at the end of the period of rule of the Frankish kings. This was linked with the existing tradition (depending on II Thessalonians 2.3) of a disappearance of political power from the Roman Empire. The literature to which his and Aelfric's contributions belong was in its turn dependent on Gregory the Great's *Dialogues*,[1] where the emphasis is upon the *senectus mundi*, the old age of the world. Gregory was also conjuring with the notion of the coming of Antichrist.[2]

When we take such a comparator, Adelard's achievement as an ordinary Englishman in going so much further, not only in terms of actual travelling but also in his intellectual journeying, is the more remarkable. He was one of a number of Englishmen, more usually connected with Worcester or Hereford, who are noted for their 'scientific' interests. Again, much of the available evidence on this points to a previous generation. Here too, Adelard comes somewhat 'out of the blue' as a surprisingly major figure.

Although we do not know how he reached that point, probably Adelard was 'employed' as a tutor to sons of the nobility. In the early years of the twelfth century Adelard took a group of pupils, including his nephew, to France to continue their studies. He seems to have spent time at Tours, with which the notorious Berengar had been associated in the previous generation. It is not impossible that he encountered the equally contentious Roscelin of Compiègne, who was at St Martin in Tours from about 1100–10. He speaks of a 'wise man of Tours' who had got him interested in astronomy. That naturally led to a curiosity about the scholarship of the Arabs, who had done far more in this area than the Latin scholars of the West.

At some stage, Adelard took his travelling company of pupils to Laon and left them there to their studies, setting off on a journey of his own in search of Greek and Arab learning. 'I left you in Laon', he teasingly tells this nephew, 'so that I could concentrate fully on the work the Arabs have done, while you with equal enthusiasm took in the shifting views of the French'.[3] The journey was profitable. He spent seven years on his 'expedition', learning about the studies of the Arabs (*Arabum studia*), and what he discovered shaped his future writing.

There is no evidence that Adelard ever proceeded to high office in the Church, and no clear indication of where he spent his last years. It is not impossible that when he returned to England he entered the royal civil service, perhaps even holding a position at the Exchequer.

Work and ideas

Adelard perceived a gap, not only of methodology but also of content, in the available textual resources for teaching science. It may have been that which sent him on his journey to make contact with Arabic learning in the first place. Adelard records that he found that his mental attitudes and methods had been so changed by the encounter with the Arabs that he could no longer talk to his pupils in the old way when he returned. 'It is difficult for me to discuss with you the nature of animals since I have learned from the Arabs my masters to go by the light of reason while you are being "led by the bridle" of the authorities,' he says.

He brought home Euclid and translated the *Elements*. In the Middle Ages, Adelard's chief fame rested on his work on the rediscovery of the text of Euclid's *Elements* and the teaching of geometry. But he also translated various texts in the field of astronomy, where the omissions from the range of classical textbooks of the liberal arts available in the West had been most conspicuous. His own original works included the handbook on the (abacus) the *Regule abaci* and *De opere astrolapsus* (*On the Astrolabe*), and he was the author of glosses on Boethius's *Arithmetica* and *Musica*.

The *Questions on Natural Science* Adelard links with his time in Antioch and his encounter with Arabic learning. There is mention of Tarsus and Mopsuestia in Cilicia. His nephew criticised his changed ideas: 'When you left me you bound me with a promise on my word that I would apply myself to philosophy. I was always anxious to know why I should be more attentive to this subject... When often you explained to me the opinions of the Saracens... quite a few of them appeared to me to be quite useless... I shall for a brief while refuse to be patient and shall take you up as you expound these opinions, wherever it seems right to do so. For you both extol the Arabs shamelessly and invidiously accuse our people of ignorance in a disparaging way.' Uncle and nephew spend time 'defining terms'.[4] The result is often penetrating, challenging.

Despite this importation of new work, there is a continuing dependence on pre-existing sets of natural questions. There was an older literature of books on 'the nature of things', from Pliny's *Natural History* to Bede's *De natura rerum* and Hrabanus Maurus's *De naturis rerum*, a compilation popular in England in the twelfth and early thirteenth centuries that is still visible in the background.

For Adelard's own *Questions on Natural Science*, he chose the form of a literary 'dialogue' with his nephew. They consciously approach the problem-solving with questions as much philosophical as scientific: 'To him who has a little experience of philosophy but had not been nourished in it completely, the question might seem to be solved, but not at all to me.'[5] This underlines a feature of the medieval scientific enterprise in all our authors. The link between natural and supernatural was clear. But the supernatural was within the scientists' frame.

Adelard assumes the theory of the four elements to be correct, but he asks tough questions about it:

> In such a way do those four simple elements compose this one body of the world that, although they exist as components in each composed object, they never appear to the senses as they are; but we assign to the composed thing the erroneous label of the name of one of its simple elements. No one has ever touched 'earth' or 'water', no one has seen 'air' or 'fire'. These composite things that we perceive with the senses are not the elements themselves, but are *from* the elements themselves.[6]

Adelard's other two books, *On the Same and the Different* and *On Birds*, to which he gives an English context, involve him in conversations with his nephew like the *Questions on Natural Science*. The first, dedicated to William, Bishop of Syracuse, is an exhortation to the study of philosophy. It is here that he describes his travels in Sicily and the Greek-speaking part of Italy (*Magna Graecia*). William is credited with mathematical interests and skills. *On the Same and the Different* is a dramatic dialogue between Philocosmia (earthly pleasure) and Philosophia, modelled on Boethius's *Consolation of Philosophy*.

Notes

1 3.38, PL 77.316C and Hom Ex.2.6.
2 *Moralia* 25.15.34.
3 Adelard of Bath, *Conversations with His Nephew: On the Same and the Different; Questions on Natural Science; On Birds*, ed. and trans. Charles Burnett (Cambridge, 1998), p. 91.
4 Adelard of Bath, *Conversations with His Nephew: On the Same and the Different; Questions on Natural Science; On Birds* ed. and trans. Charles Burnett (Cambridge, 1998), p. 95.
5 Adelard of Bath, *Conversations with His Nephew: On the Same and the*

Different; Questions on Natural Science; On Birds ed. and trans. Charles Burnett (Cambridge, 1998), p. 95.

6   Adelard of Bath, *Conversations with His Nephew: On the Same and the Different; Questions on Natural Science; On Birds*, ed. and trans. Charles Burnett (Cambridge, 1998), p. 93.

Bibliography

The First Latin Translation of Euclid's Elements, Commonly Ascribed to Adelard of Bath, ed. H.L.L. Busard (Toronto, 1983). In translation, Adelard of Bath, *Conversations with His Nephew: On the same and the Different; Questions on Natural Science; On Birds*, ed. and trans. Charles Burnett (Cambridge, 1998).

Further reading

Adelard of Bath: An English Scientist and Arabist of the Early Twelfth Century, ed. C. Burnett (London, 1987); Louise Cochrane, *Adelard of Bath: The First English Scientist* (London, 1994).

IVO OF CHARTRES *c.* 1040–1115

Life and times

Ivo of Chartres was probably born near Beauvais, or possibly in the region of Chartres. He was sent to Bec, where he was a pupil of Lanfranc and a fellow pupil of Anselm of Canterbury. He was thus 'formed' by the Benedictines. He was Bishop of Chartres from 1090 until his death. As a bishop, from 1092–4 he was much occupied with the remarriage of King Philip I of France and from 1100–04, he was involved in difficulties about the succession to the see of Beauvais. These events brought him into opposition to Philip I and Louis VI. He died in 1115.

Work and ideas

Ivo lived in a period when there was growing awareness of a need for a more coherent system of academic law to underpin and provide guidance in the handling of practical legal problems, of the sort he encountered, like any other bishop, but perhaps with better intellectual and scholarly equipment for dealing with them than most. For Ivo was an interventionist bishop, with an active mind, in an age when many other bishops appear to have been less certain about their duties in canon law. Pressing legal issues arose out of the contemporary debates on simony, clerical celibacy and lay investiture. Gregory VII (d. 1085) had heightened the general contemporary awareness during his active and reforming pontificate. He had been fond of sending papal legates to excommunicate recalcitrant bishops and even to depose metropolitans.

In his legal writing, Ivo was well aware that there was a difficulty about sources. There was no defined corpus for canon law. Would-be canon lawyers could point only to such uncertain collections as the Pseudo-Isidorian *Decretals*, in which forged texts of fictional popes were brazenly assembled as 'authentic canon law' to make up for the deficit of real material. Ivo was the author of the *Panormia*, the *Tripartita*, and the *Decretum*. The last is dependent on the *Decretum* of Burchard of Worms for much of the content but it is still a pioneering work of its time in the theory of the study of canon law. In the *Prologue* (it is not certain which work this belongs to) Ivo explains that he has tried to bring together in his immense collection materials from the letters of Popes, the *acta* of Councils, the Christian authorities and secular legislation. He has arranged everything under topic headings or titles.

Ivo warns the user that he will find things which appear to be contradictory. He should ask himself whether they really are, or whether he should be taking some to be intended to evince severity, others mercy.[1] He looked from a lawyer's point of view (with a glance sideways at the parallel Scriptural problem) at the internal economy of the problem of contradiction. He suggested a new way forward, which was to regard texts as not *adversi* but *diversi*.[2]

He also explores the law on 'dispensation', clarifying some laws as *immobiles* (from which there can be no dispensation), while others are *mobiles*, and some flexibility can be allowed. There can be occasions when they may be dispensed from, without the law being changed when this happens. For Ivo, the *utilitas* of the Church and the rule that love is the fulfilment of the law are the guidelines in deciding when this should be done.

Ivo was also the author of a large corpus of letters, more than three hundred, almost all letters of ecclesiastical business, and full of clues to the development of canon law in practice.

Influence

Ivo's *Prologue* seems to have had an influence on Alger of Liège, who took up the theme in his *Liber de misericordia et iusticia*. On Gratian, the author of the definitive *Decretum* of the twelfth century, too, he had an influence, though Gratian read for himself and independently the component parts of the *Corpus iuris civilis* of Justinian in his years of preparation for the completion of his book in about 1140. The complete text of the old body of Roman law was only now coming back into academic and practical use and interest in it was running high, at just the time when interest in the study of logic was also mounting. Gratian took such work into account too. And indeed his work went on developing during the second half of the twelfth century, as it moved into the schools and commentaries began to be written on it. Ivo stands at the head of this process for the twelfth century.

Notes

1 *A Scholastic Miscellany: Anselm to Ockham*, trans. Eugene R. Fairweather (London, 1956).
2 Cf. PL 162.226–7, Letter 222.

Bibliography

Ivo of Chartres, *Panormia* and *Prologue*, PL 161; *Prologue*, ed. J. Werckmeister, *Sources canoniques* (Paris, 1997); *Correspondance* (1090–8), ed. J. Leclercq (Paris, 1949); Ivo of Chartres, *Le Prologue*, trans. J. Werckmeister (Paris, 1997).

Further reading

M. Grandjean, *Laics dans l'église* (Paris, 1994).

MAIMONIDES 1138–1204

Life and times

Moses Maimonides was born at Cordoba where he was taught by his father, who was an expert in the Talmud, the compilation of oral Jewish teaching known as the Mishnah and of authoritative early commentary upon it. He was therefore brought up as a child in Moorish Spain at the period of the maximum intellectual interchange between Christian scholars and those of Judaism and Islam. Under the Abbasids it was an important centre of classical Greek and medieval Arabic learning. At the end of the 1140s Maimonides fled anti-Jewish persecution and settled in Fez in Morocco and then, after a short period, in Cairo, where he became a physician, the family breadwinner and something of a leader of the

Jewish community. The rest of his education was thus obtained in a wandering way.

Work and ideas

Maimonides's first book seems to have been a treatise on logic which he wrote when he was still a boy, but he was not drawn to Aristotelianism in his mature writings except as an ingredient in his interpretative mix. His chief love was Jewish thought. Maimonides's commentary on the Mishnah, which he finished in early adulthood, was called the *Siraj* (*Book of Illumination*). His code on the Talmud appeared in about 1180, setting out in an orderly way the religious beliefs of Jews and the standard interpretations, with further ethical and philosophical commentary. It served something of the purpose of Peter Lombard's *Sentences* in contemporary Christian theology, and met some of the same needs of contemporary students for summary and explanatory materials which would help them get their bearings in an increasingly complex mass of knowledge. Of his work on the Jewish law the most noted were perhaps the *Book of Commandments* and *The Book of Knowledge*.

The *Guide for the Perplexed* (*c.* 1190), an extensive work of philosophy for the educated Jew who found himself in religious difficulties, is perhaps the most significant of his works in Arabic. It assumes that the reader has a good deal of previous knowledge of Greek science and philosophy, or provides clues to such necessary knowledge. The contemporary respect of the Latin West for demonstrative method is visible in Maimonides too. His *Guide* covers the classic philosophical question: proofs for the existence of God; the nature of theological language; divine attributes; the purpose of the law in human life; the purpose of human life itself.

It is an important lesson of the work of Maimonides that medieval thought in its characteristic preoccupations is a product of the Judaic as well as the Roman and Greco-Christian traditions of late antiquity. There are differences of course. Maimonides as philosopher-theologian is concerned to assist his Jewish readers in their observance of the Old Testament Law, and as a consequence his speculative philosophical writing has a practical air not to be found in the Latin thinkers of his day in quite the same way. Where the Christian author tends to struggle with the relationship between faith and reason, that is, between things which can be 'known' only through revelation and by trust in God, and things which can be arrived at by reasoning alone, for Maimonides the division or tension is between these same rational matters and things held because they are beneficial to society (*Guide* III.27–8).

In Book III.51–4 of the *Guide* Maimonides brings to an end a general discussion of Law, and the Torah in particular, in which he has been explaining the reasons why the Ten Commandments should be obeyed. He then turns to the practicalities of fixing the mind on God and living in obedience to his Law. He gives the famous 'parable of the palace'. The Ruler is in his palace, and his subjects are distributed, some within the city, some outside it. Some are trying to reach the place where the Ruler is; others are outside the gates and looking for the way in. To persevere in this quest until one is in his presence requires a new kind of effort, Maimonides suggests.

Influence

Maimonides had a considerable influence on Albert the Great and Thomas Aquinas.

Bibliography

The Book of Commandments, trans. Charles B. Chaval (London, 1967); *The Book of Knowledge*, trans. Moses Hyamson (New York, 1974); *Ethical Writings of Maimonides*, ed. Raymond L. Weiss and Charles Butterworth (New York, 1983); *Guide of the Perplexed*, trans. Schlomo Pines (Chicago, 1963).

Further reading

J. Haberman, *Maimonides and Aquinas: A Contemporary Appraisal* (New York, 1979); M. Kellner, *Maimonides on Human Perfection* (New York, 1990); I. Dobs-Weinstein, *Maimonides and St. Thomas on the Limits of Reason* (New York, 1995); *Maimonides: a Collection of Critical Essays*, ed. J.A. Buijs (Notre Dame, 1988); B.Z. Bokser, *The Legacy of Maimonides* (New York, 1950).

RUPERT OF DEUTZ *c.* 1075–1129/30

Life and times

Rupert of Deutz was born in Liège in about 1075. He became an oblate at St Laurence, Liège and was professed there in 1091. In about 1100–05 the monastery became a Cluniac house. Rupert did not seek ordination and when he reached the proper age, in about 1105–08, he refused it. It seems that he simply wanted to be a monk, and indeed that is how he spent his life.

But he was not a quiet figure, and he enjoyed a dispute. In the period 1113–15 he was engaged in debate on the Eucharist in Liége with Alger of Liège. The controversy with Alger of Liège is touched on Book XII of *De sancta Trinitate* (On the Holy Trinity) which he wrote about this time (*c*.1113–14). In 1114–16 there was more debate, this time at Liège, on predestination, and again, over a period of time, Rupert became involved. The years 1116–17 Rupert spent in exile at Siegburg, still writing. In 1117 he produced *De omnipotentia dei*. There followed in the same year debates with the Laon masters and bishop William of Châlon-sur-Marne.

There was already a degree of 'theatre' in academic disputation. Alger had been secretary to the bishop of Liège for a decade when he made his criticisms. When he attacked Rupert of Deutz for his views on the Eucharist, Rupert responded with vigour, and there were plenty keen to watch the contest, or even to join in. At this date it could be dangerous to a writer's reputation for orthodoxy to engage in scholarly argument. In his remarks on part of the Rule of St Benedict, *In quaedam capitula Regulae Sancti Benedicti*, Rupert describes an actual incident in which he was called a heretic: 'They began to defame me as a heretic who had said that the blessed Augustine was not in the canon.' Rupert comments that others began to destroy his reputation too: *Illi me ex hoc diffamare coeperunt.*[1]

Rupert's description of this episode hints at more than one encounter, and it is possible to identify a plausible audience of students among the local clergy who seem to have contributed material for Alger's *De sacramentis*.

Rupert's polemic provoked a 'show-down'. The trigger may have been the point when he pitted his opinions against Anselm of Laon in *De voluntate Dei* (V.2). That brought him to trial for heresy in September 1116. There is some evidence that the accusations against him were quite wide-ranging, not confined to the eucharistic or predestination issues alone, though those were serious enough. Rupert was accused of being an impanationist, holding that the body and blood of Christ are present in the consecrated bread and wine by being somehow 'inside' it, and not by transforming it. He would have been condemned, it has been suggested, but for the surprise intervention of Abbot Cuno of Siegberg.

There remain questions about 'who started it' (did Alger initiate offensives against Rupert or Rupert against Anselm of Laon?), as well as uncertainties over what it was about. But what seems fairly certain is that not only Rupert but his supporters and detractors enjoyed it and saw it as legitimate debate, and the affair turned 'nasty' only when it began to appear that Rupert might find himself condemned for heresy.

There was then, in these events, a slippage between the academic and the ecclesiastical worlds, in which a lively exchange of views could become a dangerous game. Rupert escaped partly by making shrewd moves, allying himself with 'the Church' against those who challenged it, and identifying those challengers with his enemies.[2]

Rupert was not cured of disputatiousness by the experience of his trial. Later in life he was arguing with the canons regular and the Jews. Rupert was engaged in debate with the Jew Hermannus in Munster in 1128. Hermannus gave his own account of this in *De conversione sua*, and something of their talk appears to be reflected in Rupert's *Commentary on the Minor Prophets*. Hermannus describes how he first encountered and began to talk to Christians while staying in the royal household of Lothar at Mainz on business. Lothar had in his entourage Ekbert, to whom Hermannus talked. (This is perhaps a glimpse of a continuation of the royal or imperial household as the forum of exchange of ideas it had often been in the Carolingian period.)

With the zeal of a convert, Hermannus the Jew explains how he became a Christian. Many *religiosi*, men and women, have asked him to tell his story, he says. He is anxious that it be fully understood that he really struggled. This was no superficial change of position but a real metanoia. While he was a boy, 'and still enmeshed in the faithlessness of Judaism', Hermannus had had a vision, and talk of a vision is often taken to indicate that God has a special 'purpose' for the individual concerned. Hermannus says that what led him to conversion in the end was a conviction of the intellectual superiority of Christianity over Judaism. The Jews read the Scriptures for their literal sense, which was like the husk of the grain, the Christians for its sweet inner kernel.

Rupert was further involved in public disputations at Liège and Laon (provocative places to choose, in the circumstances) and elsewhere,[3] resulting in still more criticism.

Work and ideas

Rupert was a prolific author. We have already seen how he persevered steadily over many years with his writing of Biblical commentaries and the cognate works, *De victoria verbi Dei* in 1123–4 and in 1125–7 *De gloria et honore Filii hominis super Matthaeum*. *De divinis officiis* was written in about 1109–12; it is partly concerned with the problems in whose airing Rupert was himself involved, over the *materia* of the Eucharist.[4] *De Sancta Trinitate et operibus eius* dates from about 1112–15. Rupert wrote on St John's Gospel in 1114–16.

Despite the monumental character of his works of exegesis, Rupert is not one of the figures strongly associated with the development of the *glossa ordinaria*. (p. 57) His main 'project' was the depiction of the three 'ages' he saw adumbrated in Scripture, the age of the Father (the Old Testament), the age of the Son (the New Testament) and the age of the Holy Spirit, covering present history leading up to the eschaton. This was a 'programme' which was to be taken much further (and more contentiously) by Joachim of Fiore. This takes us into questions to do with twelfth-century thinking on prophecy and the temptation to trace 'ages of the world', so as to try to foretell when it might end.

The *Commentary on the Apocalypse* has traditionally been seen as an allegory of the struggle of the Church and early Christianity. Medieval monks liked it because of its familiar motif of the warfare of the soul.

Notes

1 PL 170.495–6
2 Van Engen, p. 165.
3 Van Engen, p. 202ff.
4 PL 170.33ff., Cols. 40–1.

Bibliography

Many of Rupert's works are edited in *Corpus Christianorum Continuatio Medievalis*; Hermannus Judaeus, *Opusculum de conversione sua*, ed. G. Niemeyer (Weimar, 1963).

Further reading

J. van Engen, *Rupert of Deutz* (California, 1983).

PETER ABELARD 1079–1142

Life and times

Peter Abelard was born near Nantes in northern France in 1079. He was one of the generation of 'wandering scholars' who studied and taught in the period of burgeoning interest in academic study before the formal beginning of the universities. Peter Abelard was some-times referred to in his own time as the *philosophus*.[1] His pupils followed him from place to place, not quite like those of Aristotle, who walked about while he was teaching, but enough to get him the label of 'the Peripatetic'. In Abelard's day, a 'school' might be no more than a group of pupils of a 'master' who expounded the key texts of accepted 'authors' by 'reading' them with his students. There need be no institutional structure.

At this period, wandering masters or teachers such as Abelard often attached themselves for a time to cities with cathedral schools, because there were communities of scholars there, and also prospective students who could be tempted to come and listen to a new and exciting teacher. In that way, he became Roscelin of Compiègne's pupil at Loches in about 1093–9. Shortly afterwards he arrived in Paris, where he studied under William of Champeaux. Abelard himself now began to lecture on logic. But by about 1108 he was challenging the teaching of the unfortunate William of Champeaux in Mont St Geneviève, to such effect that William was driven out by the competition and joined the Victorine canons, where he was perhaps able to continue to teach in a more peaceful environment (see p. 72).

Abelard was then tempted to apply his skills in logic to the study of theology, which at this date was known as 'the study of Holy Scripture' (*studium sacrae scripturae*). This was already where real fame lay for a teacher. In 1113, in order to get himself recognised in this new field, he went to the leading 'theological school' of Laon, where the famous brothers Ralph and Anselm were teaching (see p. 57). He says in his autobiographical *Historia Calamitatum* that he came in some trepidation, expecting Anselm of Laon to be impressive as a teacher. But he found Anselm resembled a tree whose leaves have fallen; his teaching was like bare branches. The ambitious and arrogant young Abelard announced that he himself would lecture on Scripture straight away, choosing for the purpose the book of Ezekiel, famous for its difficulty. He was able to make an impression. He appears to have given these lectures not only at Laon but again at Paris (*c.*1113–14).

By 1114 Abelard was back in Paris, now a master at the school of Notre Dame. There he lodged with one of the canons, Fulbert, who had a niece called Heloise. Although she was a girl, Fulbert was – unusually for the time – anxious that Heloise should be well-educated and he appointed Abelard to undertake the task. The education she received was of a high academic level, but they also became lovers and a son was born in 1118. Abelard was castrated by angry members of Fulbert's family. That led him from disgrace into academic controversy, first with Roscelin, and then to condemnation for heresy at the Council of Soissons in 1121.

He continued in dispute with Roscelin, and indeed it may be that his *Theologia 'Summi boni'* was composed in order to take a position on the 'tritheistic' heresy of claiming that the three Persons of the Trinity were like three gods, for which Roscelin had been condemned at Soissons in 1092. That is what Abelard suggests in his letter to the Bishop of Paris. But in the *Historia Calamitatum* he gives a different motive, stating that he intended simply to write something for his students, with no mention of Roscelin.

Roscelin was quite aggressive in his attack on Abelard's *Theologia*. He tried to get the matter taken up by the Bishop of Paris. Gilbert, the bishop, received a letter from Abelard (Letter 14) asking him to set up a disputation, which would be conducted in front of witnesses. There is no contemporary record of the Council of Soissons. The chronicler Otto of Freising says that Alberic of Rheims and Lotulf of Lombardy instigated the proceedings against Abelard. Otto explains that Abelard was accused of Sabellianism, that is, of understating or diminishing the difference between the persons of the Trinity.

Roscelin died in 1120, and his thought does not seem to have been of importance thereafter. The problem he had raised was overtaken by other questions. Nevertheless, there was a great deal of pressure to get Abelard condemned and his *Theologia 'Summi boni'* burned. He was even imprisoned by the Papal Legate at St Médard, though apparently for only a few days.

Abelard withdrew and became a monk at St Denis. But wherever he went, it seemed, disputes began. More controversy arose over Abelard's challenge to the 'authenticity' of St Denis in 1121. Abelard had to flee to seek the protection of Count Thibaud of Champagne. Abelard and Suger, Abbot of St Denis, made peace in 1122, but Abelard's monastic life continued not there but at a cell he himself founded at Nogent-sur-Seine. From there he went, in about 1125–6, to St Gildas in Brittany, leaving the 'cell', now renamed the 'Paraclete', to the use of Heloise and the community of nuns of which she was now head. It was from there that she wrote the series of letters to which we have Abelard's replies. There has been some uncertainty about the authenticity of these letters, because of the lateness and slenderness of the manuscript tradition. But their content speaks for the likelihood of their being genuine. The first is the *Historia Calamitatum*, the 'history of my troubles'. In form it is like a classical *epistola consolatoria*, a letter written (oddly to the modern eye) for the formal purpose of 'consoling' someone in trouble with the reflection that the writer's troubles have been greater still.

Abelard could not stay away from the schools. He went back to Paris, to Mont St Geneviève, in about 1133. There the controversial Arnold of Brescia joined him. Abelard was tried again for heresy at Sens in 1140 and appealed to Rome, but Pope Innocent II condemned him as a heretic. He retreated to Cluny, where Peter the Venerable gave him protection, and he died in a Cluniac house two years later.

Work and ideas

Of Abelard's logical works, his *Logica ingredientibus* and his *Dialectica* survive and contain much that was at the cutting edge when he wrote. The *Dialectica* is apparently an early work. He was unfortunate in being overtaken very rapidly by the further technical development of twelfth-century logic.

Abelard's *Theologia*, or rather his series of works on theology, were controversial from the beginning, and remained so. Abelard's *Theologia 'Scholarium'* was criticised by friends of Bernard of Clairvaux and by Bernard himself at the Council of Sens in 1140.

His *Sic et Non*, or 'Yes and No', was a collection of extracts from the authorities set side by side in opposition to one another, so that students could practice their skills in resolving the contradictions they presented. Abelard did not find all these for himself. They were already in use in the schools as examples. Existing catenas of patristic texts underlie the *Sic et Non* and the *Theologia Christiana*, but do not appear in the *Theologia 'Summi Boni'*. That may suggest that the *Sic et Non* is a later work, written at the stage when Abelard was able to make use of this kind of aid.

Abelard provided a preface to this work in which he shows an understanding (unusual for his time) that the meanings of words and the foci of controversy alter over time. Abelard's biblical commentary was a vehicle of his theological speculation, just as much as the speculative monographs themselves. In it can be observed the development which was to lead to the evolution of the *disputatio* a few years later. The earliest 'lectures' were just that. They were 'readings' of a text with helpful explanatory remarks. Yet it was gradually becoming obvious in Abelard's lifetime that the old pattern of gloss or commentary, in the form of brief explanation of the meaning of a word or of the views of one of the Fathers was no longer adequate to carry the amount of conflicting opinion which might surround a text. When Abelard came in the course of his exploration of Romans 3.25–26 to the theme of Anselm's *Cur Deus Homo* he digressed at length, for several printed pages.[2] He sets out all the arguments with which he is familiar, some of them evidently highly topical, and the subject of heated debate among the students and teachers he knew. For example, he compares Anselm of Canterbury's explanation and that of the School of Laon. The Laon view tended to allow a role to Satan. It was argued that when Adam fell, Satan had won the loyalty of humanity and mankind must therefore be wrested from him if human beings were to be restored to God. Abelard says that Satan could have no rights. Yet he does not like Anselm of Canterbury's answer much better. He sees no force in the argument that it was necessary for the Son of God to suffer and be humiliated and die on a cross side by side with 'the wicked'. How could that have repaired the damage to God's honour? God ought to have been angered more than ever by such treatment of his Son; Abelard cannot see it as a reconciliatory act. God can forgive by grace. That would have been enough.

But Abelard does not wish to deny that God became man. He therefore has to find another reason why he did. He identifies it in God's 'love' of his human creation. The act of God in sending his Son has transformed forever man's response to God. Christ has shown forth God to man and also shown man how to live a perfect human life. This 'loving example' theory seems to Abelard much more satisfactory.

One of Abelard's most original works was the *Scito te ipsum*, on the currently fashionable theme of 'knowing oneself'. This is not a book of spirituality, as the title might suggest, but of ethics, in which Abelard poses the question whether a given act is always right or wrong or whether circumstances make a difference. He concludes, at the end of an extremely subtle analysis, that the intention with which an act is done makes a great deal of difference. He goes so far as to suggest that an action is good *because* it proceeds from a good intention. That takes him back, behind that assertion, to the question whether the mere belief that one is acting rightly makes an act good, even if one is deceiving oneself. Here, Abelard believes God's knowledge of what is really in the heart is important. There is even an Anselmian echo, in the notion that the test is that the intention not only 'seems' good, but really is what it appears to be.

Sin then becomes that which is done against the prompting of conscience. This was pioneering thinking in the century before Aristotle's *Ethics* became available in the West.

Influence

Peter Abelard is an example of a scholar at the cutting edge in his day, but overtaken by developments in his field which occurred very rapidly after he had done his own pioneering work in logic. He did not exert a substantial influence after his lifetime, except perhaps upon a group of contemporary scholars who had heard him lecture and been captivated by what was evidently a compelling style of delivery.

Notes

1   *Commentarius Cantabrigiensis in epistolas Pauli e scola Petri Abaelardi I, In epistolam ad Romanos,* ed. A. Landgraf (Notre Dame, 1937); D. Luscombe, *The School of Peter Abelard* (Cambridge, 1967).
2   CCCM, XI, pp. 113–17.

Bibliography

Peter Abelard, *Opera Theologica, Corpus Christianorum Continuatio Mediaevalis*, XI, XII, XIII; A. Landgraf, *Commentarius Cantabrigiensis in epistolas Pauli e scola Petri Abaelardi I, In Epistolam ad Romanos* (Notre Dame, 1937); Peter Abelard, *Dialogue of a Philosopher with a Jew and a Christian*, trans. P.J. Payer (Toronto, 1979).

Further reading

Michael Clanchy, *Abelard: A Medieval Life* (Oxford, 1997); D. Luscombe, *The School of Peter Abelard* (Cambridge, 1967); John Marenbon, *The Philosophy of Peter Abelard* (Cambridge, 1997); Constant J. Mews, *Peter Abelard* (Aldershot, 1995).

WILLIAM OF CONCHES *c.*1080–*c.* 1154

Life and times

William of Conches was born in about 1080. He may himself have been a pupil of Bernard of Chartres. He certainly taught John of Salisbury. He appears to have been involved in the 'Cornifician' dispute John describes, between those who wanted to keep the syllabus compact and those who wanted to expand it. He retired early from the fray in the schools.

Work and ideas

As a young teacher (*c*.1120), William of Conches wrote glosses on Boethius's *Consolation of Philosophy*, on Macrobius's work on the *Dream of Cicero*, possibly on the *De Nuptiis* of Martianus Capella, as well as a *Philosophia* and glosses on Priscian. He thus displayed an aptitude for a group of semi-philosophical works more 'literary' than Peter Abelard's taste ran to, and yet not scientific in quite the way Adelard of Bath's work had proved to be. He himself had a taste for the diffused Platonism which – apart from Chalcidius's commentary on Plato's *Timaeus* – was still the only means by which Platonism could be accessed by contemporary scholars.

The *Philosophia* attempts a definition of philosophy which draws both on Cicero and on Scripture. Cicero is cited for his notion that eloquence without wisdom is dangerous (I, Prologue). But there is also a Scripturally-inspired reference to philosophy as the 'true comprehension' of things seen and unseen (I.4). William proposes to begin with the first cause of things (*prima causa rerum*), and to go on until he gets to the subject of mankind, on which he will have much to say. Accordingly he progresses through the prior question of the very existence of God, to discussion of the Trinity, almost as though he were writing systematic theology in the sequence of treatment of a Peter Lombard or an Aquinas in a later generation. Then he comes to the *anima mundi*, a theme which proved dangerous when Peter Abelard discussed it, because it was easy to fall into heresy by seeming to identify 'the soul of the world' with the Holy Spirit. That way lay pantheism. Indeed, William consciously takes the risk of opening himself up to that accusation: 'According to some the soul of the world is the Holy Spirit' (IV.3); 'Everything which lives in the world lives by the divine will and goodness which is the Holy Spirit' (IV.13). He explores the equally vexed and controversial question whether the soul of the world is somehow 'in' each living thing alongside the soul of the living thing itself, in such a way as to give it two souls (IV.13).

The Platonism of the Latin West, which had been mediated through the opening verses of St John's Gospel and early Christian writers, especially through the hugely influential Augustine, was joined in the early twelfth century by matter drawn from fresh discussion of Plato's *Timaeus*, with its interesting challenge to Genesis on the subject of the creation of the world. William's *Philosophia* is full of references to the lips of Plato (*os Platonis*) but also to comparative views of other authorities. In his later working life he wrote a *Super Platonem* on the commentary on the *Timaeus* by Chalcidius, and further work on the Roman Grammarian Priscian. Sometimes in the *Philosophia* itself he slips into pure Platonism, (noting that Plato says that there are three orders of demons in the firmament). Sometimes he moves towards scientific questions. 'Where' are the elements? William says that they are there in the composition of the human body, but they are not visible in their own right because the elementary particles are tiny. The elements are *simplae et minimae particulae* (VII.22). In the realms of natural science William is keen on tides, winds, thunder, comets, planets, stars, all the topics of the Latins and of Bede. He had no apparent sense of a conflict of cultures or traditions in that area to disturb him in making his synthesis..

William's *Dragmaticon* is largely a reworking or simplification of his *Philosophia*, made during his spell in the household of the Duke of Normandy, after he had left the schools. The *Dragmaticon* also has some claims to belong to the 'genre' of encyclopaedias.

Influence

William of Conches is associated with a group of scholars who had links with the cathedral school of Chartres, and William's focus of interests reflects the interests we find in other authors connected with this 'school'. Others – Thierry of Chartres, Gilbert of Poitiers – extended their work in other directions. For example, there was a fashion for a few decades of commenting on the 'theological tractates' of Boethius. In the *Commentary on the First Six Books of the Aeneid of Virgil*, which is certainly a Chartrian work, if not certainly his own, Bernardus Silvestris allegorised the poem. From Macrobius came the idea of identifying Virgil as a philosopher. From Fulgentius (467–532) came the idea of treating the *Aeneid* as a mirror of the stages of the human life.

The medieval vernaculars were used for serious scholarly writing up to a point, but not until later in the Middle Ages when their vocabulary and sophistication of usage had developed sufficiently. The *Summa de Philosophia in Vulgari*, which appeared in Catalan. in The *Dragmaticon* also provides a link to Ramon Llull, who was using Catalan as a vehicle for scientific writings already in the thirteenth century.

Bibliography

William of Conches, *Dragmaticon*, ed. I. Ronca, CCCM, 152 (1997); William of Conches, *Philosophia*, ed. G. Maurach (Pretoria, 1980); *Glosa super*

Boetium, ed. L.W. Nauta (Gröningen, 1999). A translation of the *Dragmaticon* is available: *Dragmaticon: A Dialogue on Natural Philosophy*, trans. I. Ronca and M. Curr in *Mediaeval Culture* (Notre Dame, 1997), vol. 2.

Further reading

R.W. Southern, *Medieval Humanism* (Oxford, 1970); Bernardus Silvestris, *Commentary on the First Six Books of the Aeneid of Virgil*, ed. J.W. Jones and E.F. Jones (Lincoln, 1977).

BERNARD OF CLAIRVAUX 1090–1153

Life and times

Bernard was born in 1090 of a good family near Dijon. His parents sent him to a school run by canons, but it was he himself who made the decision in 1113 to enter the monastic life by joining the new Cistercian Order. These were 'reformed' Benedictine monks, who had as their ideal a return to a simpler life than was often being led in monasteries of the time, ascetic, truly poor, with the main body of the monks freed for prayer and reading, by others, who as 'lay brothers' would do much of the humbler work of the community. Bernard's natural powers of exciting others with his ideas meant that he was able to take in with him more than two dozen of his friends and relatives. Citeaux, the first monastery of the new Order, quickly became a success and a string of further houses was founded. In one of these, Clairvaux, Bernard himself was made abbot two years later, still very young. The strain of his office made him ill, and he was greatly helped by his friend William of St Thierry, who was then a Benedictine himself but who came and spent time with him while he recovered.

Bernard remained at Clairvaux as its abbot for the rest of his life, but he did not stay within its walls. He became a great traveller, much in demand for his diplomatic skills from at least as early as 1128 when he acted as a secretary at the Council of Troyes and helped to win recognition for the new Order of the Knights Templar. They had been founded as an imaginative new kind of Order, both monk and soldier, dedicated to protecting Christians, especially pilgrims, travelling in the Holy Land. They were a living embodiment of a combination of traditional Christian imagery, of the Soldier of Christ and the pilgrim as seeker after union with God. In the 1130s he was much occupied with supporting Innocent II in his claims to the papacy at a period when the appointment was actively in dispute.

That won many advantages for the Cistercian Order, and its special place in the papal goodwill was if anything strengthened in 1145, when Eugenius III became Pope, for he had formerly been a Cistercian monk. In 1140, even though everyone knew he could be no match for Abelard in scholarly argument, Bernard was the natural choice to lead the party investigating the accusations of heresy against Peter Abelard at the Council of Sens. Bernard was persuaded by Peter the Venerable, the Abbot of Cluny, to preach the Second Crusade. He did this, at first, rather against his better judgement because, as he told Peter, he believed that his first task was to win the souls already in Christendom to a more serious commitment to Christ.

Work and ideas

Bernard was above all a 'monastic' writer. His great intellectual interest was in a practical spirituality. He wrote on *The Steps of Humility and Pride* as a half-humorous warning for his monks about the way in which, once the first step downhill is taken, the other steps become easier to take. He wrote a number of other monographs, on such subjects as 'loving God' (*De diligendo Deo*) and 'precept and dispensation', that is, the important question what commandments must be obeyed by a devout Christian and where some flexibility can be allowed.

Bernard was also outstanding as a preacher. His sermons, of which a considerable number survive, could be lengthy, but never dull. His most famous series of sermons, which set a fashion, were the eighty-six he preached on the Song of Songs (even then without completing the analysis of the text of this short book of the Old Testament). Bernard could tease out of a text of Scripture a thousand reflections and analogies and connections of ideas. His own familiarity with the text of Scripture was so great that it became almost impossible for him to write except in its language, with quotation and allusion moving in and out of his prose in every sentence. For Bernard, preaching was the most natural mode of exegesis, just as it had been for Augustine and the Latin Fathers.

On Consideration is, like Bernard's large volume of surviving letters, an indicator of the political Bernard at work. Bernard began to write it for Eugenius III, when he heard that the latter was allowing all his time to be taken up in hearing appeals to the papal court of appeal. He took as his model Gregory the Great's 'Pastoral Rule' (*Regula Pastoralis*) and developed for Eugenius a doctrine of a balanced life, in which the contemplative and the active should be kept in due proportion. He explained that this was particularly important for those in public life if they were also leaders of the Church. After he had sent Eugenius Book I came the failure of the Second Crusade, and Bernard found himself writing additional sections of *On Consideration* to draw lessons for Christendom from that disaster. If God had allowed a Holy War to fail, he must have had a larger purpose of strengthening Christians in the faith. In the end, Bernard developed in this work a theory of the plenitude of papal power which was to be of immense importance for the later Middle Ages. His idea was that the Pope stood in the hierarchy of heaven and earth, not only above every secular power, but also above all others in the Church. That line of thought, already present as a result of the reforms of Pope Gregory VII half a century earlier, was to lead the papacy into such grand ideas of its status as a papal monarchy as to cause a backlash in the end, both before, and during the Reformation of the sixteenth century.

Influence

Bernard's charismatic personal qualities made him immensely influential in his own time and his presence at or involvement in so many major events of the century ensured that his work was disseminated. Apart from the train of aggrandisement of papal self-image which he helped to encourage, his intellectual influence lay mainly in the realm of monastic spirituality, where his chief interest lay and which he himself believed to be the most important area of his work.

Bibliography

Bernard's *Opera Omnia* are edited by J. Leclercq, C.H. Talbot and H. Rochais (Rome, 1957–), 8 vols, and many of his treatises and sermons are in translation in the Cistercian Fathers series.

Further reading

M. Clanchy, *Abelard: A Mediaeval Life* (Oxford, 1997); G.R. Evans, *Bernard of Clairvaux* (Oxford, 2000); A.H. Bredero, *Bernard of Clairvaux: Between Cult and History* (Grand Rapids, MI, 1996); J. Leclercq, *A Second Look at Bernard of Clairvaux* (Kalamazoo, MI, 1990).

ANSELM OF HAVELBERG *c.*1100–58

Life and times

Anselm of Havelberg provides an important and unusual link with contemporary Greek thinkers. He studied at Laon, possibly as a pupil of Ralph of Laon, who took over from his brother Anselm in 1117. Anselm's time as a student at Laon gave him considerable knowledge of the topics which were of contemporary interest in theology and law and of a good range of the 'authorities'. He became one of the first followers of Norbert, the founder of the Order of Premonstratensian canons. In 1129 he was made Bishop of Havelberg. He spent some time at the imperial court, and was ambassador to Constantinople in 1135. That brought him into contact with the Greek Church. Anselm knew, or got to know, some of the small group of contemporary scholars, such as James of Venice, who had the knowledge of the language necessary to make translations of classical works from the Greek.

During his absence in the East the see of Havelberg was ravaged and that kept its bishop hovering about the imperial and papal courts. It proved dangerous to place trust in either quarter, and in about 1149 he fell into disgrace, probably the victim of bad blood between the Emperor Conrad III and the Papacy. He returned at last to his diocese and began to concentrate on the ideals of trying to live an apostolic life (*vita apostolica*) in imitation of Christ and imitating the poverty of Christ, *paupertas Christi*, which had attracted him to the Premonstratensian movement. He was helpful here to Norbert.

In 1152 Anselm returned to favour and to political life under the Emperor Frederick Barbarossa. He died in 1158 in the Emperor's entourage, at the siege of Milan.

Work and ideas

Anselm is important as an 'early ecumenicist'. He made an effort to sit down with Greek Christians in order to discuss the differences between them and see if they could be mended. In the Church, Greek East and Latin West had been divided since the schism of 1054. At that period the real reasons were probably political, but there were identifiable differences. The two Churches were divided on the primacy, the Greeks taking the view that the Bishop of Rome was not entitled to claim to be primate of the patriarchates of the East as well as of the Western Church. There was a difference of opinion as to whether leavened or unleavened bread should be used in the Eucharist. Perhaps most important was the addition to the creed made by the West in Carolingian times. For the sake of clarity the West had added 'and the Son' (*filioque*) to the original statement that the Holy Spirit proceeded from the Father. The Greeks said that even if that was theologically correct, which they disputed, it was unacceptable because it was an innovation. Nothing must be 'added' to the faith delivered by Christ and stated during the period of the first ecumenical Councils, they argued. Anselm's discussions with Greeks, using interpreters, are a first attempt after Anselm of Canterbury's *De processione Spiritus Sancti* to resolve these differences face to face.

The *Dialogues*, which Anselm wrote after his return from Constantinople, are divided into three books. He sets the scene, describing his own visit as ambassador to Constantinople under the Emperor Lothar. He says that he had helpful conversations with Nechites, the Archbishop of Nicomedia. Diplomatically, he compliments Nechites on his learning, together with others, who, 'in accordance with the custom of the educated Greeks', are knowledgeable in the liberal arts and in Scripture. In the *Prologue*, Anselm also comments on the visit Pope Eugenius had received from an ambassador from Constantinople, who had come to discuss with him various points at which Greek doctrine and rites differed from those of the Latins, citing Scriptural authorities to support the Greeks.

In the first book, his fundamental postulate is that 'unity' is what God wants for his creation. There is only one Church, one Saviour, one economy of salvation. Like Bernard of Clairvaux in his closely contemporaneous *De consideratione* sent to Pope Eugenius III, Anselm takes as his themes the operations of providence and the unity of the divine plan for creation.

He casts the first book of his *Dialogues* in the form of an exposition of the unity of faith and life from the time of Abel to the present. He sets out his explanation in terms of the seven seals of the apocalypse. There are seven ages of the Church (*status ecclesiae*) from the coming of Christ. They begin with the primitive Church and move on to the ages, respectively, of persecution; heretics; false brothers; the lingering of souls of the saints under the altar crying for vengeance the coming of Antichrist and, after many tribulations, of paradise at last.

He comments on the numerous occasions when people have come to him scandalised by the innovations (*novitates*) of their time. Some are misleading the simple. He is therefore concerned to encourage the right place for the right sort of reform. For example, the 'innovation' of founding a new religious order (like that of Norbert's Premonstratensians) may be a beneficial novelty, if it is at one with the patterns of history. Relying on Scripture, Anselm assures his readers, he has presumed to write something to address these regrettable modern trends, but at the same time to emphasise the value of the right sort of diversity. He accepts that the one body of Christ, ruled by the one Spirit reflects a diversity of gifts of grace. He is easily able to show, beginning with Abel, that God has been pleased by a variety of sacrifices down the ages. It is also possible (though here he is on more controversial ground) that those who lived before Christ, the *antiqui patres*, were saved by faith in what was to come, even though they could not know the details of the faith of Christ: 'And so the one God was faithfully served in one faith among them in any ways'.

Influence

Anselm's work found its modest place in the continuing endeavour to mend the schism and in the line of enquiry which led to Joachim of Fiore's prophetic work.

Bibliography

Anselm of Havelberg, *Dialogues*, Book I, ed. G. Salet (Paris, 1966). The majority of Anselm's work is still available only in the unreliable versions in Migne's *Patrologia Latina*.

Further reading

F. Petit, 'L'Ordre de Prémontré de Saint Norbert à Anselme de Havelberg', *La Vita comune del Clero nei sec. xi e xii* (Milan, 1962); F. Petit, *La spiritualité des Prémontrés aux xiie et xiiie siècles* (Paris, 1947).

AVERROES (IBN RUSHD) 1126–98

Life and times

Averroes, as Ibn Rushd was known to Western Latin thinkers, came from a respected Moslem family of lawyers, judges and public servants in Cordoba in Islamic Spain. There he had a sound education in the sciences, medicine, mathematics, and also in theology and law. For a long time, he enjoyed useful patronage in the family and household of the Caliph at the court in Marrakech, until the 1190s when he was accused of heresy and was sent into exile.

Work and ideas

Averroes's philosophical conversation had commended him to his prince; the Caliph had complained that he found Aristotle difficult to understand, and the translations unhelpful. He wanted someone to work on this literature, summarise it and explain its aims, so that it might be more easily read and used. Averroes was therefore commissioned in 1168/9 to work on the compilations of commentaries on Aristotle.

Averroes himself is important to our story as a commentator on Aristotle, whose views entered the Western Latin-speaking universities with the scientific and philosophical works of Aristotle himself in the thirteenth century, where some of his ideas and teachings caused a furore. His interpretation of Aristotle was infected with ideas the Arabs had drawn from late Platonism and which were diametrically opposed to fundamental Christian tenets. For example, Averroes held that as the Prime Mover, God must be entirely removed from the world and could be exercising no providential purpose within it. These were notions as alien to Islam as to Christianity, and the question whether causes were 'efficacious entities' had been the subject of long debate in Islam, but they raised more complex questions still within the wider range of issues in play in Christian theology. From his own Muslim standpoint, Averroes could avoid many difficulties by interpreting the Koran figuratively, but there still remained the question, also central to the Christian debate about Aristotle, whether on certain topics, philosophy and theology could work together in a symbiotic relationship or were simply incompatible.

Influence

When in 1255 the Arts Faculty at the University of Paris prescribed the study of Aristotle the difficulties Averroes's commentaries raised became obvious enough for the Pope, Alexander IV, to ask Albert the Great to write a refutation (*On the Unicity of the Intellect against Averroes*), which he completed in 1256. Aquinas also attacked Averroes's teaching in his *Summa* against unbelievers (the *Summa contra Gentiles*). In 1263 Pope Urban IV renewed the earlier prohibition of Averroes's opinions. Siger of Brabant, on the other hand, favoured many of Averroes's views, and the ensuing academic squabble, with Aquinas writing his own condemnation (1270), led to a formal condemnation and anathematization of Averroist errors and the excommunication of those who held them. The condemnation of 1277 was severe enough to bring 'Averroism' to an end in the university world for some generations, but his ideas were sufficiently enticing to win themselves a revival in the fourteenth century, when they were taken up by John of Jandun, and they are still found in play for some time after that.

Bibliography

See Oliver Leaman, *Averroes and His Philosophy* (London, 1998) for sources.

Further reading

Oliver Leaman, *Averroes and His Philosophy* (London, 1998); Barry S. Kogan, *Averroes and the Metaphysics of Causation* (New York, 1985).

PETER LOMBARD *c.* 1100–60

Life and times

Peter Lombard was born around 1100 in Lombardy. He may have studied at Bologna and then at Rheims. He is mentioned in a letter of Bernard of Clairvaux, written to the Prior of the house of St Victor in Paris in 1134–5. Bernard recommends Peter to Victorine hospitality while he studies in Paris, in the hope that he may be permitted to continue in Paris with the studies he began at Rheims. In 1133 he seems to have gone to Pisa, where he may have had an opportunity to make an impression on Innocent II and become 'known' in papal circles. In 1136 Peter was again studying or teaching in Paris; it is clear that Peter knew the *De Sacramentis* of Hugh of St Victor. By the 1140s he was a canon of Notre Dame, teaching in the school there from 1143–4.

It has been suggested that Peter Lombard lacked family 'connections'. If so, his rise up the ladder of preferment may well have been solely on merit. Certainly he seems to have been generally well-regarded by his contemporaries. He was one of those brought in as a 'theological expert' at the Council of Rheims in 1148, at the instigation of Pope Eugenius. In 1159 he gained high preferment when he became Bishop of Paris.

Work and ideas

The writing which won Peter Lombard his fame seems to have been produced from the mid-1130s to the late 1150s. He began in the usual contemporary way, by lecturing. He is the author of commentaries on the Psalms (before 1138) and also commentaries on the Pauline Epistles (the 'Collectanea', composed first between 1139 and 1141 and revised 1155–8). He may have glossed the whole Bible, but only these two texts appear to survive. These are not original works. There is an evident debt to Gilbert de la Porrée (Gilbert of Poitiers) and to the much earlier Florus of Lyons in the ones on the Pauline Epistles. Florus of Lyons's *Expositio epistolarum beati Pauli* (816–55) had already brought conveniently together most of Augustine's significant remarks on the Pauline Epistles in a ready-made collection.

Peter Lombard's major and ultimately most successful work was the *Sentences*. This appears to have developed out of Peter's teaching over time. He was putting a collection together before 1155 and revising it between 1155 and 1158. It was a contribution to a 'genre' of theological literature, which we have already seen emerging, but which was now, in Peter Lombard's hands, to develop into a standard work of reference.

He explains his intention: to bring together the *sententie* or opinions of the Fathers with supporting texts as an accessible collection for his students, so that they did not have to read the whole works of each author for themselves. But this was to be much more than a florilegium. It was to be a course in systematic theology. That was the important innovation. Like other twelfth-century authors, Peter Lombard borrowed a good deal from existing collections here, just as he did in his Biblical Commentaries. Ivo of Chartres, Abelard's *Sic et Non*, the *Glossa Ordinaria* do the same. It is likely that of the works of Augustine, Peter Lombard himself drew directly only on *De doctrina Christiana*, the *Enchiridion*, *De diversis quaestionibus* 83 and the *Retractationes*.[1] He was, however, consciously using some new material, notably the work of John Damascene, which he knew through the intermediary of Burgundio of Pisa. He sees John as a new *auctoritas, inter Graecorum doctores magnus*, an 'important Greek'.[2]

In their detailed structure, the *Sentences* reflect the growing practice of the mid-twelfth century of trying to bring order into the mass of proliferating arguments on theological points by setting them out neatly grouped 'on either side'. There is evidence of the development of the formal *disputatio* from the middle of the century, for example in the *Disputationes* of Simon of Tournai. This approach was clearly helpful to Peter in organising his own material. Was the incarnate Christ the adopted Son of God? (Book III, Dist. x.2). No, says Peter Lombard. Christ is Son by nature, not by adoption. He sets out the arguments for one view. Then he admits that arguments can be put the other way. He furnishes supportive authorities, from Augustine, Jerome, Hilary and Ambrose, as well as sequences of argumentation.

There is an early hint in the *Sentences* of the difficulty (noted by Aquinas at the beginning of his *Summa Theologiae*) that interesting questions may be quite small, even trivial, and make it difficult to keep clearly in view the overall balance and proportion of the questions arising. But an apparently small matter may have huge implications. For example, in Book IV, Dist. i.8, Peter Lombard discusses the question what 'remedy' for sin was available to those who lived in Old Testament times. Circumcision might then be said to have some of the functions of baptism, but that left open the question what remedy was available to women, who were not circumcised. That becomes a question about what is necessary to salvation. Peter Lombard explores various possibilities with implications immensely interesting to twelfth-century theologians: is justification brought about 'by faith' or 'by good works' or by circumcision, or by 'circumcised parentage' (in the case of women)? Is justification achieved by sacrifice? Book IV, Dist. vii.2 discusses the reasons why confirmation can be performed only by bishops ('the highest priests'), depending here upon materials in the canonical collections of Ivo of Chartres and Gratian. The theme of the distinction of the functions of the ordained ministries is taken up elsewhere, in Book IV.xxiv.1–16, as Peter Lombard discovers yet more implications.

The *Sentences* also exemplify another developing methodological device of early 'scholasticism', the technique of *divisio*. The most efficient way to begin to treat a complex question may be to break it down into its elements. Medieval academics certainly thought so. Thus Peter Lombard in Book IV, Dist. i.1 sets out 'four things to be considered' in examining the sacraments: What is a sacrament? Why was it instituted? What does it consist in? What is the difference between the old and the new Law with reference to the sacraments?

Influence

The *Sentences* were not uncontroversial; there were fierce debates about their orthodoxy and that of their author. But after a period in which it established itself as the standard textbook for students of theology, it became the subject of an immense series of commentaries throughout the later Middle Ages. Every budding master had to comment upon the *Sentences* as part of his training and early teaching career, and a good deal of this material survives. Commentaries on the *Sentences* in the later Middle Ages reflect the shifts of theological preoccupation decade by decade and place by place.

Notes

1 J.-G. Bougerol, 'The Church Fathers and the *Sentences* of Peter Lombard', in Irena Backus (ed.), *The Reception of the Church Fathers in the West* (Leiden, 1997), p. 114.
2 J.-G. Bougerol, 'The Church Fathers and the *Sentences* of Peter Lombard', in Irena Backus (ed.), *The Reception of the Church Fathers in the West* (Leiden, 1997), pp. 137, 162.

Bibliography

Sentences (Rome, 1971), 4 vols; *Commentaries on the Psalms and the Pauline Epistles* PL 191.

Further reading

J.-G. Bougerol, 'The Church Fathers and the *Sentences* of Peter Lombard', in Irena Backus (ed.), *The Reception of the Church Fathers in the West* (Leiden, 1997); M. Colish, *Peter Lombard* (Brill, 1994), 2 vols; *Mediaeval Commentaries on the Sentences of Peter Lombard*, ed. G.R. Evans (Leiden, 2001), Vol. 1.

JOHN OF SALISBURY *c.*1120–80

Life and times

John of Salisbury, perhaps the twelfth century's nearest approach to a 'humanist' in the sixteenth century sense, began his education as an English schoolboy. He had one companion in his 'village school', run by the local priest, where the level of instruction was probably modest. He proudly reports that his 'schoolmaster' unsuccessfully tried to entice him to play with the magical arts, in which the schoolmaster himself secretly dabbled (*Policraticus* ii.28). (The other boy was made of more malleable stuff).

John was, however, not put off study by this experience. Indeed, he developed an enduring enthusiasm for the life of the mind. He became a 'perpetual student'. He spent a dozen years as a student in northern France, mainly in Paris and Chartres (1135–6). He describes what it was like to be taught by some of the great names of the mid-twelfth century such as Bernard of Chartres, Thierry of Chartres, Peter Abelard and Gilbert of Poitiers.

John then became an ecclesiastical civil servant, first at the papal court. In his period in the papal *curia* (1148–52) he was at the centre of the politics of not only the ecclesiastical but also the secular world. He describes what happened when he was present at the Council of Rheims (1148), where his old master Gilbert of Poitiers was to be tried for heresy and he observed Bernard of Clairvaux making preliminary moves to ensure his condemnation.

John next became secretary to Archbishop Theobald of Canterbury. That brought him into the arena where the Becket controversy about the respective jurisdictions in the courts of King and Church was to be enacted. He served Becket as Archbishop's secretary, too, and wrote an account of events. Near the end of his life John himself became a bishop, at Chartres (1176–80).

This was in some ways a typical career-pattern of the day, which could take a talented but not especially well-connected individual from the schools to high ecclesiastical preferment by way of a period in the ecclesiastical civil service, where he could get himself noticed.

Work and ideas

Most of John's writing is in essence autobiography, for he writes again and again of the experiences of his own life. His letters reflect that experience most directly of all. They form two collections, the first extending to 1161, the year of the death of his patron, Theobald of Canterbury. John enjoyed a lifelong friendship with Peter of Celle, which is reflected in his letters. Other relationships are similarly recorded in what he himself certainly saw as a literary genre, requiring the expenditure of the utmost conscious artistry in composition.

The *Historia Pontificalis* is John's memoir of his time at the Papal Court. It purports, with the confidence we met in Ralph Glaber, to bring history up to date on the basis of the author's special knowledge of recent events.

John of Salisbury's affection for the schools never left him, but it too was infected with a certain vanity. He claims acquaintance with all the works of dialectic which 'modern scholars have been accustomed to read in the schools' (*moderni patres nostri in scolis legere consueverant*).[1] His *Metalogicon*, in which he describes his own studies in some detail, was intended as an attack on a group whom he calls the 'Cornificians', and abuses them for arrogantly 'undermining' scholarship. These *novi doctores* are more asleep than awake when it comes to reading philosophy (*in scrutinio philosophiae*).[2] They seek to innovate in every one of the liberal arts. John would have us believe they sought reforms rather of the kind introduced by Peter Ramus and his followers in the sixteenth century – that is, a crude simplification of the course requirements.

The *Policraticus* is a treatise on political theory, with moments of satire. John of Salisbury identifies a rationale (*ratio*) of the state (*respublica*). The *respublica* is like a macrocosm of the human body, in which the head and all the members have their places, and work to serve one another and for the welfare of the body as a whole. That is the model which nature affords and it respects power as coming ultimately from God. His 'source', the *Institutio Trajani*, is a work purporting to be by Plutarch, which John seeks to use as an 'authority' to give a classical antiquity to his ideas on the 'prince'.

In John's view, a bad but legitimate king should be obeyed even if he acts unjustly. A usurper is another matter because he has got his power by improper means. John explains that a prince differs from a tyrant in that a prince keeps to the law and rules the people according to the law, believing himself to be the people's servant. A tyrant acts against the interests of his subjects (*Policraticus* IV, 1). A tyrant could be amoral, the secular equivalent of the 'unworthy minister', and then public *utilitas* would suffer.

The prince indeed receives his 'sword' of secular authority from the Church. This is a theme which crops up in writer after writer from the twelfth century.

Influence

John of Salisbury's letters stand as examples of a flower of humanism, construed in terms of a sensitivity to the beauty and the 'feel' of classical literature rather than any theoretical elevation of the position of man. Yet his works had limited influence.

Notes

1   *Metalogicon*, CCCM, 98 Book III, x.
2   *Metalogicon*, CCCM, 98, p. 17.

Bibliography

The Letters of John of Salisbury, ed. W.J. Millor and H.E. Butler (London, 1955; 2nd edn, Oxford, 1986); John of Salisbury, *Historia Pontificalis*, ed. and trans. Marjorie Chibnall (Oxford, 1986); John of Salisbury, *Policraticus*, ed. and trans. Cary J. Nederman (Cambridge, 1990); John of Salisbury, *Metalogicon*, ed. J.B. Hall, CCCM, 98 (1991).

Further reading

The World of John of Salisbury, ed. M. Wilks, *Studies in Church History, Subsidia* 3 (Oxford, 1984).

HILDEGARD OF BINGEN 1098–1179

Life and times

Hildegard was first a nun in a community paired with the male religious community at Disibod. Her birth, like that of most of the thinkers in this book, was noble, for it was extremely difficult for someone not of reasonably good family to make an impact as a writer. From childhood (the story went) she had visions. In 1141 a fiery light filled her and she was given by direct illumination the knowledge of the contents of Scripture which others got only by patient reading. Ten years' work followed, at the end of which she had completed the *Scivias*. Despite the dramatic story of her education, Hildegard herself laid no claim to divine inspiration. She exemplifies in reality the difficulty women found in getting an education comparable with that of men, who could go into the schools and argue. She could hope to learn chiefly by reading, and the limitations of her academic knowledge are apparent in her writing.

She and some of the nuns broke away in the late 1140s to form a new community. It was in this way that Hildegard became founder and first Abbess of Bingen. Pope Eugenius heard of her and gave her his formal approval at Trier in 1147–8, thus encouraging her to complete the *Scivias* (short for *Scito vias Domini*, 'know the ways of the Lord').

Around 1158 Hildegard began to travel on preaching journeys. It is of interest that this was an acceptable thing for a woman to do. It was too early for the question to have become an 'issue'; the Lollard women preachers had not yet sharpened objections to women engaging in this kind of ministry. Hildegard delivered apocalyptic sermons at Cologne and Trier. Hers was not a call for radical reform, nor was it millenarianism; Hildegard did not point to the Second Coming or (like Joachim) to an Age of the Spirit. The thrust of her arguments was the more traditional one, that judgement follows inescapably upon the acts of men and women. Nevertheless, in old age Hildegard became something of a controversial figure.

Work and ideas

Hildegard of Bingen exemplifies the kind of writer especially interested in 'spirituality', that is, the task of teaching others how to 'manage the interior man' (*interior homo*) or soul. The *Scivias* makes its way through the course of salvation history, sometimes in uncertain Latin, with errors which reflect Hildegard's lack of serious formal education. There are three books, dealing with the order of creation, the order of redemption and the order of salvation. Hildegard may have been influenced here by the division in Hugh of St Victor's *De Sacramentis*, into the 'work of creation' and the 'work of restoration'. But this is also, and perhaps more closely, in line with the theme of the division of salvation history into the 'works' of the individual persons of the Trinity, a form of twelfth century Trinitarian theology to be found in Rupert of Deutz and Anselm of Havelberg as well as in the works of Joachim.

A series of visions, each beginning, 'And I heard a voice from heaven saying', is 'interpreted'. Each vision is made into an allegory, and Scriptural passages are brought in as proof texts to underpin the explanation. These in their turn are subjected to allegorical interpretation.

The *Scivias* contains a book of simple medicine (on animals, herbs, trees, gems, minerals), and a book of 'composite' medicine, which she did not finish. There is nothing quite like this among the examples of 'vision literature' of this period of the Middle Ages, and Hildegard deserves credit for a freshness of approach.

Hildegard's work thus combines the encyclopaedic exploration of Christian doctrine, ethics, cosmology, medicine and the natural sciences with spirituality, eschatology, Antichrist and the end of world history. She is also the author of surviving letters, two saints' lives, and pieces of music, including seventy liturgical songs.

Influence

Hildegard was read. She won influence by sheer popularity, and eventual notoriety.

Bibliography

Hildegard of Bingen, *Scivias*, ed. and trans. C. Hart *et al.*, *Classics of Western Spirituality* (New York, 1990); Hildegard of Bingen, *On Natural Philosophy and Medicine*, selections from *Cause et cure*, trans. M. Berger (Cambridge, 1999).

Further reading

F. Bowie, *The Wisdom of Hildegard of Bingen* (Oxford, 1997).

JOACHIM OF FIORE *c*.1135–1202

Life and times

Joachim of Fiore was a monastic scholar. He became a Benedictine at Corazzo sometime after 1171 and may have been made abbot there before 1177. He tried to bring Cistercian habits into this community and even to bring about its full acceptance into the Cistercian Order. But even the strictness of the Cistercians did not satisfy Joachim, and in 1192 he left to found an even stricter Order, the Florensians. The Florensians were given papal approval by Celestine III in 1196, and Pope Gregory IX in 1234 termed them one of the 'pillars' of the Church.

Work and ideas

Joachim wrote 'prophetic history' with an element of political satire. It is easy to see why Dante, with his taste for the cosmic and eschatological, was attracted to his work and drew on it. The *Liber figurarum*, perhaps the work of disciples near or just after the end of Joachim's life, seems to have been particularly influential on Dante. Several of its symbols appear in his writing, for example, the dog as a symbol of the clergy in the 'new age', and an arrangement of circles representing the Trinity.

Joachim drew on a tradition adumbrated in Rupert of Deutz and Anselm of Havelberg, in which the 'line of time' and the linkage of allegorical comparison or pairing, joining Old and New Testament were continued into a new 'age'. The Old Testament was interpreted as the Age of the Father, the New Testament as that of the Son and the third Age was to be the Age of the Holy Spirit. The first was the Age of Law, the second of Grace, the third of Spirit and Love.

Interwoven with Joachim's exploration of the purpose or meaning of history was a preoccupation with the Trinity and its symbolism.

The two were indeed inseparable in his historiography. But whereas history was an area where speculation might run reasonably freely, the doctrine of the Trinity was not, and there are indications that Joachim was involved earlier in his life in a debate which also put into question the orthodoxy of Peter Lombard. In the *Psalterium* Joachim seems orthodox enough, but he was condemned by the Fourth Lateran Council of 1215.

It has been suggested that the lost work *De essentia* may be the source of the material which was condemned and that it may belong to the period around 1179 (Third Lateran Council), when Peter Lombard's own Trinitarian and Christological orthodoxy was being debated. Joachim may have been taking the view that Peter Lombard was unbalancing the Trinity by overemphasising its unity; Joachim himself went some way towards investing the Persons with a 'distinctness' which seems almost to amount to distinction of substance.

Joachim depicts 'the kingdom of God in history'. Joachim's system in his various works (*Liber concordie novi ac veteris testamenti*; *Expositio in Apocalypsim*; *Psalterium decem chordarum*) is not always consistent. There are patterns of seven ages, of 'five and seven', of three *status*. In the third age there were Joachim proclaimed, to be, new orders of spiritual men. The Franciscans and Dominicans, established after Joachim's death, were naturally eager to claim that he had prophesied their coming and to use that as a defence against the charge of the 'novelty' of what they were doing. The 'spiritual' theme of the new age was to extend to an attempted 'spiritualising' of the sacraments, the Pope and everything else in the Church.

Influence

As a prophet, Joachim lent himself to imitation. Joachite works, such as the *Commentary on Jeremiah*, written thirty years after his death, involved an attack on the Emperor Frederick II. The Pharisees are the Cistercians. The new religious orders were compared to the raven and to the dove, which Noah had released from the Ark of the true Church. The story of Joachim's influence goes on a remarkably long way. In parts of twentieth-century Calabria his 'return', like that of a King Arthur, is still waited for.

As a thinker, Joachim was setting a trend which later medieval dissidents and some Reformation thinkers were to take up. What he taught gradually sharpened into a doctrine of the 'invisibility of the true Church'. That was to be perceived as a threat by the 'visible' hierarchy of the Church in the world, for there were powerful vested interests; the Church's wealth and power and influence depended upon its being visibly 'in control'.

Bibliography

Joachim of Fiore, *Concordia novi ac veteris testamenti* (Venice, 1519, reprinted 1964); Joachim of Fiore, *Dialogi de prescientia Dei et predestinatione electorum*, ed. G.L. Podestà (Rome, 1995); Joachim of Fiore, *Enchiridion super Apocalypsim*, ed. E.K. Burger (Toronto, 1986); *Adversus judaeos*, ed. A. Frugoni (Rome, 1957).

Further reading

M. Reeves, *Joachim of Fiore and the Prophetic Future* (Oxford, 1977); Stephen E. Wessley, *Joachim of Fiore and Monastic Reform* (New York, 1990); *Joachim of Fiore in Christian Thought*, ed. C.C. West (New York, 1975), 2 vols.

FRANCIS OF ASSISI 1181/2–1226

Life and times

In 1206, in the Church of San Damiano, Christ said to Francis, 'Go, Francis, and repair my house'. So relates Thomas of Celano in his life of the saint. He describes how thereafter Francis was always 'busy with Christ'. He renounced wealth and set about living in imitation of the manner in which he saw Christ as having lived and teaching his disciples to live in the Gospels. *The Legend of the Three Companions* says that Francis gave the friars admonitions. The apostolic life was one of 'wandering preaching'. Francis lived like that too, and encouraged his followers to do the same.

The group eventually became an Order, when it achieved papal approval, first of a Rule approved in 1209 by Innocent III, and then of a second Rule approved by Pope Honorius III in a Bull of 1223. Because preaching was central to the work of the friars, with it went a need for an education adequate to ensure that the preaching was sound and effective and deserving of the necessary episcopal licence. Chapter 9 of the Rule of 1223 states that: 'Friars are forbidden to preach in any diocese, if the bishop objects. No friar should... preach... unless he has been examined and approved by the Minister General of the Order and has received from him the commission to preach.'

Work and ideas

It is important to set this new preaching in its context of contemporary developments. For when Dominic and Francis embraced the call each felt to the ministry of the Word, they did it in a period of revival of the art of preaching. Since the great patristic age of preaching, when an Augustine could hold an applauding audience for hours, there had been relatively few new sermons. Monastic communities tended to content themselves with readings from the Fathers' homilies or other writings at mealtimes. An occasional exception arose, such as Anselm of Canterbury with his little analogies or *similitudines* or Bernard of Clairvaux, who could rival Augustine in charisma and eloquence. But it was not until Alain of Lille at the end of the twelfth century that a manual on how to preach a sermon was published, and not until the 1230s that the fashion caught on for providing such practical aids to preachers. In this experimental period, Thomas of Chobham and Peter the Chanter were authors of works designed to help the preacher. Francis's *Summa* of advice on the encouragement of virtues and the eradication of vices, written about 1220, is close in form and purpose to Peter the Chanter's *Verbum Abbreviatum*, and perhaps written in imitation of this work of his former master. Peter the Chanter had divided modes of instruction into *lectio, disputatio, predicatio*, and Thomas maintains this division. Thomas sets preaching squarely in the field of rhetoric when he says in his Prologue that he has set out to provide something: *magis utilem quam subtilem... magis affectabilem quam disputibilem*, more useful than subtle, more designed to 'move' people's emotions than to be the subject of discussion and argument.

It is all the more striking in view of the central place his friars were to occupy in the history of late medieval preaching, that Francis's own actual writings are few. Indeed, his legacy raises a question about what constitutes 'writing' in this period. His *Admonitions* were dictated, a practice followed by many authors of the time. Aquinas could dictate to several secretaries at once on different subjects. But Francis was doing it as an 'author' with much less learning than Aquinas, and the question must arise as to how far his amanuensis adjusted what he wrote.

Francis himself believed that his *Admonitions* were his authentic statements of his position on a number of aspects of doctrine and the living of the spiritual life. A theology is embedded in his practical advice. For example 'Good works must follow knowledge' (VII) gives guidance on the question whether it is necessary to salvation to live rightly as well as to have faith. (II) on the evil of self-will cites Genesis 2.16–7 and then comments that: 'He who eats of the tree of the knowledge of good, who appropriates to himself his own will and thus exalts himself over the good things which the Lord says and does in him'.

In the *Canticle of Brother Sun*, Francis invites all creation to praise its creator. *The Testament* was dictated close to Francis's death in 1226. He said that he did not mean to add to his original rule in this text, but in fact he was taken to have done so. The Rule which had been approved by Innocent III was simple; it contained merely Gospel texts and a few prescriptions.

Influence

Francis himself had led a life of poverty and simplicity, and encouraged his followers to do the same. The discussion about Christ's teaching on poverty which arose sharply on Francis's death divided the Church for generations, and inadvertently encouraged the taking of an 'official' position which was in the end to cause much offence with its rejection of Christ's call to simplicity of life. It was one of the developments which helped set the scene for the Reformation of the sixteenth century. This discussion will appear later in the book, but it may be helpful here to glance at the contribution of Petrus Olivi. Olivi was born in 1247–8 in southern France, and became a Franciscan in 1259–60. He studied at Paris, but probably never taught there; he was lecturing at Narbonne or Montpellier in 1270. He found his orthodoxy challenged, then and in subsequent years, over his teaching on poverty in the *Tractatus de usu paupere*. A commission was set up as a result of disputes in the late 1270s and he was censured. Yet what was he teaching? His *Quaestiones de perfectione evangelica* (Questions on Evangelical Perfection) are concerned with what one might have expected to be unexceptionable propositions – about the importance of the practice of contemplation, the role of study and vows, particularly of poverty, chastity and obedience. He goes on, it is true, to explore such questions as whether a Pope can dispense from evangelical vows and to suggest that even a bishop ought to be poor. His point is that poverty is a higher thing than wealth. His condemnation for such talk makes a striking statement about the impact of what Francis had dared to say and the dangerousness to vested interests in the Church of the vision which his followers had found attractive.

Bibliography

Francis and Clare, trans. R.J. Armstrong and I.C. Brady (London, 1982);
Thomas of Chobham, *Summa de commendatione virtutum et extirpatione
vitiorum*, ed. F. Morenzoni, *Corpus Christianorum Continuatio Medievalis*,
82B (1997).

Further reading

J. Moorman, *St Francis of Assisi* (London, 1963); *Francis and Clare*, trans.
R.J. Armstrong and I.C. Brady (London, 1982); Petrus Olivi, *De usu
paupere*, ed. D. Burr (Perth and Florence, 1992).

ROBERT GROSSETESTE *c.*1170–1253

Life and times

How did an order initially dedicated to simplicity of life become
another learned Order like the Dominicans? A partial answer lies in
the growing rivalry of the two orders in the course of the thirteenth
century, as they jostled for chairs in the universities. Indeed, the
thirteenth-century academic world is dominated by the advent of the
mendicant orders, whose intellectually powerful leading figures often
pushed the secular masters or ordinary academic writers into a
corner in their own universities and overshadowed them. It is
illuminating to look first at a writer who found that the Franciscan
Order and the learned life went together quite acceptably from the
beginning of his own experience of the mendicant way.

Robert Grosseteste seems to have been born in about 1170. If that
is correct, we have no further firm information about the first fifty-
five years of his life. But it is at the least puzzling that he should have
become visible as a scholar for the first time at such a comparatively
advanced age. He may have gone the usual scholarly route of
studying in Paris or Oxford. From 1225, in the earliest years of the
University, he was a leading figure in Oxford, at first in the secular
schools. He continued to be prominent until 1235, but now as a
Franciscan. The *Life* of Friar Hubert shows us a Grosseteste of
smooth manners, who enjoyed dispensing hospitality. In 1235 he was
elected bishop of Lincoln, where he remained for eighteen years until
his death in 1253.

Work and ideas

Grosseteste was inventive and experimental in his interests, translating from the Greek in an age when few knew enough of the language to try; and he was apparently up to the minute in scholarship on the study of the Bible, as well as on Aristotle. Grosseteste draws on Origen (via Jerome) but also the *glossa ordinaria* and Peter Lombard's commentary on the Pauline Epistles. Grosseteste was something of a polymath, producing, as well as Biblical commentary, writings on 'scientific subjects' arising in the context of the study of Genesis, such as optics, light, astronomy, meteorology and the movement of the tides. His *Hexaemeron* was probably written after 1225. The tradition of using the account of the six days of creation as a row of pegs on which to hang scientific studies was well-established. Grosseteste appears to have made use of Basil the Great, and we have seen Ambrose engaged in a similar enterprise. Henry of Langenstein was still doing it in the fourteenth century.

The *Proemium* to Grosseteste's *Hexaemeron* seems to be almost an independent work. It is a commentary on Jerome's Letter 53 to Paulinus, in which Jerome sets out his view of his purposes in translating the Bible. Grosseteste recognises Jerome's letter for what it is, as a prologue to Jerome's text of the whole Old and New Testaments. Jerome wanted to encourage his correspondent to go to good teachers to help him study the Bible. Such teaching is necessary unless the reader has direct guidance from the Holy Spirit. All arts need a teacher if they are to be mastered.

In the body of *On the Six Days of Creation*, Grosseteste can be seen to be wrestling with the 'new' science. He holds, in a manner clearly influenced by his study of the *Posterior Analytics*, that each science has its distinctive subject matter and first principles. He insists on creation *ex nihilo*, for the advent of Aristotle's scientific writings was reopening questions about the origins of things which had been prompted in the twelfth century by reading Plato's *Timaeus*. He discusses the conflicts of authorities on the time it took to create light, and the familiar problem of where in the Genesis story the creation of the angels took place.

Grosseteste recognises the difference between astrology and astronomy, which Jerome tends to blur. Grosseteste is clear that astrology is misleading, 'a deceit of the demons'. He keeps clear of such 'dubious science' and provides instead monographs on such solid and respectable scientific topics as *Physics*, *De Luce* and *De Sphaera*.

Contemporary debate in the schools on the Law of Moses was lively. In *De cessatione legalium*, Grosseteste wrote on the question whether the Law ended with the coming of Christ. The central question is whether the Old Law must continue to be observed in the era of the New Law. *De decem mandatis*, Grosseteste's treatise on the Ten Commandments, sees 'love put into practice' as the only reliable interpreter of the senses of Scripture. He seems to mean by this a 'love' properly ordered to God and neighbour.

Grosseteste made an original attempt to reconstruct the debate in the primitive Church about judaising tendencies. His exposition of Galatians must have been made before he became Bishop of Lincoln in 1235, when he was still engaged in disputations. It is probable that he learned Greek after about 1230, so it has been suggested that the echoes of Greek sources in the *Expositio* may indicate a date in the early 1230s. There are references to John Damascene's *De fide orthodoxa* and also, suprisingly, to the homilies of Chrysostom and the *catena* of Theophylact of Bulgaria. Chrysostom was not translated before the sixteenth century, so Grosseteste may have had to read the homilies in the Greek. If he did, that was enterprising, and it also says something about the level of his attainment in the language. It is perhaps more probable that he had an *expositor*, or crib, with a catena of extracts from the Greek Fathers, and that his direct source was perhaps Theophylact.[1]

Grosseteste's *Tabula* is an index of the Bible and the Fathers, with some secular authors and Islamic writers. It consists of topics arranged under nine headings or *distinctiones* ('On God', 'On creatures', and so on). He gives cross-references to a large number of texts, using a unique system of signs. This device belongs perhaps with a body of reference-work literature of the late twelfth and early thirteenth centuries, but the typographic symbols are of Grosseteste's own invention.

For Grosseteste, as for Peter the Chanter in *De tropis loquendi*, the best way to reconcile apparent contradictions is to examine the language closely. In language and logic, Grosseteste was one of the scholars of his generation to be stimulated by the challenge presented by the arrival of Aristotle's *Posterior Analytics*. John of Salisbury had remarked on its difficulty and given the impression that few could cope with it. It had the attraction of offering the possibility of a method of argumentation, the demonstrative method, whose conclusions could be regarded as certainties. It was, in essence, the method used by Euclid, and it could strictly be applied only to geometry. It meant taking the self-evident first principles of each subject and building on them by a process of argumentation so as to arrive at further equally reliable truths.

Euclid built a tower of theorems in this way. Aristotle in the *Posterior Analytics* saw the possession of distinctive first principles as a constituent feature of a true 'subject' or 'discipline'.

There are indications that Grosseteste sought to bring back the habit of reading the authorities, the source texts of the medieval intellectual endeavour, as a whole, instead of in the 'extracted form' of *florilegia*.[2]

Notes

1 L. Rizziero, 'Robert Grosseteste, Jean Chrysostom et l'expositor Graecus (=Theophylact) dans le Commentaire Super Epistolam ad Galatas', RTAM 59 (1992), 166–209.
2 See on the *Originalia patrum*, M.A. Rouse and R.H. Rouse, 'Authentic witnesses: approaches to medieval texts and manuscripts' (Notre Dame, 1991).

Bibliography

Grosseteste, Hexaemeron, ed. R.C. Dales, S. Gieben (*Auctores Britannici Medii Aevi*, London, 1982) and *On the Six Days of Creation*, tr. C.J.F. Martin, *Auctores Britannici Medii Aevi*, (London, 1996); *De cessatione legalium*, ed. R.C. Dales and E.B. King (*Auctores Britannici Medii Aevi*, (London, 1986); *De decem mandatis*, ed. R.C. Dales and E.B. King, (*Auctores Britannici Medii Aevi* (London, 1987); Robert Grosseteste, *Expositio on Galatians*, ed. J. McEvoy and *Glosses on the Pauline Epistles*, ed. R. Dales, R. McEvoy *et al.*, Corpus Christianorum Continuatio Medievalis, 130 (1995); *Commentary on the Posterior Analytics*, ed. P. Rossi (Florence, 1981).

Further reading

R.W. Southern, *Robert Grosseteste* (Oxford, 1986).

ROGER BACON *c.*1214/20–92

Life and times

Roger Bacon was born in England in about 1214/20. He studied first at Oxford. Around 1245 he want to Paris to teach, where he was one of the pioneers of the teaching of the 'new' Aristotle, the works of science and metaphysics. Around 1250 he became a Franciscan. He may have had access to Grosseteste's papers in the Oxford community of Franciscans after he himself went back to Oxford and entered the community there in 1257; so he could have been influenced by Grosseteste and that would make him one of the closest witnesses to Grosseteste's life. Bacon may have been stimulated in this way into the marked interest he displays in the scientific questions Grosseteste had been exploring.[1] He 'invokes' Grosseteste, albeit to criticise him and to say that he believes that he himself has gone beyond what Grosseteste has achieved. For whatever reason, by 1267 he had woken up to the interest of the subject and begun to write about it. During the 1280s he disappears from view, possibly in trouble for 'suspected novelties'.[2]

Work and ideas

Roger Bacon's 'Great Work', the *Opus Maius*, was written around 1267 and, like later works, he sent it to Pope Clement IV in the hope that his blessing and patronage would assist it to make its mark. The Pope's view of the Great Work is not recorded. The 'Third Work' (*Opus Tertium*) is described by Bacon as the third work he has sent to Pope Clement IV. The 'Compendium of the Study of Theology' (*Compendium Studii Theologiae*) was written in 1292 in the last years of his life and forms a summary of what he felt that he had spent a lifetime trying to say. Again, Bacon himself maintains at the beginning of the *Compendium* that Pope Clement has enjoined him to write and that he was gratified to be asked.

Bacon set himself the highest objectives. 'What is the purpose of study?' he asks in the *Opus Tertium*. The *utilitas philosophiae*, the benefit or value of philosophy, must, he believes, be to theology, in encouraging the conversions of unbelievers. It will thus also be a reproof to those who do not find themselves converted. That does not mean that he was only interested in theology. Among the branches of philosophy, he believes that the sciences of the origins of things and of elements have been especially neglected. He mentions geology and metallurgy. The result, he says, is ignorance of all that arises from these beginnings; man, animal, vegetable.

Bacon was a systematiser. He wanted to write an encyclopaedic book for beginners in philosophy (*Opus Tertium*, p. 56). He wrote very fully, *in extenso*, trying to map the elements by locating them within large complexes of study so as to show how they were interrelated. This pattern-making activity was not matched by an instinct for intellectual economy. He can be self-indulgently prolix as he explains his methodology. Yet Bacon had a real interest in *methods* of learning. He says in the *Opus Tertium* that it is in the nature of the human mind to move from the general to the particular; that it needs the wider setting in which to lodge its knowledge of specific issues.

Roger Bacon recognised a number of things in the same basic working materials which others of his day did not notice. Or perhaps it would be more accurate to say that he had a different approach to what were at root the same basic questions. Like Aquinas, Bacon was concerned at the number of ways in which people could go astray in their faith. He tried to assemble systematically all known errors of faith, and the way to rebut them. Aquinas simply set about assembling characteristic errors of those who do not hold the orthodox Christian faith and explaining how to answer them and put those in error back on the right track. Bacon looks at the deeper sources of those errors, the wrong intellectual habits which might cause people to fall into the: relying on weak authority, trusting long-standing mistaken practice, relying on the opinion of the ignorant mob, and so on.

Like Aquinas, Bacon deplores the recent proliferation of 'disputed questions', but while Aquinas sets about putting them into an orderly framework, Bacon suggests abandoning the whole exercise and returning to the study of Scripture.[3] He suggests that children should begin with the more straightforward books of Scripture and those which contain moral teaching, even the versified Bible, rather than with such unedifying classical poets as Ovid.

Bacon was unusually insistent for his time on the value of the study of languages,[4] as distinct from 'language' (that is, the well-trodden medieval ground of the study of grammar and the theory of signification). Perhaps Grosseteste's achievement in acquiring Greek had thrown down a challenge to his successor and admirer to do the same thing.

Experimental verification was another of Bacon's interests. This is startling because of the still pervasive presumption that an idea could not be overturned just by its failure to be borne out by when it was tested in the ordinary circumstances of the created world. Bacon identifies a *scientia experimentalis*. Arguments prove nothing unless they are supported by the results of experiments (*Opus Tertium*, p. 43). This is an astonishing claim. The whole economy of the intellectual system Bacon inherited assumed that the ideas or forms are more real than any particular exemplifications of them, which are subject to change and decay and to imperfections. So to conduct an experiment with objects in the created world is to base the test on inherently unreliable materials. No such experiment ought to be able to overturn a hypothesis which answers to reason. Bacon conjures with a related idea about 'Christian evidences', proofs which prove truths of faith (the *probatio fidei Christianae*). He balances 'all the works of experimental science (*scientia experimentalis*) and other wonders (*mirabilia*)' carefully against magical arts (p. 51).

Notes

1 R.W. Southern, *Robert Grosseteste* (Oxford, 1986), p. 14.
2 *Analecta Franciscana* 3 (1897), p. 360.
3 *Opus Tertium*, p. 54.
4 *Opus Maius*, Part III, *Opus Tertium*, p. 56.

Bibliography

Roger Bacon, *Opus Maius*, ed. J.H. Bridges (London, 1900), vol. 1; Roger Bacon, *Compendium of the Study of Theology*, ed. and trans. Thomas S. Maloney, *Studien und Texte zur Geistesgeschichte des Mittelalters* (Leiden, 1988); Roger Bacon, *Opus Tertium, Opera*, Rolls Series, ed. J.S. Brewer (London, 1857); Roger Bacon, *Opera Hactenus Inedita* (Oxford, 1920–40), vols 1–16; Roger Bacon, *Moralis Philosophia*, ed. E. Massa (Verona, 1953); Roger Bacon, *The Greek Grammar*, ed. E. Nolan (Cambridge, 1902).

Further reading

Roger Bacon and the Sciences: Commemorative Essays, ed. J. Hackett (London and New York, 1997); P. Kibre, *Studies in Mediaeval Science* (London, 1984); *The Life and Works of Roger Bacon: An Introduction to the Opus Maius*, ed. H. Gordon Jones (London, 1914); S.E. Easton, *Roger Bacon and His Search for a Universal Science* (London, 1952).

BONAVENTURE *c.* 1217–1274

Life and times

Bonaventure was born about 1217 at Bagnorea near Viterbo. He became a Franciscan probably in his late teens. Before 1245 he was a student at Paris, where he studied under Alexander of Hales. In 1248 he began to lecture in theology. This was the period of the battle for supremacy at Paris, when the secular masters were trying to exclude the Franciscans and Dominicans. There was some support from the papacy for the mendicants. In 1256 Pope Alexander IV instructed the University of Paris to accept both the Franciscan Bonaventure and the Dominican Aquinas as doctors in the University. Bonaventure became Minister General of his Order. In 1273 he was made Bishop of Albano and a cardinal. He died in 1274 at Lyons.

Work and ideas

Bonaventure's main periods of active writing were in 1250–9, during his teaching career and from 1267 to his death (the period of the controversy over the University of Paris). From 1250–5 dates his commentary on Peter Lombard's *Sentences*; from 1255–7 the *Breviloquium*; from 1257 *De mysterio Trinitatis* and *De scientia Christi*; from 1259 the *Itinerarium mentis in Deum*.

In 1267–8 Bonaventure gave various *collationes* or seminars at Paris, including the *Collationes in Hexaemeron* (1273). He was far from uninvolved in the controversies which were dividing his contemporaries. The battle in Paris over the teaching of certain Aristotelian, and especially Averroist, ideas was visible early in the thirteenth century and it was to lead to the condemnations of particular opinions in 1270 and 1277. One of the most heated of these debates was about the eternity of the world. It was important to Christian orthodoxy that the world should not be deemed to be eternal, for the Bible said that the Christian God had created it. The theme comes up in Bonaventure's *Commentary on the Sentences* and also in his work on the *Hexaemeron*.

This kind of thing is important in illustrating the difference between Bonaventure's response to the new Aristotle and that of some of the Dominicans in particular. Where they actively sought to embrace it and create a synthesis, he sought to contain its implications and even to stand a little away from it.

Bonaventure strove to hold together two modes of thinking and writing which were tending to diverge in his day, the spiritual and contemplative and the rational and 'academic'. Anselm of Canterbury had done the same, but he had not had to achieve this in the context of a pressing university life. This position became associated with some of the Franciscans. Bonaventure describes at the beginning of his *Itinerarium mentis ad deum* how he withdrew to a quiet place to contemplate and there reflected on various ways by which the soul ascends to God. He recollected the miracle of Francis's vision of a winged seraph in the form of the crucified Christ. He saw at once that this vision represented rapture and contemplation.

Bonaventure uses the image of the six wings of the seraphim for the six levels of illumination by which the soul can pass upwards into peace. He divides perceptions into sense-perceptions, perceptions within the self (spiritual) and perceptions above the self (*mens* or mind). God is Alpha and Omega so he can be seen in two ways, and by each of three methods, which means in six ways. Just as God made the world in six days and rested on the seventh, so man has six stages of illumination to pass through before he 'rests' in the quiet of contemplation. There is much that is Anselmian in his approach to his theme. Happiness is no more than the enjoyment of the highest good, which is God. There is an Anselmian 'ascent' through the goods human beings know, though with a more developed spiritual-epistemological slant.

In *The Tree of Life*, Bonaventure describes a tree watered by an ever-flowing fountain which becomes a great and living river with four channels, watering the garden of the entire Church. There are twelve branches adorned with leaves, flowers and fruit. The leaves are medicine for sickness. The flowers arouse the desire for God. The text covers the birth of Christ, the humility of his life, the loftiness of his power and the plenitude of his piety.

The *Legenda Maior* is a life of St Francis. Bonaventure says he visited the sites of the birth, life and death of Francis. He describes Francis's charitable generosity even as a young man, and depicts vividly the defining experiences of Francis' life.

Bibliography

Bonaventure's *Opera Omnia* are edited in the Quarracchi series (Rome, 1882–). Bonaventure, *Breviloquium*, trans. E.E. Nemmers (St. Louis and London, 1947); Bonaventure, *On the Eternity of the World*, selections, trans. P.M. Byrne (Marquette, WI, 1964); Bonaventure, *The Soul's Journey into God*, trans. E. Cousins (London, 1978); *Les six jours de creation*, trans. M. Ozilou (Paris, 1991).

Further reading

Francis and Bonaventure, ed. Paul Rout (London, 1996); J.G. Bougerol, *Saint Bonaventure: études sur les sources de sa pensée* (Northampton, 1989); *Celebrating the Mediaeval Heritage: A Colloquy on the Thought of Aquinas and Bonaventure*, ed. David Tracey (Chicago, 1978).

ALBERTUS MAGNUS *c.*1192/1200–1280

Life and times

Albertus Magnus (Albert the Great) was born in Swabia *c.*1192/1200, of a knightly family. He probably got his elementary education from the local clergy or at the cathedral school at Ulm. As a young man he went to Lombardy (where he had an uncle), and studied the liberal arts at Padua. Joining the friars was attractive to able young men such as Albert; the chief question was whether to become a Dominican or a Franciscan. Albert was one of the promising students recruited by Jordan of Saxony on a journey which took him through Padua. Jordan wrote that he had found ten, two of whom were sons of German counts, and one of those was almost certainly Albert. In 1223 he became a Dominican.

In the thirteenth century the universities were becoming fully institutionalised, and the Dominicans were to play a leading role in the process of their also becoming hotbeds of academic controversy. To replace the rather casual acquisition of a knowledge of key texts which in the twelfth century a student such as John of Salisbury might acquire as the mood took him, by choosing his lecturer and set books for himself, they began to develop something closer to a formal syllabus.

It was also an expanding syllabus. The additional works of Aristotle on logic, in addition to those transmitted by Boethius, the *Categories* and *On Interpretation*, had become available during the twelfth century. That had its effect in stimulating much more sophisticated work on logic, leading on from the *logica vetus* to the *logica nova* to the *logica moderna*, taking up quite fresh topics. Now Aristotle's works on natural science began to appear on the scene in the West, together with the work of Arabic commentators, and to cause a good deal of upset as attempts were made to integrate their challenging assumptions into the existing system of Christian thought. Avicenna's prologue to his commentary on Aristotle's book *On the Soul* is not merely a commentary on Aristotle but a fresh analysis of the subject from the Moslem point of view. Yet there was curiosity among Christian thinkers about such work. A Latin translation of Avicenna contains a dedication to the Archbishop of Toledo, making reassuringly Christian protestations about the importance of the subject, but indicating that the translation from this Arabic thinker has been made at the Archbishop's request.[1]

Not only degrees but higher degrees began to be awarded. The statutes of the University of Paris in 1274 required candidates in medicine to be licensed in the arts already, and to have attended lectures in medicine for five and a half years. The higher degrees were not research degrees but taught courses in medicine, law or theology, at an advanced level, and they too began to have syllabuses. For medicine, at this period in Paris, the basis of instruction was Greek medical theory, in renderings into Latin or accessible through the Arabic tradition. Hippocrates's *Aforismi* was being copied in the eleventh century. For Galen the Arabs were useful, and Avicenna's canon of medical texts was favoured. A student would also encounter Theophilus's *On Urines* and other items collected into an anthology known as the *Ars medicina*.[2]

This is not to say that the Dominican influence was exclusively 'learned'. They were preachers, communicators, even popularisers. Vincent of Beauvais is a case in point. Vincent was born 1184–94 and studied in Paris with the Dominicans around 1220. He moved in about 1229 to Beauvais, and after a time seems to have become intimate with the King of France, Louis IX, and to have found favour at court, teaching, preaching and lecturing to the royal family. He is the author of the largest of the medieval encyclopaedias, the *Speculum maius*. Like Cassiodorus, he was concerned, as he says, with the decline of standards in his own day and it may be that one of the motivators for the writing of encyclopaedias throughout these centuries was this anxious pedagogic urge (modified to meet the needs of each age) to protect and conserve a precious heritage. Science is declining, teaching is dull, says Vincent, and so he has compiled an encyclopaedia. The work was completed in the late 1250s, about the time when Paris was at the beginning of the furore over the new Aristotle. With his different (spiritual rather than intellectual) priorities, Vincent offers his *Speculum* as a remedy for three things. The first is ignorance (for ignorance destroys the divine image in us). The second is concupiscence (which erases the divine likeness). The third is infirmity (ills of the body) for which the mechanical arts provide practical remedies. The *Speculum* has three parts: *naturale* (the heavens and the created world); *historiale* (a chronological survey of the story of the creation of Adam and Eve and of history since); and *doctrinale* (including the seven liberal arts and other subjects of academic study).

By 1228 Albert himself had been *lector* in a series of houses of the Dominican Order in Germany: Hildesheim, Freiburg-im-Breisgau, Regensburg, Strasbourg. In 1241 he was sent to Paris to study theology. He became Master of Theology in 1245. From 1245–8 he was holding one of the Dominican chairs there; he was again at the forefront of a trend, for the friars to become leaders of academe. His courses seem to have been popular. Aquinas was one of his students and he evidently won Albert's respect. 'You call him a dumb ox, but I tell you the bellowing of this ox will one day be heard around the world'.

In 1248 he was sent to Cologne, to the new *studium generale* for Germany. Albert was to be its rector and Aquinas went with him. In

1254 he was elected Prior Provincial of the Teutonic province, which stretched from Holland to Hungary. He did not cease to set an example of humility despite this preferment; indeed he was notable for travelling about the province a great deal on foot. That enabled him to indulge the interest in natural history whose results are reflected in his writings.

In 1256 he defended the mendicant orders before a commission of Cardinals at the papal Court at Anagni in Italy. He seems to have impressed the pope's circle, for he remained at the Curia to lecture on the New Testament, and to chair debates, in which he refuted the arguments of Averroes. In 1259 Albert was appointed to a working party to draw up a standard course of studies for the Dominican order. In 1260 he was made Bishop of Regensburg. This was not a post he aspired to, and he conspicuously refrained from being a rich bishop. He walked about the diocese on foot much as he had walked about the province. In 1261 Pope Alexander IV died, and Albert felt himself free to return to non-episcopal life.

In 1261, he was sent by the Order to preach the crusade to German-speaking peoples. There followed more periods of teaching at Wurzburg and Strasbourg, and a return to Cologne in 1271. He died in 1280, outliving his pupil Aquinas.

Work and ideas

This was a lifetime which spanned a period of prime importance in terms of what was happening in the world of learning. Albert the Great had had a long and fruitful scholarly life at the time when the new Aristotelian materials were just coming into use, and he became greatly interested in Aristotle. He wrote commentaries on all Aristotle's known works, with the apparent intention of bringing them into use in the schools as elements in a new enlarged syllabus. He was so intent on completeness that he added materials from various sources to fill gaps in subjects on which Aristotle had provided nothing, such as falconry. Albert sought in vain for a treatise by Aristotle on alchemy which he could use. He relies on the twelfth-century Moslem scholar Avicenna where Aristotle fails him, even sometimes on supposititious Avicenna, including *De Anima in arte alchemiae*, a treatise on the possibility of transmutation of metals.

This was the matter issue in the famous search for the Philosopher's Stone, which was believed to be capable of turning base metals to gold. Albert was interested in this enquiry at a rather different level – that of possible 'immediate efficient causes existing in the material and transmuting it'. 'Action at a distance' was another of Albert's themes. One body acts on another by touch. Can it act at a distance? Causation theory was an important preoccupation of thirteenth century writers working on Aristotle, especially where they had been reading Averroes.. The main ideas had been in play throughout the Christian Middle Ages in the West. There were final (ultimate), formal and efficient causes of things, which could be identified with the Father, Son and Holy Spirit. There was a material cause, which was the matter God had created from nothing. But the advent of preoccupations bred by reading the newly arrived scientific works of Aristotle was greatly to complicate the picture, sometimes with disturbing questions, such as the one about the eternity of the world, sometimes simply with matters of compelling philosophical interest. Writing on physics, for example, Albertus discusses whether a place actually exists in nature. Does it remain the same thing when different bodies move into and out of it? Is the place an entity distinct from the things it contains? It is a kind of receptacle (*receptaculum*) of any body which happens to be in it?[3]

The task of digesting the newly arrived texts, seeking to fill the gaps in the range of text-books available to cover the syllabus, and providing an introduction for students to the whole corpus of learning as it now stood, was to prove indispensable in laying the groundwork for the labours of the next generation. Yet Albert was not a mere synthesiser. He noted some of the fundamental questions which others were to take forward. It had been a development of the twelfth century to begin to take an interest in what makes an individual distinctive, a 'person', rather than in what makes him characteristic of his human 'species'. Until then, since the ancient world, the emphasis had been on typicality. A good king ought to be much like another good king; that is how one would know that he was a good king. A good Christian or a good citizen would be likewise a 'type'. Albert's commentary on the *Sentences* reveals an interest in the concept of the individual, which he also discusses in the *Summa de creaturis*. The problem is that it is difficult to identify anything which can be in a individual which is not also in the blueprint of the species, except the individuation which makes the individual a separate specimen.

It was Albert's view that a species includes all that is to be found in the members of it: *species est totum esse individuorum*. This kind of approach puts an emphasis on man as a species of animal, and indeed (without losing sight of the Christian insistence that mankind is not *merely* one among other animals), Albert follows Aristotle in regarding man as an 'animal'. Human characteristics and ailments can be described alongside those of other animals. His *De animalibus* was written in about 1258–62. His interest in animals and wildlife generally was manifest from his youth, for he liked to observe nature on his long walks. He seems to have been the first to describe certain creatures, such as the dormouse, the weasel and the rat. Some fish and squirrels were identified by Albert for the first time. Albert's natural scientific bent led him to some surprisingly modern activities. He conducted experiments, for example with bivalve molluscs. The medical remedies he suggests were of the sort which indicate borrowings from popular medicine: burned dog's head, olive oil, dog fat.

Notes

1 *Avicenna Latinus, Liber de Anima*, ed. S. Van Riet (Leiden, 1972).
2 P. Kibre, *Studies in Mediaeval Science* (London, 1984).
3 Albertus Magnus, *Opera Omnia, Physica*, IV, tract.1.c.2, p. 202.

Bibliography

Albert's *Opera Omnia* are available (Aschendorff, 1952–). Albertus Magnus, *Summa Theologiae*, ed. D. Diedley, *Opera Omnia* (Aschendorff, 1978); Albert the Great, *Man and Beast*, trans. J. Scanlon (New York, 1987); Albert the Great, *The Book of Secrets* (Oxford, 1973).

Further reading

S.M. Albert, *Albert the Great* (Oxford, 1948); *Albert the Great, Commemorative Essays*, ed. F.J. Kovach and W. Norman Shahan (Tulsa, 1980); *Albert the Great and the Sciences: Commemorative Essays*, ed. J.A. Weisheipl (Toronto, 1980); J.A. Weisheipl, *Thomas d'Aquino and Albert His Teacher* (Toronto, 1980); H. Wilms, *Albert the Great*, trans. A. English (London, 1933); Astrik L. Gabriel, *The Educational Ideas of Vincent of Beauvais* (Notre Dame, 1956).

THOMAS AQUINAS 1224/5–74

Life and times

Thomas Aquinas was born of a 'good' family in about 1225, and sent to school at the great Benedictine house of Monte Cassino. He then went to the University of Naples. There, in the early 1240s, he joined the Dominicans. This decision displeased his family, who had him waylaid when the Order sent him to Paris two years later. The family had ambitions for him to become abbot of Monte Cassino. Aquinas was kept in imprisonment for a year before he was free to follow his vocation.

In 1246 he arrived in Paris and began to study under Albert the Great, at the time when the latter was engaged in his huge task of synthesising the newly arrived scientific works of Aristotle with the Christian tradition. In 1248 both scholars went to Cologne, where Aquinas remained for four years, studying under Albert.

In 1252 they returned to Paris, and Aquinas began his own teaching career. They returned to the controversy which was reaching its height in the university about the position of the mendicants. The secular masters and students had gone on strike in March 1229. They had returned in 1231 to find two Dominicans lecturing in Paris. During the 1230s and 1240s resentment about this grew among the 'seculars', those masters who were not Franciscans or Dominicans. The mendicant masters continued to number only three, two Dominicans and one Franciscan, out of a mere handful of a dozen possible positions in total (three places being reserved for canons of Notre Dame, including the Chancellor), but they were proving more productive and more successful. The mendicants were increasingly suspected of being in the pockets of the papacy and of seeking to foster papal policy. Although the university was a 'pontifical' institution under the papal charter of 1215 and enjoyed various papal privileges, it was nervous of being controlled by the pope. So Aquinas's arrival to take the second Dominican chair thrust him into the heart of this lingering dispute; for he discovered that the Dominican chair he had come to fill was no longer available; the Dominicans' allocation had been reduced to one. He became involved in the ensuing pamphlet warfare. At this period he wrote his commentary on the *Sentences* of Peter Lombard and *De veritate*, which was his first substantial collection of disputed questions.

Aquinas became a master in theology in 1256. He stayed in Paris until 1259, beginning his *Summa contra Gentiles* there. In 1260 he was back in Naples; 1261–4 he spent in Orvieto, the location of Urban IV's papal court, and 1265–8 in Rome, where he was charged with the task of setting up the house of studies for the Dominican Order there. There was a pattern in the Order of establishing *studia* (which might move from place to place within a province of the Order, following the master. These are *studia provincialia*, not *studia generalia*).

Aquinas was only forty when he was sent to Rome, and he had to work largely on his own. He may have had as assistant a bachelor to 'respond' in disputation (to enable the students to see how each question ought to be analysed), and a lecturer to help with the task of reading the commentary on Scripture, but probably no more. He seems to have imitated the methods and system of the *studia* he had known at Cologne and Paris under Albert, including in his teaching both lectures and discussion of topics arising from the texts, in the form of formal disputations. It was about this time that Aquinas wrote his only book on the relations of Church and State, *De regimine principum.*

There was a third period in Paris from 1269–72, when Aquinas became involved in a controversy with the Averroists. This was the period of his major commentary on Aristotle's *Metaphysics*, and of some Scriptural commentary.

The *Summa theologiae* was begun in 1266, but not completed by Aquinas himself. A second part was the work of his second Paris 'regency', or period as a Regent Master (1269–72) and the rest was almost entirely written at Naples in the period before 6 December 1273, when Aquinas stopped writing altogether.

This was a period of massive productivity and overwork. Aquinas was writing, teaching, praying; and not sleeping. Bernard Gui testifies to his dictating in his cell to three or four secretaries on different subjects at the same time, it was said even dictating in his sleep if he fell asleep in the middle of a sentence. It has been suggested that signs that something was changing in him as a result are visible in the contrasts between Part I and Part II of the *Summa Theologiae*. At last, he was struck by a sudden perception that everything he had written was 'like straw'. He was unable to continue. Eventually others finished the work for him, according to what was known of his plan for the content of what remained to be written. Aquinas died in 1274 on his way from Naples to the Council of Lyons.

Work and ideas

Aquinas was directed by his Order to provide teaching materials, and his work is in many ways a summary of the Dominican positions of his day. He lived at the end of the period of twelfth-century and early thirteenth-century pioneering activity, and much of what he has to say amounts to stock-taking of his work, with a 'Thomist' resolution or 'angle', in which he moved beyond his master

Albertus's preliminary synthesis of the newly-arrived Aristotle with the persisting Christian academic tradition of the medieval West.

The real difficulty was to know where to 'put' the new texts in the scheme of reliability. Even the traditional texts were still causing difficulties. Aquinas does not speak of 'Fathers of the Church', *patres ecclesiae*, only of 'doctors' *alii doctores ecclesiae* and *sancti doctores*. His 'Fathers' extend beyond the first few centuries. Aquinas accepts that some authorities may be less reliable, or at least that opinions may differ. In the *Preface* to 'Against the Errors of the Greeks', *Contra errores Graecorum*, he warns that: 'Since certain statements in the works of the Fathers seem dubious, they can become occasion for error.' Aquinas tackles this problem by setting out first to explain what it is that is uncertain, and then to show how to use such doubt-inducing statements in defence of the faith. In order to accommodate this possibility he conjures with the notion of *adiaphora*, things which are 'indifferent', so that faithful Christians have a choice whether to accept them or not. 'In things which do not belong to the faith we may have different opinions' (*Quodlibeta* XII.a.26 ad 1). Aquinas realises that doctrine comes to be 'officially' defined only when an assumption is challenged by being disputed, so a Father may well have got it wrong if he was writing before a matter had been properly aired in the Church: 'For the old doctors and holy men were so eager to rebut errors about the faith that they can seem to slip into the contrary error.'[1] Aquinas commented (unusually for his period) on Boethius's *De Trinitate* and *De hebdomadibus*. These had been popular books on which to lecture for two or three decades, especially at Chartres, in the middle of the twelfth century, but had now fallen somewhat out of fashion because there was the newly arrived Aristotle to read. Aquinas commented on Ps-Dionysius's *De divinis nominibus* too.

To admit the new Aristotle and his Arabic intellectual satellites onto this already uncertain ground was to create quicksands. Aquinas tackled the problem valiantly. He commented on Aristotle's *De interpretatione, Posterior Analytics, Physics, De Caelo, De generatione et corruptione, Meteora, De anima, De sensu et sensato, De memoria et reminiscentia, Metaphysics, Nichomachean Ethics* and *Politics*. Soaking himself in Aristotle gave Aquinas, and his contemporaries, a familiarity with the deep themes and assumptions of Aristotelian thought, for example that it is helpful when trying to determine what something is, to ask what it is for (teleology). It also warned him of areas where the assumptions could not simply be adopted, at any rate not by a faithful Christian. Aristotle's *Politics* takes man to be a political 'animal'. But Augustine had said he is truly only a social animal, created to live in communion with God and other blessed souls for eternity. The 'politics' involved in systems of control and government became necessary only after the Fall, to keep the consequences of sin under control and to protect the weak from the powerful. That conflict of views had to be resolved, and every thinker who wrote on themes of political thought from the thirteenth century had to take a view of this dilemma and come down either for Augustine or for Aristotle.

Aquinas 'commented' on the 'Book of Causes', *Liber de causis*, in fact an anonymous Muslim compilation, but included in the Arts curriculum in Paris as Aristotelian. Aquinas himself realised, because he had seen William of Moerbeke's new translation of Proclus, that it was not Aristotle at all, but from Proclus's *Theological Elements*. Aquinas was responsive to the controversy around him. Faced with the opinion that all intellect is one intellect, he wrote *De unitate intellectus contra Averroistas*, chiefly to defeat Siger of Brabant, though Siger is not named in the work.

The *Summa Theologiae*, seeking to draw much of this together, was begun in 1266–8. Aquinas's stated intention was to provide a work for the use of the (academically relatively mature) 'beginners' in theology, eliminating the proliferating questions of the day, putting things in a systematic order and generally helping the student find his way through the thicket of contemporary theological studies. Neither the Bible itself, which is far from being a textbook of systematic theology, nor, in Aquinas's view, the *Sentences*, provided this kind of systematic approach. The overarching organising principle is to trace the *exitus* of all things from God and then the *reditus* of all things back to God.

Aquinas's complementary *Summa contra Gentiles* also approaches theology systematically, but beginning this time from the question how a teacher is to deal with the false teachings and errors about the faith which he may encounter in the mouths of various sorts of unbeliever. It should be remembered here that the Dominicans were founded as an order of preachers against heretics. Aquinas takes all kinds of errors, dividing them not according to the affiliation of those who hold or historically have held them, but according to their location in the theological theme. An example may be helpful. For example, he deals with the type of heresy which would seem to make evil a 'something', even a first principle (particularly the dualism of the Gnostics, Manichees and Cathars), by arguing that the intention of an act is always good. Therefore when the result of an act is evil, the evil happens without intention (III.iv). Evil cannot be caused by evil because evil is not, it does not exist, and that which is not cannot be the cause of anything. So evil is caused by some good (III.x). Evil must reside in some good. It cannot exist by itself because it has no essence. It must be in some subject and every subject will be a good (III.xi). There is no highest evil which is the principle of all evils (which is what the Manichees and Cathars teach). A highest evil would, by definition, have to exclude all association with good. But we have shown that evil resides in some good (III.xv). The end of everything is a good (III.xvii).

Providence governs all things but it does not prevent defects or stop evil from operating in the world. A defect may occur in the secondary active cause without there being a defect in the first cause, which is God (that is, the craftsman himself makes no mistake but his tool is defective) (III.lxxi). Similarly, divine Providence does not exclude contingency or impose necessity. The sun shines, a plant grows, the plant bears fruit, but the plant can fail to thrive and then there will be no fruit (III.lxxii).

Divine Providence does not exclude freedom of choice. The heavenly bodies are not the cause of our willing and choosing (III.lxxxv): 'In this way we counter the opinion of the Stoics, who held that all things happen of necessity according to the order of infallible causes' (III.lxxiii).

In *De regimine principum*, Aquinas favours the Ghelf or papalist theory of papal plenitude of power, against the Ghibelline view that all temporal power comes from God through the consent of the governed, and that the Pope cannot exercise even spiritual power in the temporal domain without that consent. This adversarial approach of contrasting irreconcilable theories constitutes a departure from the 'each to his own sphere' solution painfully arrived at in the Concordat of Worms in 1122, where it was pragmatically agreed that there were temporalities and spiritualities and the State should have charge of the one and the Church of the other.

Influence

After Aquinas's death, Averroism was growing fashionable in Paris. The condemnation of thirteen Averroist theses by Stephen Tempier in 1270 proved ineffectual. In 1277, 219 propositions were listed by Tempier and condemned, an action directed in part against Siger of

Brabant and Boethius of Dacia. Some of Aquinas's views were included in the condemned list. That is striking, in view of his endeavour to ensure that he taught only what would keep souls safe, and it underlines how dangerous the times were for a writer.

Aquinas had few former pupils capable of ensuring that his teaching was immediately influential. Something of an 'Augustinian revival' occurred in the half century after his death changing the fashion against him. However, in the early fourteenth century his work acquired an 'official' status in the order. Aquinas's importance grew in the sixteenth century. So in the end, Aquinas's importance was huge, but, curiously, perhaps less because of what he did in his own day, as because he became the hero of the Dominican Order in later centuries (especially from the sixteenth century).

Notes

1   *Nam antiqui doctores et sancti, emergentes errores circa fidem ita persequebantur, ut interdum viderentur in errores labi contrarios, In Evang. Ioannis* I lectio 7 n. 174.

Bibliography

Opera (Rome, 1952–); *Summa theologiae* (Oxford, 1964–).

Further reading

The Cambridge Companion to Aquinas, ed. N. Kretzmann and E. Stump (Cambridge, 1993); Brian Davies, *The Thought of Thomas Aquinas* (Oxford, 1992); Anthony Kenny, *Aquinas* (Oxford, 1980); J.A. Weisheipl, *Friar Thomas D'Aquino* (Oxford, 1975); Leo J. Elders, *The Philosophy of Nature of St. Thomas Aquinas: Nature, Universe and Man* (Frankfurt, 1997).

SIGER OF BRABANT *c*.1240–*c.* 1284

Life and times

Siger of Brabant represents a group of thinkers and university teachers who did not belong to one of the mendicant orders. He was born in the 1240s. He arrived in Paris as a student in the Arts Faculty around 1255–60, at a stage when the arrival and synthesis of the philosophical works of Aristotle, and the integration of the commentary and discussion of Aristotle's ideas by Arab scholars, were challenging old assumptions. As a result of a decision of the provincial synod of Paris in 1210, Masters of Arts were being prevented from commenting on the *libri naturales* of Aristotle, his books on natural science. That prohibition continued in force until the early 1250s. Then there was something of a crisis, in the form of a movement of resistance. The attractions of the new material were too strong for it to be easily ignored. In 1252 the 'English nation' in the Faculty of Arts formally added Aristotle's *De Anima* to the syllabus. It was a gesture. It was as controversial as was expected. In 1270 thirteen articles were condemned by Stephen Tempier, Bishop of Paris.

One way of addressing the danger was to seek to 'contain' the effect, by taking a fresh overview of the philosopher's task, asking what philosophy was and how it related to other disciplines, especially to what we should now call 'theology'. That is one of the first questions Aquinas tackles in his *Summa theologiae*. This was of importance in clarifying the scope and nature of philosophy, and it encouraged thinking about content and method.

Siger himself, a 'Picard' by 'Nation' at Paris, is first heard of in 1266. He was keen on the newly-arrived Aristotle to a degree such that his ideas seemed to contemporaries seriously to threaten the integrity of the faith.

Work and ideas

Siger won a name for himself as a leader of those in favour of a 'rational' approach, which seemed to their opponents to put Christian orthodoxy in danger. And indeed it might, since reason could lead to conclusions in tune with Aristotle as easily as to those in keeping with the Christian faith. Siger advocated a fearless use of reason to compare and evaluate the new ideas, regardless of the implications for settled ideas about the faith.

In 1269–70 Siger produced his *Quaestiones in Physicam*. After the death of Aquinas, a question Siger had been discussing became more controversial still: whether creatures have an essence which is different from their existence. Siger claimed to be unclear what Aquinas had been teaching on this subject.

What danger did Siger represent to justify the condemnations of the 1270s? There were held to be four main 'errors': his views on providence, on the eternity of the world (this asserted that the world had always existed and that therefore God did not create it in time and *ex nihilo*), on the unicity of human intellect (that is, that there was a single intellect shared by all mankind, derived from Averroes's discussion of Aristotle's *De Anima* 430a17–23), and on moral freedom.

Influence

Siger of Brabant was seen as a dangerous influence by his contemporaries, but his long-term influence was modest.

Bibliography

Siger of Brabant, *On the Eternity of the World*, trans. Lottie H. Kendzierski (Marquette, 1964); Siger of Brabant, *Quaestiones in Metaphysicam*, ed. W. Dunphy (Louvain, 1981); Siger of Brabant, *Quaestiones in tertium De Anima*, ed. B. Bazan (Louvain, 1972); *Les quaestiones super librum de causis de Siger de Brabant*, ed. A. Marlasca (Louvain, 1972).

JOHANNES DUNS SCOTUS *c.* 1265–1308

Life and times

The Scottish Franciscan Johannes Duns Scotus was ordained priest in the diocese of Lincoln in 1291. It may be inferred that he was probably born in 1265–6; that would have brought him to 'canonical' age for ordination at the right time. His ordination in England rather than Scotland seems to require explanation. There was a sequence of changes in the mid-thirteenth century, which first gave the Scottish Franciscan friaries an independent vicariate and then restored them to subjection to the English province.

Scotus was at Oxford in 1300, probably having begun his theological studies there in 1288. In 1298–9 he would have been commenting on the *Sentences* of Peter Lombard, by now a routine stage of an academic's training. He may have been briefly in Cambridge in 1301–2. By 1302–4 he was in Paris, commenting again on the *Sentences*. During this period, in 1303, he was sent into exile, with others, for refusing to give his support to King Philip IV in an appeal against Boniface VIII to the General Council. He was allowed to come back in 1304 and to finish his Commentary on the *Sentences*. In 1304, too, he was made Regent Master of the Franciscans in Paris. This led to his chairing disputations, and he produced his *Quodlibetal Questions* in 1306–7. (Quodlibetal questions were questions on any subject the questioner liked to raise.) His name is also found as *lector Coloniae* at Cologne in 1307, taking him to a fourth university.

Work and ideas

How did such a relatively short-lived scholar make his way into the ranks of the well-known? One reason may lie in the prominence of his opponents, for there is nothing like a high-profile battle to make a man famous. The effect is rather like that of the pamphlet warfare of later centuries in its capacity to bring names to prominence. For instance, Henry of Ghent is cited in order to be refuted. Once noticed, Scotus won respect for the refinement of his arguments, and he was accorded the title of *doctor subtilis*. The Franciscans in particular were instrumental in making his reputation, even (or perhaps especially) those who wished to mar it by disagreeing with him. Two of those indebted to his work who themselves became notable were Peter Aureoli and William of Ockham, both Franciscans, one French, the other English. Scotus made his mark in virtually all the areas of contemporary concern, particularly the discussion of the unity and unicity of God, their connection with the proof of his very existence, and their implication for God's perfection.

Scotus produced at least two commentaries on Peter Lombard's *Sentences*, one while he was at Oxford and one during his time at Paris. Scotus asks whether there is in the realm of beings a thing which is infinite. He develops Aristotle's argument about the Prime Mover in fine the *Physics* (VIII.x, 266a, 24–266b,6). But he was not only interested in this type of proof of the existence of God. He reviewed the arguments for the existence of God (Book I, Dist. 2.i.2) in an attempt to determine the still more difficult question whether the existence of God is known *per se*. In favour of the opinion that it is self-evident that God exists, he cites John Damascene's statement that the knowledge of God's existence is implanted in everything by nature; and Anselm of Canterbury's contention that the existence of that than which no greater can be thought is known *per se*. He concludes that these two thinkers cannot be right. What is self-evident cannot be denied, but the Fool of the Psalms said in his heart that there is no God. So God's existence can be denied and is therefore not self-evident. So far he is close to Aquinas.

Scotus goes on to explore what is meant by self-evidency. In his view the notion does not exclude there being some cause of the 'knowledge', but any 'reason for holding a proposition to be self-evident' must, by definition, be included within the terms in which it is expressed. Those terms include the thing defined and also its definition. That takes him into Aristotle's *Posterior Analytics* and the *Physics*, and thus to authorities beyond the reach of the twelfth-century authors who struggled with this question. Yet he is left with the task of explaining away the opinions of the respected Damascene and Anselm. In the case of John Damascene, he suggests that the argument looks different if it is taken to refer to the cognitive powers we have by nature, which enable us to make inferences about God's existence from the existence of creatures. The knowledge is therefore not self-evident but derived by inference. In the case of Anselm, he contends that he is not really arguing that his proposition is self-evident; he is saying something subtly but importantly different.

Duns Scotus is thus one of the medieval thinkers to make a contribution to the question of the proofs for God's existence. He seeks to establish that there is God, but only one God, for it might otherwise be made to follow from his proofs that there is a multiplicity of Gods. Indeed, he acknowledges that there are those who hold that the unicity of God is a matter of faith and cannot be proved. He identifies intelligence and possessing a will as 'absolute' properties of God. He takes a line already visible in Augustine and Boethius, that what in a creature would be a mere attribute is, in God, of his essence.

Can man have a natural knowledge of God? In other words, is it possible for the human intellect to understand what God is like in any way but by analogy with things within its grasp? Duns Scotus did not believe it to be possible for the intellect of a creature to have an intuitive or 'direct' knowledge of God as he really is in this life, but he did hold that there are concepts of God which the human mind may lay hold on, and that it can do so 'properly'. The technical sense of 'properly' here is 'not merely by comparison'.

Scotus is also the author of surviving *disputationes* and the *Quaestiones quodlibetales* and *Collationes Parisienses et Oxonienses*. There are other collections of 'questions' attributed to Scotus, and a *Tractatus de primo principio*. He wrote on metaphysics and epistemology and the theory of action and on ethics.

Bibliography

Duns Scotus, *Opera Omnia*, ed. C. Balic (Vatican, 1950–); Duns Scotus, *God and Creatures: The Quodlibetal Questions*, trans. Felix Alluntis and Allan B. Wolter (Princeton, 1975); *Duns Scotus on the Will and Morality*, trans. Allan B. Wolter (Washington, DC, 1986).

Further reading

B.M. Bonansea, *Man and His Approach to God in John Duns Scotus* (London, 1983); A. Broadie, *The Shadow of Scotus: Philosophy and Faith in Pre-Reformation Scotland* (Edinburgh, 1995); M. Sylwanowicz, *Contingent*

Causality and the Foundations of Duns Scotus' Metaphysics (Leiden, 1996);
A. Wolter, *The Philosophical Theology of John Duns Scotus* (Ithaca, NY, 1990).

DANTE ALIGHIERI 1265–1321

Life and times

Dante was born in Florence. When he was nine years old he set eyes on Beatrice Portinari, still a little girl, in fact slightly younger than himself. Nine years later he met her again, and he says that 'child as he was', he loved her from that moment. She died about nine years later, at the age of twenty-five. Beatrice was married when she died in 1290, but not to Dante. Dante, taking these events and the intervals of nine years which recur in the story to be of immense significance, broken-heartedly put together his poems about her in the *Vita Nuova* (c. 1294). Yet Dante did not expect, or even want, to marry Beatrice himself. This was 'courtly love', which had had its conventions since the twelfth century. One of these conventions was the idealisation of an inaccessible lady, for whose smile or favour the lover performed tasks of daring or great virtue. This was the world inhabited by Lancelot and Guinevere in the Arthurian legend. The 'beloved' became an inspiration to high endeavour, rather than a prospective future wife. For Dante, Beatrice was an inspiration to a poetic spirituality which reached its ultimate expression in the *Divina Commedia*.

During this time of his young manhood, Dante was suffering political as well as amatory reversals. Florence was a city state, given to the ebb and flow of faction warfare and of crises of governance. In 1284 all noble Florentines were disenfranchised. It was possible to get the franchise back by joining an appointed 'gild'. Dante was able to advance within the new political structure and to become actively involved in the government of the city. Early in 1300 the Guelfs, his faction, split into two, the Blacks and the Whites. The Blacks called for papal intervention, but merely got outside intervention in the form of the brother of the French King, Charles of Valois. The Whites, including Dante, were deprived of their property and driven into exile, accused of anti-papal activities. Dante remained in exile, bitter and sick for home, until his death nineteen years later. It was this experience which perhaps helped to crystallise for him the view that the world needed the protection of an Emperor to override the pretensions of contemporary papal monarchy. In 1310 the Emperor Henry came to Italy and Dante had hopes of being able to return to

Florence. Henry laid siege to Florence, but his death put an end to the project. In 1315 the sentence against Dante was renewed. He ended his days at Ravenna.

Work and ideas

Dante was 'formed' by a wider than usual range of reading, or it may be that he was attracted to unusual aspects of what he was taught. He 'responded' to Boethius, to the Victorines, to the 'courtly' literature of love, to the story-traditions to be found in such works as the 'Matter of Brittany' (*Matière de Bretagne*), as well as to Virgil, and although it is Virgil he chooses to be his companion in the first parts of the *Divina Commedia*, the others are there too in their shadowy way. Dante's writing was all done after he had read Aquinas, and so he also had an academic tradition in his mind. Dante's synthesis raises unprecedented questions about the syncretism of medieval writing.

The 'New Life' (*Vita Nuova*) is the story of a love affair. Dante describes the emotional impact it had upon him when at the ninth hour of the day, nine years since he had first seen Beatrice, she glanced at him and greeted him. Yet there is conscious art and conscious use of symbolism, with other threads woven into an account of something which goes far beyond a lover's autobiography. In the *Vita Nuova*, Dante speaks of going astray in a 'dark wood'; perhaps of heresy as well as hopeless love?

The *Divina Commedia*, for which Dante chose Italian as the language of composition, is his most important work. It is the story of a journey through hell, purgatory and heaven. Dante does not go alone. For the first two stages of the journey he is accompanied by the poet Virgil. Virgil is the natural choice, because in his *Aeneid* (Book VI), he describes a journey into the underworld. He can therefore be taken to be a knowledgeable guide. A commonly quoted tag was the opening line: *facilis est descensus Averni*, which warns that it is easy to go down into the underworld but difficult to climb out again. The device of providing himself with a companion allows Dante to use conversation as a means of explaining what he is seeing. Beatrice appears at the end of Purgatory, where Virgil leaves Dante's side (Canto XXVII). For when Dante gets to the threshold of heaven, Virgil can take him no further; Virgil was not a Christian. Beatrice takes over, and here the meaning of her name becomes significant. She is one of the 'blessed', who dwell in the realms he now enters.

Dante's cosmos had the geography that medieval thinkers would have expected. It begins with a supernatural dimension which sets the context. God is the single first principle of things. In the one God are three Persons, Father, Son and Holy Ghost. From the Godhead streams out creation. God did not need to make things. He is complete in himself. But he is generous; his creation brought into being creatures who would not only reflect his glory but also enjoy contemplating and loving him. With these creatures, we cross the border which, to modern eyes, lies between the supernatural and the natural, theology and science. It was not that medieval thinkers did not see it there. They did, however, see no reason not to pass backwards and forwards across it in the course of either theological or scientific discussion, and certainly in poetry.

God made everything from nothing. It was important to establish this, since Plato in the *Timaeus* describes a God who is more like a craftsman, taking pre-existing matter and forms and putting them together into 'created things'. There was a clearly understood hierarchy of being, with inanimate matter at its lowliest point; the vegetable creation next (having life but not movement); then the animal creation (having life and movement); then human beings, who have rational souls and angels who are pure rational spirit.

Hell is under the earth, at the centre. The earth is composed of four elements, earth, water, air and fire, the four 'humours' of medieval medicine, which need to be kept in balance for health. Round the earth circle the seven planets, each carried on a transparent sphere, and revolving east to west every twenty-four hours. At the same time each planetary sphere is moving west to east on its own motion, in epicycles. The sun's movement is a simple circle. Beyond lies the sphere of the fixed planets. Further out still comes the *primum mobile*, the crystalline sphere beyond which is heaven. Or, more strictly, there is nothing, for 'beyond' implies a spatial relationship and heaven is outside time and space.

Dante's universe is, however, far from mechanical. He understands that there can be beauty in hell, indeed there must be, for hell is part of God's creation. Purgatory, however was something relatively 'new', largely an invention of the penitential system of the twelfth century. It met a pastoral need for an explanation of what was to become of the vast majority of human beings who clearly do not die in a condition of sanctity but whom it seemed hard to write off as destined for hell. Ordinary people wanted a hope of heaven and the doctrine of purgatory suggested a way in which they might be purged of the uncompleted penalties of their sins after death, and ultimately enter heaven.

The *Divina Commedia* is perhaps the supreme example of the genre of medieval vision literature. It is a comedy and a tragedy, at the same time satire and serious philosophy and theology. The *Convivio* is Dante's 'Symposium', a philosophical work on wisdom and goodness, in which the inspiration of Beatrice is still hovering. The soul of divine philosophy, it is suggested, is love and the beauty of her body is morality. The noble intellectual soul and the power of reason is a fair woman.

The *Monarchia* of 1320 contains Dante's argument for a single world government. It is known to have been circulated in at least forty copies and was used in 1329 by the publicists of Ludwig of Bavaria. The choice of Latin for this work may be significant, if it tells us that Dante meant it to be taken for a solid 'academic' work of enduring importance. In the *Convivio*, Dante discusses in a sequence of chapters the proper use of each language. Latin is lasting; it is a better vehicle for abstract ideas; it is more beautiful because (as Dante mistakenly believed, because he could not take the overview we now can of the development of Latin since classical times), it is not constantly changing like a vernacular language. On the other hand, Dante clearly did not envisage a solely academic or scholarly readership for his Latin. His Latin can be rich and rhetorical, designed to move men of the world. He was not writing just for theorists. He wanted the *Monarchia* to have political effect, to bring about an imperial world government in reality. The question how much academic learning underlies it is harder to answer. Dante did not like the lawyers. He found them to be greedy power-brokers. So he does not make more than the briefest explicit reference to the legal ideas which nevertheless underlie his scheme, and with which it is apparent in the *Convivio* that he was perfectly familiar.

Bibliography

Dante Alighieri, *Vita Nuova*, trans. W. Anderson (Harmondsworth, 1964); Dante Alighieri, *Monarchia*, ed. and trans. Prue Shaw (Cambridge, 1995); Dante Alighieri, *The Divine Comedy*, ed. A. Mandelbaum (Berkeley, CA, 1980–2); Giovanni Bocaccio, *The Life of Dante*, trans. V.Z. Bollettino (New York, 1990).

Further reading

W. Anderson, *Dante the Maker* (London, 1980); P. Boyde, *Philomythes and Philosopher: Man in the Cosmos* (Cambridge, 1981); Mazzeo, *Mediaeval*

Cultural Tradition in Dante's Comedy (New York, 1960); Dorothy Sayers, *Further Papers on Dante* (London, 1957).

RAMON LLULL *c.* 1233–*c.* 1315

Life and times

Ramon Llull is an unusual example of a scholar who entered the world of learning late and from a courtly environment. The tradition that the academic life, the life of a 'clerk', is the life of a *cleric,* was strong. Llull came from Majorca, and began his adult life as a courtier and poet. He changed direction after he had a vision of Christ and believed himself to be called to write the 'best book in the world'. He was, it seems, 'moved' by hearing a Franciscan preacher. He gave up his family and worldly goods and went on pilgrimage, and then on to systematic study. He is notable for encouraging the study of oriental languages, and for his medical knowledge and interests. He also served as a missionary on more than one occasion, and he probably lectured for a time at Paris.

Work and ideas

In his attempts to write the best book in the world Llull became prolific. He was more experimental with form and style than many who had gone only through the usual scholarly channels. He says in the prologue to this that he wanted to find a new method and new reasons for faith, so that those in error might be shown the path to glory.

Llull evinced a Christian Neoplatonism, producing 'mystical' writings and perhaps dipping into alchemy. His *Principia Philosophiae* (*First Principles of Philosophy*) was begun in Paris in 1299. His contention is that there is a fundamental accord between philosophy and theology. Philosophy is the *effectus* of the First Cause, who is God himself. Philosophy is the *instrumentum* and the *speculum*, the tool and the mirror, with which mankind attains theological knowledge. It is therefore, he suggests, a sound plan to examine the first principles of philosophy and theology and see if they agree. He devises something resembling a Venn diagram: let philosophy be a white circle, containing within itself potentially all the divisions of other circles. He also proposed a version of Aristotle's *Categories* with nine rather than ten categories. One asks what the thing is, where it comes from, why, how big it is, what kind of thing it is, when and where it is, how it is, and in what company it is.

Llull wrote a certain amount in Catalan, using the vernacular for philosophical purposes in a pioneering way. Most vernaculars were only gradually becoming adequate vehicles for serious thinking, as their vocabulary and structures reached a sufficient level of sophistication. The *Blanquerna* is his vernacular *Confessions*. Lull is personified as the Court Fool or Lover, Blanquerna. In his *Book of the Lover and the Beloved*, he provides a verse *locus* for each day of the year, in which a love of paradox is prominent. One or two examples may give the flavour of Llull's version of a fundamentally Franciscan type of 'ascent to God' spirituality: 'Many lovers come together to love One only, their Beloved, who made them all to abound in love. And each one had the Beloved for his possession and his thoughts of him were very pleasant, making him suffer pain which brought delight.'[1] 'Love is an ocean; its waves are troubled by the winds; it has no port or shore. The Lover perished in this ocean, and with him perished his torments, and the work of his fulfilment began.'[2]

Lull wrote his own 'Life', the *Vita coetana*, around 1311.

Influence

In 1332, sixteen years after Llull's death, a *Testamentum* appeared, linked with Llull's name, but this is probably the work of a Catalan alchemist living in London.

Notes

1 *Late Mediaeval Mystics*, ed. R.C. Petry (London, 1957), pp.157ff.
2 *Late Mediaeval Mystics*, ed. R.C. Petry (London, 1957), pp.157ff.

Bibliography

Ramon Llull, *Opera* in *Corpus Chistianorum Continuatio Medievalis*; *Selected Works of Ramon Lull,* ed. and trans. A. Bonner (Princeton, 1985), 2 vols; Ramon Llull, *Principia Philosophae*, ed. F. Domínguez Reboiras (1993).

Further reading

Mark D. Johnston, *The Spiritual Logic of Raymond Lull* (Oxford, 1987); Mark D. Johnston, *The Evangelical Rhetoric of Raymond Lull: Lay Learning and Piety in the Christian West Around 1300* (New York, 1996); *Late Mediaeval Mystics*, ed. R.C. Petry (London, 1957).

MEISTER ECKHART *c.*1260–1327/8

Life and times

Eckhart was a Dominican all his adult life. He was born in about 1260 at Hocheim in Thuringia, in Germany. He entered the Dominican order at Erfurt when he was a boy. In 1277 he was sent, briefly, to the Dominican *Studium* in Paris. He may have studied in Cologne with Albert the Great before 1280. He was lecturing on the *Sentences* in Paris in 1293. From 1294–1300 he was prior of the Dominican house at Erfurt and simultaneously vicar of the Dominican house in Thuringia. In 1302 he was back in Paris as a teaching master.

From 1303–11 Eckhart was the Provincial of Saxon, and that of Teutonia in 1310. From 1310–14 he reappears in Paris. From 1314 to the end of his life he was preacher, and sometime advisor, to Dominican nuns and Beguines, the new 'lay' women religious of the day.

Despite this solid record of service and the high reputation he enjoyed for a time, Eckhart ended his life on trial for his opinions. The Inquisition set up to look into what he had been teaching in 1326 found 150 propositions which suggested that he might be a pantheist or an antinomian. In 1327 Eckhart appealed to the Pope and a Commission considered twenty-eight of his propositions, which were, rather inconclusively, condemned as heretical 'on the face of things' (*prout verba sonant*).

Work and ideas

In the 1290s Eckhart wrote his *Counsels on Discernment*, his first German work. Around 1302 he was writing his Paris disputations. He was thus contributing both in conventional academic fields and in innovatory ways.

There were new trends in mysticism in the Rhineland in Eckhart's lifetime. Hildegard of Bingen had been succeeded by the Beguines: female, generally lower-class 'would-be religious'. The Beguines often sought a place to live close to a Dominican or Franciscan priory. They had been forced to find a place for themselves somewhat outside the system, which tended to place high-born ladies in the high positions in conventional abbeys for women. Mechthild of Magdeberg is an important example.

In advising such communities, Eckhart developed his own ideals and practices of spirituality. He encouraged Christians to seek an interior transformation. Meister Eckhart suggests in his sermon on the contemplative life that Martha, whatever her faults, had nobility of nature and unflagging industry to her credit. Mary was Martha before she was Mary. She was not yet Mary when she sat at the feet of our Lord. She was Mary in name but not yet in nature. She had to learn to serve. In the sermon on the eternal birth (on the text of Luke 2.49), Eckhart considers the text 'I must be about my Father's business'. 'The whole life of Christ instructs us in this matter and the lives of his saints as well'. We must preach the Word:

> the inborn secret word that lies hidden in the soul... If a person is quite unoccupied, his mind is stilled, God becomes controller... and is himself begotten in the passive intellect... The active intellect cannot pass on what it has received... when God acts in lieu of it he begets many ideas or images... all your resources for good take shape and gather at the same instant to the same point.

But there are paradoxes here, and paradoxes can easily be misunderstood. Eckhart might have meant something spiritually profound when he said, 'Even he who blasphemes against God praises God,' yet that was an assertion easily misread as heretical. In fact, it was among the articles condemned in the Bull of John XXII. The same danger lay in his love of negative theology. He might suggest leaving behind Augustine's teaching in *De Trinitate* (about the memory, will and understanding in each person, which form a trinitarian image in each soul), only to encourage a fresh look at what it takes to find Christ by beginning from what we do not know about God. There was a dangerous combination of passion and opacity in much of what Eckhart wrote.

Alongside his *Divine Comfort*, his *On Detachment* and his *Talks*, there were also in circulation texts which purported to be his but which are of doubtful attribution, again to his peril.

Bibliography

Meister Eckhart: A Modern Translation, trans. R.B. Blakney (New York and London, 1941); Meister Eckhart, *Selections*, ed. H. Backhouse (London, 1992); Meister Eckhart, *Selected Treatises and Sermons*, trans. J.M. Clark and J.V. Skinner (London, 1994).

Further reading

C.F. Kelley, *Meister Eckhart on Divine Knowledge* (Yale, 1977); B. McGinn, *Meister Eckhart and the Beguine Mystics* (New York, 1994); Stephen E. Ozment, *Homo Spiritualis* (Leiden, 1969); F. Tobin, *Meister Eckhardt, Thought and Language* (Philadelphia, 1986).

THOMAS BRADWARDINE *c*.1295–1349

Life and times

Thomas Bradwardine, born in Chichester or Sussex in the late thirteenth century, was a Fellow of Balliol College, Oxford in 1321. By 1326 he was a Master of Arts and a fellow of Merton. He was Proctor in 1325 and 1326, when there was a town and gown dispute over the moving of a pillory. As Proctor, acting in a legal office on behalf of the University, Bradwardine was involved in lengthy litigation with the Archdeacon of Oxford about the spiritual authority the Church had over the students of an independent university. The case went to the courts and the University won autonomy from episcopal interference, which was to be very important for its future. Bradwardine was also involved in his Oxford period in a formal disputation with Baconthorpe on foreknowledge and free will.

Bradwardine left Oxford in 1335 and he joined the Bishop of Durham, Richard de Bury, the great book collector and author of the *Philobiblon*, who had become his patron. Richard de Bury seems to have liked to have a household of scholars about him, rather as Grosseteste did when he was bishop. Bradwardine was only one of several such scholars. The link may go back to his youth: Richard de Bury had been at Chichester cathedral in the early fourteenth century. In the bishop's circle were a number of other Mertonians, including Holcot. They seem to have held disputations in the evenings.

In 1337 Bradwardine became Chancellor of St Paul's in London. Until Bury's death in 1345 he continued to act as the latter's agent. Bradwardine was appointed chaplain to King Edward III, and went to France in 1346 with the English expedition which led to the battle of Crécy; and finally in 1348 he became Archbishop of Canterbury. He died of plague in 1349.

Work and ideas

Most of the mathematics and logic and natural philosophy of Bradwardine belong to his Oxford period, notably the important *Geometria speculativa* and the *Tractatus de proportionibus.* This geometrical work was significant.[1] The syllabus of mathematics in the Statutes of the University of Oxford before 1350 included chiefly Boethius's *Arithmetica*, Euclid, Books 1–6 of the *Compotus*, the *Algorismus* and Sacrobosco's *De Sphaera.* Euclid had come into use relatively late in the Middle Ages. He was much respected. Grosseteste says that natural philosophy cannot be understood without his work, as does Bacon.

There was also an active interest in its uniquely successful demonstrative method, and the question whether that method could be adapted to other subjects. This was seen to be desirable because the demonstrative method proceeded from self-evident truths to necessary conclusions, which was obviously better than dealing with mere probabilities as ordinary syllogistic arguments did. Bradwardine was drawn, like his contemporaries, to the elegance of the Euclidean demonstrative method and made the same connection as others had, between Euclid and Aristotle's *Posterior Analytics.* In the spirit of *Posterior Analytics* I.2, he uses definitions, first principles or 'immediate' propositions, depending on no others, which he identifies with major premises (*maximae propositiones*) and postulates (*posita*). Yet there was not the same energetic development of the methodologies as had happened in developing the merely 'probable' arguments of logic.

Bradwardine was unusual in attempting to prove new geometrical theorems. The *Geometrica speculativa* was probably written in the 1320s, before Bradwardine began on the *Tractatus de proportionibus.* It is unusual for its time in that it is not merely a commentary but a fresh treatise. It does not expect the reader to know Euclid already. But it is not merely an elementary manual of introduction to Euclid. Bradwardine was a confident geometer. He succeeded in arriving at Euclid's 32nd proposition in only five of his own.[2] It has new topics, such as star polygons and operimetry. Bradwardine develops the concepts of ratio and proportion, using Aristotle as well as Euclid as a stimulus and starting point. For Aristotle was full of themes of potential mathematical interest to medieval thinkers: the properties of the void, speeds of movement, intensities of heat in a body and proportion, as we have already seen in Albert the Great.

Bradwardine's *De proportionibus* (On Proportion) is a treatise on mechanics. It draws on Gerald of Brussels's work the 'Book of

Motion', *Liber de Motu*. Bradwardine explores Aristotle's ideas about the relationship between forces and times and distances. He found mathematical inconsistencies. Insisting on the use of mathematical principles, he discovered a novel way of relating these variables in a theory of movement. He hit on the notion of 'instantaneous' velocity to replace Aristotle's 'completed change'. Aristotle had claimed that velocity varies according to the proportion between the power of the mover and the power of the thing moved. Averroes had added the view that it was necessary to begin from a force resistant to the moving power. The fact that movements in the heavens take time could then be taken to show that a force is present which is resistant to the moving power. The key to Bradwardine's insight was the identification of the question how changes (here 'motions') take place in time. He thought out a rule for representing uniform acceleration by its mean speed. One quantity is taken to be capable of definition in terms of a relationship between two others. This has been held to be the first statement of a law of physics involving more than elementary mathematics.[3]

Romans 9.16 stresses man's dependence on God, if he is to do anything good. Bradwardine became interested in the implications of this idea, and got involved in the contemporary revival of the Pelagian debate of the time of Augustine about the balance of grace, human free will and divine predestination in deciding how human beings will act. This led him into the work which resulted in the *De causa Dei*. Other surviving works which may be attributable to him surround this theme, a work on predestination and another on future contingents.

Bradwardine's *De causa Dei* was finished in 1344, after he had left Oxford. There have been various attempts to 'place' Thomas Bradwardine, on the basis of the idea he expresses in this work, perhaps as a 'determinist' in the Pelagian controversy of the fourteenth century, perhaps as a 'pre-reformer' who influenced Wyclif and in due course Luther. A group of related issues within this discourse occupied him: the sovereignty of God and divine foreknowledge and will; free will and necessity; predestination and prescience; justification by grace alone.

In forming his views on free will and necessity, Bradwardine seems to have resisted the so-called 'Ockhamist' division between past and present on the one hand and future on the other. This was nothing new. It was of concern to Aristotle at the end of *De interpretatione* (and consequently to Boethius in commenting upon it) that it is possible to be sure of the truth of statements in the present and past tense in a way it is not possible to be sure of the truth of those in the future tense. A statement in the future tense can apparently be true only in a contingent sense, for it depends on how things will be at a time which has not yet come. Bradwardine approaches this long-standing difficulty, inherited from the classical world, but especially important for Christians who believe in an omniscient and omnipotent God, from the vantage point of his own strong position on the sovereignty of God. There was a contemporary notion that something may be a future contingent in a way which is itself an absolute, in the sense that it *has been previously known* to God from the moment when it enters the present and thus ceases to be a 'future contingent'. Bradwardine sought to show that God's prescience may indeed be 'necessary', without its coming into conflict with free will. God himself remains free. There is no coercion. People making decisions are moved by God but they are unaware of that and so, from their own point of view, they act freely.

Bradwardine also enters territory which was to become immensely important with the advent of the Reformation debates. He explores the question whether predestination is 'caused' by God's will, and is thus a free gift, or whether it is earned by a person's own good works. He thinks it must be a free gift because if it depends on the actual performance of good works by the individual in question that would make it uncertain, and that is impossible with God.

The pastoral implications of this dilemma were already apparent. Bradwardine disapproved of two schools of thought of his day, the 'Cainites' who despaired of forgiveness because they had committed such serious sins, and the 'Judaeans', who believed they could not be forgiven because they had committed so many sins. Both fears seem to him to place in doubt the infinity of God's goodness and mercy. He tends to the view that man first comes to repentance and then merits grace and justification by means of his repentance. But there are many shadings here, as he was well aware. Most important was the question whether a man or woman must first make his/her own decision to repent, at which point grace acts to confirm his/her choice, or whether the action of grace is necessary first, so that even making the decision to repent depends on divine aid.

Influence

That Bradwardine had some general fame is clear. Chaucer's 'Nun's Priest's Tale' links Bradwardine with Boethius and Augustine.

Bradwardine's *De proportionibus* came to be widely used in Paris and throughout Europe in the fourteenth and fifteenth centuries. It found its way onto the syllabus of the Universities of Vienna and Freiburg at the end of the fourteenth century.

Notes

1 Crosby,
2 G. Molland, *Mathematics and the Mediaeval Ancestry of Physics* (Aldershot, 1995).
3 Crosby, p. 12.

Bibliography

Three Logical Treatises Ascribed to Thomas Bradwardine, ed. L. Nielsen, N.-J. Green-Pedersen and J. Pinborg (Copenhagen, 1982); Thomas Bradwardine, *Tractatus de Proportionibus: Its Significance for the Development of Mathematical Physics*, ed. and trans. H. Lamar Crosby (Madison, WI, 1955).

Further reading

G. Leff, *Bradwardine and the Pelagians* (Cambridge, 1957); G. Molland, 'The Geometrical Background to the "Merton School"', *Mathematics and the Mediaeval Ancestry of Physics* (Aldershot, 1995); H.A. Oberman, *Archbishop Thomas Bradwardine: a Fourteenth Century Augustinian. A Study of his Theology in its Historical Context* (Utrecht, 1957).

WILLIAM OF OCKHAM *c.*1285–1347

Life and times

Ockham was a Franciscan from his youth, and in 1306 he was ordained subdeacon of Southwark in the diocese of Winchester. That would put him in Oxford as a student of theology in about 1309–15. He lectured in the usual way on Scripture (1315–17), and on the *Sentences* (1317–19). It seems that he may have been prevented from ever becoming a Regent Master by university politics, which probably also got in the way of his obtaining a chair. Ockham seems to have spent the next few years in London, teaching in the studium of the order there and writing his 'non-political' works.

Lutterell, a previous Chancellor of Oxford University and an adherent of the views of Aquinas, was deposed by the Bishop of Lincoln at the wish of the University, and became a bitter enemy of

Ockham thereafter.[1] There is some correspondence from King Edward II in 1322 refusing Lutterell permission to leave England, and instructing him not to bring the reputation of the University into disrepute by taking its internal quarrels abroad. Nevertheless, in 1323 Lutterell was allowed to go to Avignon, where he brought accusations against Ockham. Before the Pope-in-exile, Lutterell said that Ockham had been preaching heretical doctrines. The Pope listened; he had before him a list of 56 theses taken from Ockham's writings. The Pope summoned Ockham to Avignon to explain himself, probably in 1324. In 1328 the Pope set up a commission to examine what Ockham had been teaching in his *Sentences* commentary, and Lutterell's articles containing his accusations became the basis for two acts of condemnation prepared during the next two years. No formal condemnation actually took place, but on 51 of the 56 points Ockham's views were held to be open to censure.

While he was lingering at Avignon waiting for matters to be resolved, Ockham became entangled in the controversy about Franciscan poverty. The Franciscans were divided in their view of the question whether Christ and his apostles possessed property. The majority, led by Michael of Cesena, General of the Order, took a radical position and opposed the ruling of Pope John XXII in his Constitutions. In the Bull *Quia quorundam* of 1324, John XXII condemned those who rejected the earlier Bull of evangelical poverty, *Inter nonnullos*. It was natural for Michael of Cesena to require Ockham to give the matter some thought while he was at hand. Ockham noticed that John XXII's ruling differed from that of earlier Popes. He supported the General of the Order.

In these muddied waters the Pope called a General Chapter of the Franciscans and ordered it to elect a new General. Michael of Cesena left Avignon. In 1328, Ockham joined him, with a few others, and they fled to the Emperor Ludwig, elected in 1314 in a disputed election. John XXII had excommunicated Ludwig in 1324 for refusing to let the Pope examine what had happened and decide whether to approve the election. In indignation, Ludwig invaded Italy in 1327.

Once in Munich the Franciscan renegades settled to the attack on the Pope and thus Ockham became one of the leaders in the power struggle between Emperor and papacy in his day. In 1328 the group, now settled at Munich, were excommunicated by the Pope and by the Order, but they had the seal of the Order with them, and when Michael died in 1342, Ockham kept hold of it, remaining at Munich where he continued to write on poverty and the question of the respective powers of Church and state, and their relationship to one another under God.

The Emperor died in 1347, and on this loss of his protection Ockham tried for reconciliation with the Pope and with his Order, even sending back the seal. He sent a submission, in which he asserted that he believed 'that the Emperor has no authority to depose the Pope', promising obedience and saying that he now held his former teaching (except his early work in Oxford which is not mentioned) to have been heretical. It is not known whether this was the work of his hand or whether he merely signed it. He died almost at once thereafter.

Work and ideas

Ockham's writings naturally fall into a series of main groupings. The first is the *reportatio* or transcript of the lectures he gave on the *Sentences* in 1317–19. The second is the series of *Expositiones* and commentaries from 1321–3, on Aristotle's *Sophistici Elenchi*, *Perihermeneias*, and the revised *Sentences* commentary. From 1324 survive the *Summa logicae* and the treatise on *The Predestination and Foreknowledge of God with Respect to Future Contingents*. There are also works on physics and the problem of quantity. The *Opera Politica* date from after 1324, when Ockham turned his attention to political problems.

Boehner isolates the following 'guiding principles of all Ockham's work'.[2] All things are possible for God, except those which involve a contradiction (*Quodlibeta* VI, q.6). Anything God can produce by means of secondary causes – that is, through the laws of the created world – he can produce immediately (directly) (*Quodlibeta* VI, q.6). He can make an oak tree directly or out of an acorn. God can make any reality by itself and apart from any other reality. (*Reportatio* II, qq.19ff). Statements ought not to be held to be true unless they are self-evident or 'revealed' or known from experience or deduced by reasoning from a revealed truth or a proposition verified by observation (e.g. *Ordinatio* d.30, q.IE). Boehner suggests that this is the real meaning of 'Ockham's razor', the principle that things are done in vain in a more complex way if they can be done by fewer steps (*frustra fit per plura quod potest fieri per pauciora*).

Ockham took it that few propositions about God can be 'demonstrated', that is, shown to be self-evident or to follow from revelation or observation. One of these is God's very existence (*Ordinatio* and *Questions on Physics*). He takes issue here with Duns

Scotus's line of argument. One of the things which Scotus had sought to show was that God is the efficient Cause, but an infinite regression of efficient causation is impossible, so God must stand at the head of it. Ockham proposes a refinement of this idea, by way of a notion of causation almost as a 'container' of that which it causes. That produces an embedding rather than a chain and it is a way of looking at the question which, unlike the 'chain of causation', is not a natural borrowing from Aristotle.

Ockham goes hand in hand with Scotus in accepting that some divine attributes are 'necessary', in the sense that without them God could not be God, for example, God's intellectual nature. Ockham sees creatures as unavoidably contingent; no creature can be 'necessary'.

Ockham's ethics turns on an assumption that an act is made good or bad solely by God's will on the subject. It follows that God can never will or ordain evil because by definition that which he wills and ordains is good. The task of the rational creature who wishes to be good is therefore to obey the will of God. Ockham thought that God *could* bring it about that a person did not love him, or even make one of his creatures hate him, but that would create a paradox. The creature which obeyed the order not to love God would be obeying God and therefore acting out of love of God. So it would be, even if not a logical impossibility, an ethical impossibility. For ethical laws are not propositions but commands.

From 1328 Ockham was writing polemical works on politics, especially ecclesiastical politics. When we can observe a practised academic move in this direction, polemic can be seen as an extreme of the diputations of the university world.

Between 1332 and 1334, Ockham was writing the *Opus nonaginta dierum*, a huge work seeking to make a balanced presentation of the issues in the 'poverty' debate. The debate had moved to a new pitch of seriousness in 1279 with the Bull of Nicholas III, *Exiit qui seminat*. Nicholas held that the poverty of Christ and the Apostles is part of the apostolic faith. John XXII issued a series of Bulls in the 1320s rejecting the theory under which the Friars had latterly been operating, that they merely had the use of property which was 'owned' by the Pope. Thomas of Celano and Ockham were naturally concerned by the implications, and that was what they had been objecting to when the rift occurred. Ockham focussed his criticism on the attempt to distinguish 'use' of property from 'lordship' over it. In *The work of ninety days*, Ockham tried to get behind to the prior question of the state of innocence which Adam and Eve enjoyed before the fall. The Pope argued from the statements in

Genesis that because Adam and Eve had lordship (*dominium*) over the earth, fish, birds, and so on that this lordship was primeval and divinely sanctioned.

In *A letter to the Friars Minor* (1334) Ockham says that it took him four years at Avignon to 'see through' the Pope. He did not want to be too quick to believe that someone placed in such a great office could have fallen into heresy. But once he had come to that conclusion, Ockham pulled no punches. He suggested that the Pope's thinking was tainted with heresy. He grew more bold still and ventured to say that the Pope was a false pope. That may have been in reaction to the papal challenge to the Emperor's position, for the Pope had accused the Emperor of being a false Emperor. But it proved to be important that this kind of thing was being said. It struck a chord with Joachim of Fiore's talk of the Antichrist.

Ockham was posing a real problem of some ecclesiological importance in an age when Papal claims to plenitude of power and to something like infallibility had risen very high. If a Pope can fall into heresy, the papacy is not under divine protection to the degree which has been claimed for it; it may not be such a high office as it looks. The question then arises whether such a Pope has to be obeyed, for the subjects of an excommunicated king or emperor were under no obligation to obey him. The *Compendium Errorum Joannis Papae XXII* raises the question of whether it is possible for the Pope to slip into heresy or to err against the faith. This was the most recently topical aspect of another long-running question as to whether the Pope has what Bernard of Clairvaux called 'plenitude of power'. Ockham disposes of that briskly. The *Tractatus contra Benedictum*, written in late 1338 or after, sets out to continue the battle against John's successor, Benedict XII. Book II takes up the contemporary debate about what it will be like to gaze on God in heaven. Ockham's point is that even if Benedict's views on this matter may be sound, his holding them is not what makes them so. The truth was the truth before he proclaimed it. Mere human declaration does not make truth, even if it is made by the Pope. Ockham unfolds a theory that it is in Scripture that divine guidance was given to the human race about what to believe. Whoever errs against Scripture, not the person who disagrees with a Pope, is a heretic. This was of course an immensely important principle with vast repercussions in the Reformation debates.

It also takes Ockham into the equally important question what is necessary for salvation. Those who know someone is a heretic should separate themselves (as he and his friends have done) for their salvation's sake. The *Dialogus* (III, Tract 1, Book 3) contains a discussion of the writings which can be relied on as necessary to salvation. In Chapter 8 it is asked whether a General Council can err. Councils were important; Ockham says a Council should regard itself as being guided by the Holy Spirit, but not blindly. It applies human reasoning and the tradition of the interpretation of Scripture. There is the related question (Chapter 11) of the necessity to salvation of consistently holding particular interpretations of Scripture: 'Many things are contained in the divine Scriptures whose true first and literal meaning is not at all times necessary to salvation.'

Ockham was interested in the political implications of questions about the power of the Pope. In his *On the Power of the Pope*, he explains the Aristotelian background discussion of the relationship between the small community of the household and the larger one of the village and the greater one of the city. He describes the six types of Aristotelian constitution. There Ockham departs from Aristotle's conclusions. In his own view, the best form of governance for the Church is a single ruler. A single supreme authority was for the common good (*Breviloquium de potestate papae*, IV.xiii), for 'greater unity and harmony are thereby fostered'.

Ockham asks what is the origin of the supreme civil power. Does it come directly from God? He asks this in the context of a discussion of the 'two swords' question. On one contemporary view, the Pope possesses the fullness of power in things temporal and spiritual alike. All power is therefore held as from him. To Peter were given the keys of the *imperium* of both heaven and earth. Ockham disputes this and sets out a sequence of errors.

The group of political treatises overlaps because Ockham was working from a stock of points and authorities in writing them in his 'exile'.

Influence

It is always a good question whether a thinker *intends* to be controversial. Ockham, it seems, set out to be clear and rational and to uphold the deep truths of faith. Politics affected both the focus and the notoriety of his later works. The 'nominalist' movement of the fourteenth and fifteenth centuries is also sometimes labelled 'Ockhamist'.

Ockham's politics were stimulated by the heat of the circumstances in which he found himself. He was not a political theorist by choice, but the source of materials on the problem of the balance of power between Church and state as it manifested itself in the debates of his own day. Yet the political writings made Ockham 'known' and gave him an influence he might not otherwise have enjoyed. His influence on later dissident movements was considerable.

Notes

1 F. Hoffmann, 'Die erste Kritik des Ockhamismus durch den Oxforder Kanzler Johannes Lutterell', *Breslauer Studien zur historischen Theologie, Neue Folge Band IX* (Breslau, 1941), pp. 1ff.
2 P. Boehner, *William of Ockham, Philosophical Writings: A Selection* (New York, 1964), pp. xix ff.

Bibliography

Ockham, *Opera Philosophica et Theologica* (St Bonaventure, NY, 1974); Ockham, *Compendium Errorum Joannis pape XXII, Opera Politica*, ed. H.S. Offler (Oxford, 1997); Ockham, *Quodlibetal Questions*, trans. A. Freddoso and F.E. Kelly (Yale, 1991), 2 vols; Ockham, *A Letter to the Friars Minor and Writings*, ed. A.S. McGrade and J. Kilcullen (Cambridge, 1995); P. Boehner, *William of Ockham, Philosophical Writings: A Selection* (New York, 1964).

Further reading

Marilyn McCord Adams, *William Ockham* (Notre Dame, 1987), 2 vols; F. Hoffmann, 'Die erste Kritik des Ockhamismus durch den Oxforder Kanzler Johannes Lutterell', *Breslauer Studien zur historischen Theologie, Neue Folge Band IX* (Breslau, 1941), pp. 1ff.

BALDUS OF UBALDIS *c.*1319–1400

Life and times

The continuing contribution of the lawyers was important, although most of the pioneering work in setting up law as an academic discipline had been completed in the twelfth and thirteenth centuries, the era of Ivo of Chartres, Gratian and the succeeding generation. Baldus of Ubaldis was born in about 1327 at Perugia, the son of a medical doctor. He studied at Perugia and possibly at Pisa. He was taught Roman law partly by Bartolus of Sassoferrato. His master in canon law was Petruccius.

Baldus became one of the great jurists of his time. From about 1351 he was lecturing at Perugia. As a professional teacher of law at

Perugia, Pisa (1357–8), Florence (1359–64), Perugia again (1365–76), Padua, Perugia once more and then Pavia again from 1390, he became a leading canonist and jurist of mid- and late fourteenth-century Italy. He held public office at Perugia, as the retained advocate of the gild-republic. He was also on occasion Perugia's ambassador to the Emperor. When the Great Schism began he was lecturing at Perugia, but he then moved to the University of Padua. He died at Pavia in 1400

Work and ideas

Baldus's 'legal opinion' was frequently sought. Indeed more *consilia* survive for him than for any other medieval jurist. Some of Bartolus's *consilia* are on political matters, such as government, politics and public law. His was a practical, case-based political theory. He did not write tracts on political thought; his political thought emerged from his legal work. But he was concerned with topics of immense contemporary importance, politically and academically.

Baldus brought together the notion of the corporate person, made up of many real bodies but a 'body' in its own right for legal purposes, with the Aristotelian concept of a natural, political man.[1] He sees the Pope and Emperor as the *universal* sovereign authorities, with kingdoms and city-republics beneath them, having a local territorial sovereignty. Here the lawyer was looking at the principles, for the actual power of the Emperor did not match the claims to universal authority which could be made under Roman law. When the Emperor Charles IV came to Italy in 1355, the city-states nevertheless came to him eagerly, wishing to buy from him the privileges which would confirm their liberties and their constitutions. That would seem to make the sovereignty of the Emperor predominantly a power of legitimising rather than ruling.[2]

Papal claims had been advanced more actively in the last two centuries. The papal claim to plenitude of power (*plenitudo potestatis*) delineated by Bernard of Clairvaux in his *De consideratione* in the mid-twelfth century had been adopted and developed with enthusiasm by the papacy ever since.

The sovereignty of the city-republics gave them a 'local' autonomy, below the level of sovereignty. Baldus raises the question whether the people who make up such a city-state may create their own legislation, whether 'each people makes its own law'. He takes their law-making to need a validation from a *princeps* unless their custom is clearly otherwise.[3]

Baldus held a 'consent' theory according to which legislation is made by a people by consent (which may be tacit).[4] The *populus* as corporate legal person (*civitas, commune, communitas, corpus*) was a familiar concept of the period in city and gild governance. So was a notion of the *sanior* or *melior pars*. Commentators had explored the dilemma that a corporation is both a body composed of a plurality of human beings and an abstract or intellectual unitary entity, a fictional 'person'. Some among the Glossators (for example, Accursius) resisted the latter, saying that the corporation was 'nothing other than the men who are there'. Baldus himself was drawn to the alternative model of the *corpus mysticum*. This had ecclesiological overtones because Church was seen as invisible and thus less easily overseen by the powerful in the visible ecclesiastical hierarchy.

Notesa

1 J. Canning, *The Political Thought of Baldus de Ubaldis* (Cambridge, 1987), p. 197.
2 J. Canning, *The Political Thought of Baldus de Ubaldis* (Cambridge, 1987), p. 19.
3 J. Canning, *The Political Thought of Baldus de Ubaldis* (Cambridge, 1987), pp. 93ff.
4 J. Canning, *The Political Thought of Baldus de Ubaldis* (Cambridge, 1987), p. 100.

Bibliography

There is no modern critical edition of the writings of Baldus, though there are numerous early printed editions.

Further reading

J. Canning, *The Political Thought of Baldus de Ubaldis* (Cambridge, 1987); R.N. Swanson, *Universities, Academics and the Great Schism* (Cambridge, 1979); B. Tierney, *Foundations of the Conciliar Theory* (Cambridge, 1955).

JOHN WYCLIF *c*.1329–84

Life and works

Wyclif probably began to teach at Oxford in the 1350s. His first writings on logic survive from 1361–71, and he was then already making a name. He perhaps encountered no real challenge at Oxford from anyone who could argue him down. Much of the hardest intellectual effort of the day was now going into discussion of the Great Schism, which was keeping the papacy in exile at Avignon, and that may have allowed Wyclif to get away for a time with publishing what was already noticeably radical material without being condemned by a Church too wrapped up in its divisions to focus squarely on what he was saying.

Nevertheless, Wyclif was being drawn into politics and controversy. He entered royal service in 1371 or 1372. In 1376 he went to London, called by John of Gaunt, it seems, to preach against Wykeham and the Good Parliament. He was summoned by the Bishop of London in 1377 to give account of himself over his preaching. He escaped because the king died, and when Richard II succeeded to the throne attention turned to other matters. In 1377 Bulls of Pope Gregory IX reached London, in which nineteen errors of Wyclif were listed. In 1378 there were unsuccessful attempts in England to get him condemned. In 1378 he published his *De veritate Scripturae Sacrae* (On the Truth of Holy Scripture) and his *De ecclesia*; in 1379 *De officio regis* and *De potestate papae* appeared, considering respectively the powers of king and pope, and *De Eucharistia*.

In 1380 an Oxford University Commission was set up to discuss Wyclif's teaching on the Eucharist. Wyclif was finally driven out of Oxford in 1380, at the age of about fifty, and he lived out his life in retirement at Lutterworth parsonage from 1381.

That was not the end of controversy. In 1382 a Council at Blackfriars condemned ten propositions of Wyclif, and his followers thought it politic to flee the country. Wyclif carried on writing. In 1382 his *Trialogus* was completed and in 1384, the year of his death, the *Opus Evangelicum* was finished.

Work and ideas

Wyclif's teaching and the reaction to it falls into a category of which we have seen a number of examples, of the writer or academic who gets into trouble with the ecclesiastical authorities. Wyclif's ideas became controversial, partly because he taught in a university world where very public controversy was possible. Oxford had long been something of a centre of discontents and challenges. Richard Fitzralph (at Oxford from about 1315, a Fellow of Balliol before 1325 and Chancellor of the University of Oxford from 1332–4 before becoming Dean of Lichfield in 1335), Thomas Bradwardine and

Thomas Buckingham had all been involved in controversy in their day. Richard Fitzralph, who came to be thought of as a 'Lollard Saint', left a collection of sermons and anti-mendicant writings and something approaching a cult formed. Wyclif was certainly influenced by his thinking on the poverty of Christ, in *De pauperie salvatoris* (*c*.1350–6).

Wyclif also became famous because he became notorious. Dissent was not tolerated at any time in the Middle Ages.[1] This was not an age which valued freedom of expression or ideas that seemed novel. It often took time to identify opinion as unorthodox where the ideas were new and it was not at first clear whether they were acceptable, or conformed with the existing orthodoxy at all. The patristic way with uncertainty had been to work through the medium of ecumenical Councils, which ultimately defined the faith on a disputed matter. Thus was produced the Niceno-Constantinopolitan creed of the fourth century. But the era of the ecumenical councils was long past, and since the schism with the Greeks it was no longer possible to hold councils of the universal Church. A series of Lateran Councils had been held from the twelfth into the thirteenth century, so that at least the bishops of the West could meet. A thinker such as Wyclif was much harder to deal with at a time when the leadership of the Church was in dispute because of the Great Schism and when the conciliarist movement, which had hoped to restore the leadership of the bishops, was running into difficulties.

Wyclif had begun by lecturing on metaphysical subjects. His position was that of a 'realist' of a moderate to extreme persuasion. For Wyclif, all that exists has an 'intelligible being' which God eternally 'knows'. He thought it followed that all things which actually exist also have an 'ideal' being. The ideal being is eternally 'present' to God in its essence. There was an incipient fundamentalism inherent in this, and when Wyclif moved on to Biblical studies it began to emerge.

As early as 1371–3 Wyclif was being noticed with disapproval in Oxford. His ideas on time and being were attacked by John Kenningham, a rival and controversialist who was then Carmelite master in theology at Oxford. He complained that Wyclif believed that it was its antiquity which gave Scripture its high authority; that other writings are the more false as they are the more recent.[2] Kenningham argued that there are many famous poets of the date of the book of Judges while Socrates, Plato, Aristotle and Pythagoras lived after the captivity in Babylon; yet these poets are now of no moment while the philosophers are. So antiquity is no guarantee: *Ergo antiquitas non auctenticat*, he concludes.

But that was a misrepresentation of what Wyclif was actually saying, as Kenningham half concedes a little later. Wyclif begins from the principle that God perceives past, present and future as though they were equally 'present' to him. He argues that what God perceives must exist. So what was was and what will be also 'is', in the sight of God.[3] Wyclif is alleged to have been saying that antiquity is a main cause of truth, and of its authority. Wyclif is here seen to be taking 'antiquity' to be the eternity of God. By 'antiquity', Augustine means age 'in time'; Wyclif means the 'antiquity' of 'eternity'.[4] He takes many other 'truths' to be eternal in the same way, indeed all statements in the present tense such as 'I sit', 'John speaks', including statements which are not Scriptural.[5]

Wyclif takes antiquity to be a cause of truth (*causa veritatis*). He argues that an older charter (for a monastery) or notary's *instrumentum* would have more authority for lawyers than a more recent one. (Though he stresses that Kenningham reasonably points out that in common usage we do not use 'antiquity' as an explanation of causation.) The blessed Laurence did not die of old age ('antiquity'), for he was young and strong when he was martyred.[6] Kenningham's argument from charters proceeds from an analogy which will not bear the weight (*ab insufficienti similitudine*).[7] But Wyclif did not really want to be sidetracked into this debate. He says that it is not a theologian's job to get into the habit of defending charters; he should rather be studying how the Word lives and reigns through all ages, as it was in the beginning, is now and ever shall be.[8]

Kenningham identifies the *principale propositum* on which the question turns, and that is whether the whole of Scripture is true *de virtute sermonis*.[9] There is discussion of the claim of the prophet Amos that he was not a prophet: *non sum propheta* (Amos 7.14). Gregory the Great says that Amos bears truthful testimony to himself when he says he is not a prophet. Otherwise he would not be a prophet, for as a prophet he must be telling the truth. (But of course that would mean that he was not a prophet, for that is what he says.) The question is whether he is saying the words, *signa*, or saying what the words mean.[10] That is a characteristically medieval way of resolving such a paradox.

It has been suggested that Wyclif's position on the Bible is an extreme fundamentalism. It is the material form of the Word. It is thus a divine exemplar and it existed before the actual writing of the

Scriptures. Wyclif regrets the modern habit of taking the Bible too lightly, with *impertinencia*. Wyclif takes 'Scripture alone' to be the *locus* and source of all authority. Legislation promulgated by popes is 'mannis law'. He dislikes 'sensory' interpretation, by which he means figurative interpretations.

Yet it is not clear that Wyclif's strict fundamentalism is really the same thing as an insistence upon the literal sense.[11] Wyclif asks Kenningham to explain why Scripture so often employs tropes and the figurative mode of speech, and especially in extension of time. Kenningham concedes that this is sometimes *ad designando aeternitatem* ('before Abraham was, I am', John 8.58) sometimes to imply certainty (John 3.18), sometimes just at the whim of the translator: *solum placitum translatorum vel interpretem*.[12] Towards the end of his life, Wyclif came close to a doctrine of *sola scriptura*. It seems to him, in the end, that to follow that what is not in Scripture directly or by inference is the teaching of Antichrist.

Wyclif's *Postilla super totam bibliam*, which he finished in 1375–6, pointed to the poverty and humility of the early Church, and allowed Scripture to set the standard for his own time. *De civili dominio* (1376–8) also includes an emphasis on poverty. Here Wyclif expounded his ideas on dominion and on grace. *De ecclesia* (1378) sets forth what was by now a fairly revolutionary doctrine of the Church. For Wyclif grew more polemical as he grew more angry.

From at least the mid-1370s, Wyclif's ecclesiology was political. He was interested in power and the abuse of power. Thus he writes on 'dominion' that no one can hold true dominion over others, or over possessions, while in a state of mortal sin. That does not mean that they may not in practice have such control. But it does call into question for Wyclif the legitimacy of the actions and legislation of the world's 'authorities', whether civil or religious.

Wyclif also held that Christ forbids his followers to exercise civil dominion, so that all ecclesiastical exercise of civil power becomes improper. He saw such exercise as corrupting. Here his thinking chimed with a tradition which had been strong since at least the beginning of the Waldensian movement at the end of the twelfth century. The Waldensians had challenged corrupt and overmighty prelacy well before Wyclif's time. Wyclif even reopens the 'unworthy minister' question, which had been resolved in the patristic period in favour of an acceptance that divine grace can work through even the most corrupt of ministers. Wyclif is saying that some think that if a priest leads an evil life that may take from him the power to administer the sacraments.[13]

Wycliffites, like the Waldensians, were especially interested in 'ministry' in the Church. They saw it as a spiritual office, not to do earthly works but to feed upon the contemplation of God. The minister is the vicar of Christ in that he feeds the people with the Word of God. So the preaching office is primary. The minister is to set an example by visibly surpassing others in grace. Wycliffites wanted to see ministers chosen according to God's law and not at the behest of princes or for money.[14] The wrong people, chosen for the wrong reasons, may be subject to avarice and worldly love, given to simony, and above all, eager for power.[15]

Wyclif and his followers particularly disliked what he called the 'sects', by which he meant the religious orders. He saw them as claiming to be a superior order of Christians. The sects divide the Christian community and thus the unity of Christ's order. There are really only two 'sects', that of Christ and that of worldly men, but Wyclif subdivides the class of the worldly into monks, canons and friars. The encouragement of diversity in the religious life is also an encouragement to quarrelling and division.

Another feature of the 'sects' which the Wycliffites mistrusted was their novelty. They are 'newe mannys ordres', and therefore of human invention. That means that people are following human leaders instead of following Christ. It means they are adding to the teaching of Christ new 'requirements' for salvation. They also bring in a form of slavery, for they keep some out of orders to which others may belong. They require unnecessary 'observances' such as the wearing of habits.

In the controversy on the Eucharist of 1380–1, William Barton, one of Wyclif's enemies, contrived a means of getting the University to make a public condemnation of Wyclif's teaching. He brought together a 'commission' of twelve doctors for the purpose, and this, as we have seen, brought about Wyclif's downfall.

Influence

Wyclif was probably instrumental in bringing the study of the Bible back into a central position in teaching in Oxford. Wyclif's name became associated with an increasingly popular movement, probably during his last years at Lutterworth. His secretary John Purvey did a good deal to encourage this. Nicholas Hereford, Philip Repton and John Aston were also important in spreading Wyclif's ideas. Repton was an Augustinian canon, the others secular clerks. All except John Purvey had been attracted to Wyclif at Oxford and had become fired by him with reforming zeal.

Wyclif perhaps did not set out to lead such a trend. But what he was saying chimed in with a long tradition of anti-clerical, anti-establishment thinking, going back at least to the Waldensians. John Purvey had a ready and receptive audience for the notion that too much property is bad for the Church and distracts it from its proper purpose; and that reform is essential, by secular authority and by force if necessary.

Wyclif may be regarded as the inspiration of the contemporary vernacular translation of the Bible. In the *Opus evangelicum* he remarks that even the simplest person can learn the words of the Gospel according to his simplicity. All Christians should have a knowledge of the Bible so as to be able to defend their faith. The arrival of so many manuscripts of Wyclif in Prague suggests that the Hussites of Bohemia were reading him.

Notes

1 For a useful general discussion, see John Guy 'Perceptions of Heresy, 1200–1550', in *Reformation, Humanism and 'Revolution'*, ed. G.J. Schocher (Washington, DC, 1990), pp. 39–61.

2 *Ingressus Fr. J. Kynyngham Carmelita contra Wicclyff, Faciculi Zizaniorum*, ed. W. Waddington Shirley, Rolls Series (1857), pp. 4–5.

3 *Ingressus Fr. J. Kynyngham Carmelita contra Wicclyff, Faciculi Zizaniorum*, ed. W. Waddington Shirley, Rolls Series (1857), p. 9.

4 *Acta... contra ideas Magistri Johannis Wyclif, Fasciculi Zizaniorum*, p. 15.

5 *Acta... contra ideas Magistri Johannis Wyclif, Fasciculi Zizaniorum*, p. 15.

6 *Acta... contra ideas Magistri Johannis Wyclif, Fasciculi Zizaniorum*, p. 17.

7 *Acta... contra ideas Magistri Johannis Wyclif*, Fasciculi Zizaniorum, p. 18.

8 *Non pertinet at theologum induere habitum defendentis cartas, sed magis studuere quomodo verbum vivit et regnat per omnia secula seculorum sicut erat in principio, et nunc, et semper. Acta... contra ideas Magistri Johannis Wyclif, Fasciculi Zizaniorum*, p. 15.

9 *Acta... contra ideas Magistri Johannis Wyclif, Fasciculi Zizaniorum*, p. 20.

10 *Acta... contra ideas Magistri Johannis Wyclif, Fasciculi Zizaniorum*, p. 24.

11 *Acta... contra ideas Magistri Johannis Wyclif, Fasciculi Zizaniorum*, p. 28.

12 *Acta... contra ideas Magistri Johannis Wyclif, Fasciculi Zizaniorum*, p. 31

13 *English Wycliffite Sermons*, ed. Anne Hudson and Pamela Gradon (Oxford, 1983–96), vol. 4, p. 114.

14 *English Wycliffite Sermons*, ed. Anne Hudson and Pamela Gradon (Oxford, 1983–96), vol. 4, p. 115.
15 *English Wycliffite Sermons*

Bibliography

Anne Hudson, *English Wycliffite Writings* (Cambridge, 1978); *English Wycliffite Sermons*, ed. Anne Hudson and Pamela Gradon (Oxford, 1983–96), 5 vols. Wyclif's works are available in the nineteenth century Wycliffite editions.

Further reading

Anne Hudson, *The Premature Reformation* (Oxford, 1988); Anthony Kenny, *Wyclif* (Oxford, 1985); Anthony Kenny, *Wyclif In His Times* (Oxford, 1986); John Guy, 'Perceptions of Heresy, 1200–1550', in *Reformation, Humanism and 'Revolution'*, ed. G.J. Schocher (Washington, DC, 1990), pp. 39–61; J.A. Robson, *Wyclif and the Oxford Schools* (Cambridge, 1961); E.H. Robertson, *John Wycliffe: Morning Star of the Reformation* (Basingstoke, 1984); K. Walsh, *Richard Fitzralph in Oxford, Avignon and Armagh* (Oxford, 1981).

PIERRE D'AILLY 1350–1420

Life and times

Pierre d'Ailly spent his working life chiefly at the University of Paris. A few dates are known. From 1364–78 he was studying at the College of Navarre. He became a bachelor of arts in 1367. Thus during 1368–9, his first year of study of theology, he was also lecturing in the *artes*. He preached to the Synod of Paris in 1374 and to the College of Navarre in 1377. 1378–84 was the period of build-up to the Great Schism, and a time of controversy in Paris. Among the masters of Paris, Pierre d'Ailly became a keen defender of the idea of a General Council. His *Epistola diaboli Leviathan* is a diatribe masquerading as a letter written by Satan against the calling of a General Council. In May 1381 the four Faculties held a meeting to agree the University's opinion. It was decided to support the call for a General Council and Peter was chosen to tell the Court what the University felt. He was not, however, sent with the next delegation, and in 1384 he was back in Paris as head of the College of Navarre. He was Chancellor of the University from 1389–95.

In 1395 Pierre was made Bishop of Le Puy, and then of Cambrai in 1397. In the years 1398–1403 the University withdrew its obedience from the Pope and Pierre was still active in the debate, speaking and writing partly from his see. In 1407–8 he was among the members of an embassy from France to Benedict XIII and Gregory XII, to try to get active papal involvement in an attempt to end the Schism. When the attempt failed, he shifted his allegiance to the conciliarists, now seeing there a better hope for the future of the Church. In 1409 he was at the Council of Pisa. In 1411 he became a Cardinal. He was an energetic commentator under Pope John XXIIII until the beginning of February 1415, and took an active part in the Council of Constance. If he had had ambitions to be the next Pope, he was unsuccessful.

Work and ideas

Pierre d'Ailly wrote during the period of the development of the *via moderna*. The 'old way' (*via antiqua*) was the 'realist' way, but it was out of fashion since Ockham had opened up some of the obvious anomalies in Aquinas's thinking. Pierre is the author of a surviving early work (*On Concepts and Insolubles*), written perhaps in his early twenties. It deals with two issues of great contemporary importance. The first is the semantic paradox, of the 'Cretan liar' type. There had been new work on paradoxes in the 1320s, to which Ralph Strode, Gregory of Rimini and William Heytsbury had contributed. Of special interest in the thirteenth and fourteenth centuries was the apparent paradox in Amos 7.14 where a prophet says 'I am not a prophet'. Various solutions had been advanced, including the argument that even an authentic prophet is not necessarily speaking prophetically in every utterance and that when he said this he was not in his prophetic mode. Nevertheless, the contradiction nagged. One view of *insolubilia* of this sort was that to utter such a sentence is in fact to say nothing, since it has no meaning.

Nominalism holds that there are no universally recognised common concepts or entities. The problem is that this makes it hard to understand how there can be any general or shared knowledge between minds. The nominalists were much interested in Pierre d'Ailly's other theme, the notion of mental language. Ockham and his followers took the view that the 'terms' of mental language are 'concepts', its 'sentences' judgements and that mental language is about the relation between thought and the world.

Pierre d'Ailly was a loyal university man, too. He found himself prosecuting Blanchard, the Chancellor of Paris, over the charging of a fee for the licence to teach, *licentia docendi*. That had been happening as early as 1172, but the practice had been prohibited by Pope Alexander II as 'depraved'. Blanchard raised the fees and levied them systematically. He invented new rules allowing him to fine people for not obeying his rules. In about 1386 Pierre d'Ailly wrote two texts against the Chancellor of Paris, accusing him of selling degrees for money. Money, he says, is the root of all evil and today that root runs everywhere, even into the venerable corporation of the University of Paris. It is leading to two scandals. The first is the selling for money of the 'free gift of knowledge' and of degrees. The second is the heresy of claiming that that is acceptable.[1] He claimed that he was moved by no wish to injure the Chancellor but only by the desire to save and protect a just cause.[2]

There follows an important discussion on whether to give and receive money for the licence to teach is the exercise of a spiritual authority, and therefore simony. In the view of his opponents, it is perfectly proper for the Chancellor to receive payment in return for granting the *licentia docendi*. In Peter's view, it is against both divine and natural law. The use of the power to grant a licence, the *usus potestati licenciandi*, was comparable with the use of the power to prophesy, the *usus prophetie*.

A second text, 'Truth conquers all', *Super omnia vincit veritas*, pursues many of the same issues, but it also goes into the question of the special privilege conceded to the University of Paris and the question of the Chancellor's benefice. If he is given a benefice to keep him in order that he may discharge the licensing office (*propter officium licentiandi*), and he is greedy enough to seek to add to it by charging fees, he is living dishonestly and he is a sinner.

Pierre d'Ailly's theological writings concentrate on issues raised by the Great Schism, which occurred early on in his time as a theological student. It was again and again in the arena of church–state relations that the nascent discipline of political thought was emerging. He wrote on the question, 'Whether someone unlearned in divine law can justly preside over the Church' and a 'Letter of Satan the Leviathan'. By the early fifteenth century he was writing more statesmanlike works, such as *De materia concilii generalis* of 1403 and the *Propositiones utiles* of his period of transfer to the conciliarist position.

Notes

1 A. Bernstein, *Pierre d'Ailly and the Blanchard Affair* (Leiden, 1978), p. 198.

2 A. Bernstein, *Pierre d'Ailly and the Blanchard Affair* (Leiden, 1978), p. 198.

Bibliography

Pierre d'Ailly, *Imago mundi*, ed. E. Buron (Paris, 1930), 3 vols; Pierre d'Ailly, *Insolubilia*, trans. Paul Vincent Spade (Dordrecht, 1980); Pierre d'Ailly, *Concepts and Insolubles: An Annotated Translation*, ed. P.V. Spade (Dordrecht, 1980).

Further reading

P. Guenée, *Between Church and State: The Lives of Four French Prelates in the Late Middle Ages*, trans. A. Goldhammer (Chicago, 1987); Francis Oakley, *The Political Thought of Pierre d'Ailly: The Voluntarist Tradition* (Yale, 1964).

JEAN GERSON 1363–1429

Life and times

Jean Gerson was born in 1363 in the Ardennes, in Champagne. His early schooling probably took place nearby, where there was a local priory. He then moved to a school attached to the mother house, the Abbey of Saint-Rémy at Rheims. Afterwards, in 1377, he went to the College of Navarre in Paris, which was then notable for 'ideas' with an air about them of early French humanism. There he met Pierre d'Ailly, who was at first his master.

Gerson stayed in Paris throughout his academic career. In 1381 he became a Bachelor of Arts and in 1387 a Bachelor of Theology. He lectured as others did on the Bible and the *Sentences*. In 1394 he became a Doctor of Theology. He was Proctor of the French 'Nation' (the association of French students) from 1383–4.

The links between academics and royal or imperial affairs in the later Middle Ages are striking in the stories of many of the writers in this volume. The University of Paris was of immense importance in Gerson's lifetime; it had a central position in the ecclesiastical world and close associations with the royal court. It enjoyed the special protection of the French kings, who asked its advice in affairs of state as well as making use of its academic theologians as personal confessors. Gerson was chaplain to the Duke of Burgundy from 1393. It was not thought inappropriate for the University to hold solemn assemblies to discuss the way to end the Schism, or for Gerson to consider it his business to do all he could to that end. The

University often had representatives on the royal council. Gerson wrote (in French) to accompany one delegation of the rector and his deputies, 'la piteuse et très miserable complainte de la fille du roi ma mere, l'université de Paris', this 'daughter of the King, fountain of knowledge, light of our faith'. The University is the King's daughter 'by royal adoption' and now she turns to the King for royal protection 'in the customary way'.[1]

Gerson was clearly recognised at an early date as being of exceptional ability; here Pierre d'Ailly's patronage may have been important in drawing the 'right kind of attention' to him. In 1388, at the age of only twenty-four, he went with the embassy from the University to the Pope in exile in Avignon, to explain to the Pope the University's reasons for wishing to see a condemnation of the Dominican Jean de Monzon. Pierre d'Ailly was also among the delegates. The embassy was successful, and the Dominicans were expelled from the University of Paris until 1403.

In 1395 Gerson succeeded Peter D'Ailly (who had now been elevated to the episcopate) as Chancellor of the University. Although he worked for the opposite outcome, in 1398 a synod of bishops, clergy and University officials voted to withdraw obedience in the hope of ending the schism. The move was ineffective and Gerson became discouraged. In 1399 he left Paris and retreated to Burges. There he remained for more than a year. Although he did return to Paris later in the year, in February 1400 he wrote to Paris giving his reasons for resigning as Chancellor. He complains of being misconstrued and criticised by factions at the royal court. He is under duress (*cogor*). His mind is being distracted from his religious obligations. His letter exemplifies all the bitterness and pettiness of academic strife. He also believes that standards are slipping in the University. He is forced as Chancellor to award degrees to students who are ignorant and not possessed of the intellectual skills a degree ought to recognise; he is obliged to listen to theological opinions which are potential stumbling blocks to the faithful. When he preaches, he finds his audience apathetic and unreceptive to sound doctrine.

His return to Paris in 1400 was a courageous attempt to bring about reform. He describes in letters to Pierre d'Ailly and the College de Navarre what he hoped to achieve. There was to be a drive to get theological studies properly focussed once more, and to discourage the taste for frivolous argument. There was to be a return to the study of the Bible and respectable authors such as Anselm of Canterbury, Bernard of Clairvaux, Richard of St Victor, Bonaventure and Thomas Aquinas.

Gerson continued to work towards the ending of the Schism, an endeavour which ate into his time for preparation of sermons, but which seems to fit with the assumption of those involved with the work of the University that it had a responsibility to try to help. In 1403 he went to Avignon with a deputation of six masters and with requests for the Pope. The election of a new Pope, Alexander V, in 1409/10, by the arguably irregular Council of Pisa, had Gerson's support. As a device to bring about the ending of the schism, it was a failure. Neither of the existing 'Popes' would resign. This 'Pisan' Pope was replaced in 1410–15 by John XXIII, who called the Council of Constance in 1415, with a wish to end the Schism once and for all. John XXIII suddenly left the Council in 1415, and it was again Gerson the peacemaker who tried to restore calm..

In 1415 Gerson finally left Paris. In the aftermath of the Council of Constance it was not in any case safe for him to return to France, where the Duke of Burgundy was in power. He went to Austria and spent some time at the University of Vienna. In 1419 he was back in France, but settled in Lyons where he remained until his death ten years later, still writing actively. In his work during the period 1415–29 he may have been affected by the aftermath of the Hussite controversy.

Work and ideas

Gerson wrote a treatise against Jean de Monzon in 1389. No other writings survive from the early years except for some sermons. From his time as Chancellor come a series of harangues, or addresses delivered to those graduating in medicine, law and the arts, *Pro licentiandis in medicina, Pro licentiandis in decretis, Pro licentiandis in artibus* (*Oeuvres*, vol. 5)

During his time at Bruges Gerson had done more than think. He had been writing for ordinary people (*simples gens*) and in the vernacular. These were spiritual writings such as the *Mountain of Contemplation* and works on the Ten Commandments, on temptations, on mortal and venial sin.

There was a mystic as well as an academic in Gerson. His *De mystica theologia speculativa* explores the theme of the return of the soul to God in the course of a human life (*regressus ad deum in via*). Yet his spirituality is cerebral. He identifies a series of powers of the soul, all distorted by the consequences of sin: simple intelligence, which receives illumination directly from God; the cognitive power of the soul which deduces conclusions from premises; sense, the power of the soul which makes use of bodily senses; synderesis or conscience, an appetitive power of the soul with an inclination to good; rational appetite and sensual appetite.

When in 1409 a group of dissident cardinals from both the 'papal courts' called the Council of Pisa, Gerson saw the need for an *apologia* for this unusual and 'extraordinary' move, and he wrote treatises in its defence.

Gerson's *De consolatione theologiae* was modelled, in the literary sense, on Boethius's *Consolation of Philosophy*. There was a further sense in which it was an appropriate precedent, written as it was in a time of political crisis. Gerson ends his 'Consolation' with a call for the establishment of the *pax dei*. This is a book, he says, for *peregrini*. The treatise begins with a reflection on Romans 15.4, 'Whatever things have been written have been written for our instruction'.

The speakers in the dialogue are not the author and a personified 'Theology', but Volucer and Monicus. Volucer says that he has been at Constance for the 'General Council', so it may be that this figure is intended to represent Gerson himself; but equally he could be taken to represent Everyman. Monicus can be interpreted as a 'monk' or professional religious. Nevertheless, Gerson clearly does not believe that the monastic life affords the only way to perfection. He says as much in *De consiliis evangelicis et statu perfectionis* (*c*.1400). It was a leading idea of Gerson's that the *vita apostolica* is open to everyone. The *peregrinus* or pilgrim is therefore any Christian seeking to ascend towards God.

Notes

1 *Contre Charles de Savoisy, Oeuvres*, Vl.7 (Paris, 1966), pp. 326–7.

Bibliography

Gerson, *Oeuvres complètes* , ed. P. Glorieux (Paris, 1960–73), 10 vols.

Further reading

D. Catherine Brown, *Pastor and Laity in the Theology of Jean Gerson* (Cambridge, 1987); J.G. Burrows and M.S. Burrows, *Jean Gerson and the De Consolatione Theologiae* (Tübingen, 1991); S.E. Ozment, *Homo Spiritualis: A Comparative Study of the Anthropology of Johannes Tauler, Jean Gerson and Martin Luther (1509–16) in the Context of Their Theological Thought* (Leiden, 1969); G.H.M. Posthumus Meyjes, *Jean Gerson, Apostle of Unity: His Church Politics and Ecclesiology*, trans. J.C. Grayson (Leiden, 1999).

NICHOLAS OF CUSA 1401–64

Nicholas of Cusa was educated by the Brothers of the Common Life at Deventer in Holland. In 1416 he went to the University of Heidelberg and in 1418 to Padua to study canon law. Padua was also a centre of scientific learning, and would have been an attraction for that reason alone. He received his doctorate in canon law (*doctor decretorum*) in 1423. He then went on to Rome. In 1425 he returned to Germany, where he spent a year at Cologne studying theology, living on a benefice he held at Trier. At this time he was able to study the work of Aquinas under Hymeric Van den Velde.

Nicholas prepared a legal document for the cathedral chapter of Cologne, and did this well enough to gain the attention of Cardinal Giordano Orsini, who took him into his service. The Cardinal had humanist tastes, and he introduced Nicholas to Poggio Bracciolini and Antonio Loschi.

Nicholas's background of formal study made him an appropriate choice in 1437 to be summoned as an academic canon lawyer, acting on behalf of the minority party of the Council of Basle. The Greeks were to be asked to come to Ferrara, to the Council which was to discuss the reunion of the Church of the East with that of the West.

In 1438 Nicholas separated himself from the conciliar movement and gave his full support to the papal party. His lifetime therefore extended from the period of the Great Schism to that of the burning of John Hus, one of the forerunners of the sixteenth-century Renaissance.

Works and ideas

Ecclesiologically, Nicholas was a 'conciliarist' with somewhat extreme ideas about the body of Christ, which he envisaged by analogy with the *universitas* or gild of the day, as a 'corporation' which should be run democratically by its members. Unity was a leading idea and key theme of Nicholas of Cusa's theological as well as ecclesiological and political work. God he sees as the *unitas complicans*, the unity which embraces all things and makes them one. *De concordantia Catholica* (1432–3) was written as a result of his attendance at the Council of Basle. In it he sketches a picture of the Church as a divine cosmos. Within it grace flows from Christ to humanity. In the Church's hierarchy the Pope, bishops and priests all have a role, and the bishops are successors of Peter just like the Pope. Nicholas of Cusa advocates that the Pope be made responsible to a Council, for in his view, consent is necessary; obedience to ecclesiastical laws is not a blind requirement. It was a work which attracted a good deal of attention and helped to make his name.

Nicholas's enthusiasm for unity took him in another direction as well. He wrote *De pace fidei* on religious pluralism, or 'interfaith dialogue'. His idea was that all religions share a fundamental harmony and he suggested that unification with Christianity would require no more than an acceptance of Christ, the Trinity and the Church. This was of course no small recipe, but the interest lies in his attempting to tackle the issue at all.

In the *De li non aliud* and *De docta ignorantia*, Nicholas of Cusa was writing in the tradition of Ps-Dionysius, Proclus, Eriugena and Eckhart. Here his arguments are often incoherent and sweeping, but there are striking notions and images. He was one of the first to suggest that the earth moves. He conjured with the notion occasionally to be found earlier in the Middle Ages that God is the sphere whose centre is everywhere and his circumference nowhere. Nicholas seems to have got this from Meister Eckhart; he liked it enough to use it six times. He enjoyed paradoxes, and liked to break the mould of the scholarly method of the day. He plays with the literary conversation, in which one of the interlocutors, the abbot of St Justine of Sedazium is said to be working on Plato's *Parmenides*, while he himself has expertise on Ps-Dionysius to offer. This kind of thinking is never far from mysticism, and there are aspects of the *devotio moderna*, the currently fashionable rather methodical spirituality of the interior life, in his thought.

Bibliography

Nicholas of Cusa, *The Catholic Concordance*, ed. and trans. P.E. Sigmund (Cambridge, 1991); Nicholas of Cusa, *Unity and Reform: Selected Writings*, ed. John Patrick Dolan (Notre Dame, 1962); *Nicholas of Cusa on God as Not-Other*, trans. J. Hopkins (Minneapolis, 1979); Nicholas of Cusa, *Of Learned Ignorance*, trans. G.Heron (London, 1954).

Further reading

On Interreligious Harmony, ed. J.E. Biechler and H. Lawrence Bond (Lewiston, NY, 1990); J. Hopkins, *A Concise Introduction to the Philosophy of Nicholas of Cusa* (Minneapolis, 1978).

GABRIEL BIEL *c.* 1420–95

Life and times

Gabriel Biel was born in Speyer. He was ordained priest, when he was in the Heidelberg Faculty of Arts. He remained there to teach for nine years. In 1442/3 he was briefly in Erfurt. In 1451 he returned to Erfurt, probably to begin his studies in theology. He can be linked with both the *via antiqua* and the *via moderna*. He must have had his licence to teach theology by 1474.

From about 1460–84, Biel won some prominence in the Church. He belonged to the Brethren of the Common Life (the *devotio moderna*), who regarded the formation of the person as an important part of education. Until 1468 he lived at the house of the Brethren at Marienthal on the Rheingau. By 1471 he had brought about a General Chapter of the Brethren Houses on the upper Rhine. In Mainz he was cathedral preacher, and a series of Mainz Sermons survives. The preaching got him into local Church politics to such a degree that he was obliged to flee Mainz for a time.

In 1484 Biel was appointed to Tübingen's new theology faculty, where the *via antiqua*, the *via moderna* and the new humanism all had their place, but the old-fashioned ways seem to have been dominant. Biel was rector of the university of Tübingen from 1485–9. He retired to the Brethren House of St Peter's at Einsiedel, where he died in 1495. This was an unusual religious community and 'house' in that representatives of all three 'estates', nobility, clergy and burgesses, lived there together.

Work and ideas

The writing of the *Defensorium obedientie apostolice* (1462) came out of the controversy at Mainz. Biel was opposing the attack made by the archbishop-elect on the papal see. This was the period when conciliarism was in decline. Councils had been tried in the early fifteenth century, but they had not worked. The *Bull execrabilis* of 1460 seemed to have put a stop to attempts to challenge papal ascendancy. No Council attempted it again until the University of Paris did so in 1518, in appeal against the *Bull execrabilis*. That was belated, and again ineffective, for in 1520 *Exurge domine* was promulgated against Luther.

Biel – realistically – took a position less hostile to the use of the skills and presumptions of the canon lawyers in their support of papal prerogatives than Pierre d'Ailly and Jean Gerson had been. He used canon law. He was prepared to assert that: 'What the Holy Church, our Mother, defines and accepts as catholic truth, must be believed with the same reverence as though it were stated in Scripture'.

Yet he is not far from Nicholas of Cusa in his confidence that the authority of the Church depends on its unity. It is just that he believes the hegemony of the See of Rome is essential to the preservation of that unity. Only St Peter was entrusted with this high pastoral care, and he passed it on to his successors. Biel approved of Bernard of Clairvaux's *plenitudo potestatis* formulation, and he quotes it. He seems to restrict papal power by saying that papal authority can be used only for the edification of the Church; it is not an absolute and unfettered power, and yet he holds that the authority to interpret Scripture has been entrusted to the Church. This is an awkward balancing act, but what is important is that it *is* a balancing act.

Why did the Canon of the Mass need expounding? The *Canonis Missae Expositio* begins with an *accessus* which notes that there are numerous scholastic disputes about the meaning of the liturgy. Here we see Biel the solid scholastic, engaged in the same kind of balancing exercise as in his commentary on the *Sentences*. Biel was perhaps trying to be a 'safe pair of hands'.

Influence

Biel was a disciple of Ockham. He was also an significant influence on Luther. Yet he was sufficiently 'of all parties and none' to be read with respect by both sides in the sixteenth-century debates.

Bibliography

Gabriel Biel, *Canonis Missae expositio*, ed. H.A. Oberman and W.J. Courtenay (Wiesbaden, 1963); Gabriel Biel, *Defensorium oboedientiae apostolicae*, ed. Heiko A. Oberman, D.E. Zerfoss and W.J. Courtenay (Cambridge, MA, 1968); Gabriel Biel, *Quaestiones de justificatione*, ed. C. Feckes (Aschendorff, 1929); Gabriel Biel, *Collectorium circa quattuor libros Sententiarum*, Prologue q.2.a1.Bed. W. Werbeck and U. Hofmann (Tübingen, 1973), 4 vols.

Further reading

H.A. Oberman, *The Harvest of Mediaeval Theology* (Cambridge, MA, 1963).

INDEX